ERNST BARLACH, AN ETCHING BY LEONARD BASKIN

THREE PLAYS
BY ERNST
BARLACH

translated by **ALEX PAGE**

The University of Minnesota Press
MINNEAPOLIS

PRINTED IN THE UNITED STATES OF AMERICA AT
THE LUND PRESS, INC., MINNEAPOLIS, MINNESOTA

FRONTISPIECE AND TITLE PAGE REPRODUCED BY
THE MERIDEN GRAVURE COMPANY, MERIDEN, CONN.

Library of Congress Catalog Card Number: 64-8671

Published in Great Britain, India, and Pakistan by the Oxford University Press, London, Bombay, and Karachi, and in Canada by the Copp Clark Publishing Co. Limited, Toronto.

FOR MY PARENTS

Acknowledgments

I WAS introduced to Barlach by Leonard Baskin, and he was the one to inspire me to do a translation. As much as anyone, he has kept urging me to complete a sometimes despairing task. As well as for many other things, I am grateful to him for permission to use his portrait of Barlach which appeared in the Autumn 1963 *Massachusetts Review*.

Additional encouragement came from Anne Halley and the editors of the *Massachusetts Review*. Anne Halley translated Parts I and II of *The Flood*; Parts II and V were printed by the *Massachusetts Review* in Spring 1960 and then reprinted in booklet form by the Gehenna Press of Northampton, Massachusetts. The version of Parts I and II of *The Flood* in the present collection is substantially Miss Halley's and is reprinted with her permission, though I have made changes to give the work a unified style and must therefore take responsibility for all of it. Miss Halley also read *The Genuine Sedemunds*; many of her suggestions have been incorporated. I heartily thank Dr. Naomi Jackson Groves, who is *prima inter pares* in everything pertaining to Barlach, for generously sharing her great knowledge. Many other readers have helped to improve the translation but none with such infinite care as Vera Lachmann. It is also a pleasure to acknowledge the help, solicitude, and expertise that the editorial staff of the University of Minnesota Press has lavished upon this work. Finally, I express my gratitude to the University of Massachusetts Research Council whose grant and whose continued services have helped in the completion of the manuscript.

My translation is based upon the excellent edition of Barlach's dramas published by R. Piper & Co. Verlag of Munich in 1956 and

ACKNOWLEDGMENTS

edited by Friedrich Dross and Klaus Lazarowicz. It is the first volume of a three-volume collection of Barlach's writings, entitled *Das Dichterische Werk* (1956–59). The sculpture on the front cover is Barlach's *Das Grauen* (1923), used with the permission of R. Piper & Co. Verlag, and the sketch that introduces each play was suggested by Barlach's *Der Berserker* (1910).

THREE PLAYS BY ERNST BARLACH

Translator's Introduction

ERNST BARLACH'S fame as a sculptor of the first rank is well established throughout the Western world. His writings, however, especially his dramas, have suffered relative neglect in all countries but Germany, where they were staged soon after they appeared. The first performances usually evoked sharp reactions, were widely discussed, and exerted important influences on younger playwrights. His best-known play, *The Flood,* won the coveted Kleist prize in 1924. Since the war there has hardly been a year that has not seen a new production of one of the plays, and a number have become part of the national repertoire. Studies of them have proliferated in Germany. It is now commonly acknowledged by the German theatergoing public and by readers, critics, and scholars that Barlach's dramatic works provide a major achievement of the German theater of the second and third decades of this century and that his intimate connection with the German Expressionist movement endows them with an added historical interest. But his literary reputation abroad has lagged. The difficulty of his highly individual language is perhaps one reason; another, the unusual nature of his ideas and themes. The three plays here translated, *The Flood, The Genuine Sedemunds,* and *The Blue Boll,* are from his middle period, about 1918 to 1924; they were chosen because they afford a somewhat more direct introduction to his dramatic techniques and the world of his ideas, but it is not easy to decide which are his best.

Ernst Barlach was born in 1870 at Wedel in northern Germany to a middle-class family that could trace its settlement in that region back

3

to the seventeenth century. He was the oldest of four children. As a young boy he often accompanied his father, a doctor, on his rounds and learned something of the hardy peasant humor and of the fortitude with which pain and suffering were met. He was an unusually sensitive child. In the very first pages of his *A Self-Told Life* he attributes his "melancholy nature" to his grandmother and alludes to an early awareness of "something other" beyond himself, a notion that became central to his work: "My brother [and I] . . . sensed around us a number of remarkable things to which it became necessary to pay attention, things which one could neither see nor hear but which were certainly real. 'It' could arrive or not, we agreed, as we lay in bed in daylight summer evenings — 'you look at the room, I'll watch the wall,' because we soon realized that 'it' could also enter through the walls." [1]

His father died when he was fourteen. After some training in art schools in Hamburg and Dresden, he spent the years 1895–97 in Paris, his time there divided among drawing "the reality of the streets," visits to the Louvre, and his first sustained efforts at writing a prose fantasy. The first exhibition of his graphic works took place in Berlin in 1900. A few years later he traveled with his brothers Hans and Nikolaus to Russia, a journey that became a turning point in his artistic career. The figures of Russia's poor, especially the beggars and vagrants, seen against the endless steppes and humble settlements overwhelmed him as truths he had long felt; they gave him "symbols for the human condition in all its nakedness between heaven and earth." Upon his return an "unheard of" realization struck him: "You may dare to attempt fearlessly all that is yours, that which is on the very outside, and that which is deepest within, the attitude of piety, the disfigurement of rage, because for everything there is expressive form, just as either or both were embodied in Russia." [2]

At this time he also began to work on his first drama, *The Dead Day*, which has certain autobiographical elements. He won custody of his son Nikolaus, the offspring of an unhappy liaison. In 1909 he made the last of his major journeys, this one to Florence, as the recipient of the Villa

[1] Ernst Barlach, *Das Dichterische Werk*, Friedrich Dross, ed. (Munich, 1958), II, 15. This and all subsequent quotations are my translations.
[2] *Ibid.*, II, 55.

4

Romana fellowship; there he met the Expressionist poet Theodor Däubler with whom he formed a warm, lifelong friendship. Upon his return he chose Güstrow, a small town east of Lübeck, as his residence, and there he spent the rest of his life, in semi-seclusion. In the meantime his first sculptures were becoming known. The following year he met Paul Cassirer, a well-known art dealer and later a publisher, entering into a contract with him that assured a regular income. He was soon recognized by such Expressionists as Lehmbruck, Kirchner, Trakl, Sorge, and Kollwitz as their leader and their honored master, although he kept himself aloof from the manifestoes, pronouncements, and intrigues that characterized much of the day-to-day progress of the movement. But his letters to his friends and family provide an extraordinary collection of insights and commentary upon art, his own and others', and upon the major preoccupations of the times — quite apart from revealing a deeply concerned, passionate, and magnificently humanistic temperament; these letters have as high an artistic and critical value as, say, the letters of Keats. The following two decades, especially the twenties, proved to be Barlach's most productive and creative period, the years of his major sculptures and of all his dramas, of two novels and much else besides. One glimpses his ever-youthful Faustian cast of mind in the following letter, written when he was sixty-two: "I crave ever higher vantage points. . . . Clinging to safeguarded possessions seems to me pathetic. One must dare to take the chance of heedlessness." [3]

With the coming to power of the National Socialists in 1933 Barlach found himself in growing official disfavor. His famous war memorials, all of them anti-war, were removed one by one; his sculptures, woodcuts, and drawings were withdrawn from the museums and sent back to his studio, if they were not destroyed; and finally even his favorite work, the bronze angel hanging in Güstrow Cathedral, was taken down — the hardest blow of all. He was beset by financial worries and by rapidly declining health, but he continued to work until his last months. His final note was to his brother Hans, written while he lay on his deathbed in a Rostock clinic in 1938; he asked him not to visit him because he feared his brother himself was incapacitated by influenza: "You would only have an uncomfortable visit since I am of course in no

[3] Ernst Barlach, *Aus Seinen Briefen* (Munich, 1947), pp. 76–77.

state for conversation. . . . I hope for an early and complete recovery."[4] He died three weeks later, at the age of sixty-eight, and was buried in Ratzeburg amid the eulogies of his many friends.

The Flood (1924) is essentially a long dialogue between two men who hold very different views of God. Noah joyfully submits to a God who "is everything and the world nothing," while Calan sees him as "a glimmering spark . . . who creates and his creation creates him anew," yet a God to whom he too can express gratitude. The dialogue gains its energy from the attempt to understand evil — random, man-made, and even divinely-sanctioned evil. Barlach's invention of Calan as the great taunter of Noah, as the one who glows with independence and freedom gained by an enormous assertion of selfhood, serves to render the biblical account highly dramatic, if not tragic. But to regard the play as a dialogue between these two figures no doubt reduces it too much: their views are not only stated and restated with increasing elaboration but are also embodied in their characters and in their relations to their offspring. An insistent question that occupies Barlach in most of his dramas is how much a son *owes* to his father, how much the son's life is fated and determined, and by how much the son may surpass him, the crucial relation between God and man serving as a paradigm for that between a human parent and his children. Throughout his life, most forcefully in his woodcuts, Barlach showed an intense concern for the Moses theme, Moses as a lawgiver (a father), and as having brought man's relation to God to a kind of perfection. Noah sees himself as a true son of his God; he has unbounded faith in him, a nearly total submissiveness, a belief that whatever happens must be God's will. His own sons, however, are a wrangling, self-seeking threesome who are not going to maintain the closeness to, and the immediate apprehension of, God that are Noah's outstanding gifts. But the sons are not evil or bad: merely "average." Barlach leaves no doubt that Noah's great obedience to God can become a ready cover behind which all sorts of dubious traits find shelter: lust, indecisiveness, the toleration of cruelty to innocents, and acquiescence in expediency especially where his sons are concerned. Perhaps because of the stirrings of his own desires for

[4] Ernst Barlach, *Leben und Werk in Seinen Briefen*, Friedrich Dross, ed. (Munich, 1952), p. 252.

Awah, he cannot refuse Japheth's insistent demands for "fat Zebid," a coarse, hypersexed, heathen woman. Noah will not kill, but neither will he show mercy when it may prevent suffering and death. To regard oneself as the executor of God's will, Barlach says, can become an act of pride resembling that of the openly proud, skeptical, self-assertive Calan. Frequently enough Noah cuts a decidedly ridiculous figure. Keenly disappointed by the manner in which various directors presented Noah on the stage and by the critics' interpretations of him, Barlach wrote: "I thought of Noah as a substantial landowner who is rather easy on himself, with a hardly noticeable paunch, walks with a stick and has his little failing, – a trifle condescending in his affability. . . ." [5]

In contrast to Noah, Calan is a free spirit, with absolute faith in his own abilities and strength and the right they give him to order his life and the lives of those dependent upon him. Barlach spares no effort to impress us with his masterliness, his generosity, his integrity. Being free, he can forgo Noah's uneasy wavering between two sets of standards. More than Noah, he is able to feel the widespread misery of mankind. He commands from his servant Chus (who is perhaps his natural son) a loyalty and a love which none of Noah's sons evinces for his father. So too does one feel the depth of Calan's love for Awah; and his giving her up to Noah in fulfillment of a vow, and Noah's subsequent passing her on to Japheth for wife, rankle more than he consciously realizes – these deeds provide in part the energy for teasing, taunting, and testing Noah's faith in his God, although the argument takes place on a far more rational level. Calan's intelligence drives him to understand, and by understanding to vanquish, the last threat to the exercise of the self in all its finality. He fails, but his vision before his gruesome demise is of a God whose demand of man is not that he submit but that he develop his potentialities to the fullest, a God, as it were, who wishes his creation well in its "becoming," its flourishing, instead of keeping a tight, capricious control over it.

Barlach vigorously denied that in Calan he had presented the spirit of nihilism. He explained that he saw in him an instance of "a dissolution into something higher . . . in which the full consciousness of the self is contained and retained." And he goes on to say, as much about

[5] *Ibid.*, p. 121.

himself as Calan, that the latter "envisions a God who has no more shape. By this he releases his self — that self that has reached the utmost of its possibilities, that has become so ripe as to join a higher community. With that, man is destroyed as a thing in himself. I have often maintained that the greatest fortune is to transcend oneself, the temporary attainment of a state beyond the everyday. Everyone feels it at times. Give man a high ideal and he is relieved (if he is seized by the ideal) of the suffering of the self, of his limited individuality." [6] For that reason, Calan's defeat is only partial. He knows that Awah carries his child, and if the sojourners in the Ark survive the catastrophe so will his seed. And that holds for Zebid, who has sullenly consented to become Japheth's wife in Awah's place. Both will reassert Calan's spirit after the flood: one, his tender, openhearted, perceptive side; the other, sensuous, aggressive, and brutal.

Barlach has not in any philosophical or theological terms pretended to offer a solution to the problem of evil. He comes closest to it by having Noah's God admit to a blunder, but then he says in the letter earlier referred to that "the Noahs need a Heavenly God Jehovah, who is as much their creation as they his. . . . I would even believe that he is a fact, but no more than a first-rate Lear-like master — a helper and rather irresponsible. Evil has a deeper source." [7] In the end Barlach is less concerned with God than with the noble and ignoble elements warring in the individual. His play attempts to trace their genesis.

If the struggle in man's innermost being is the recurrent concern of *The Flood*, its achievement lies in the working out of the theme, in the details, and in the secondary characters. God, for example, as he appears in several guises (especially in that of a beggar), conveys a sense both of immense power and of cross-grained irascibility. His power is made vivid by two angels who in their role of a marmoreal divine chorus are like overconscientious servants deploring their master's peccadilloes. In a moving scene between Noah, who has been apprised of God's imminent arrival, and God, who comes as an old beggar claiming by and by to be Noah's long-dead real parent, the relations between the two are most sensitively explored: Noah's great expectancy, mingled

[6] *Ibid.*, pp. 156–57.
[7] *Ibid.*

with an old man's near-senile testiness, is only partially fulfilled, since he is never sure of the beggar's identity; but the elation and excitement he feels give proof that on a deeper level he has recognized his nondescript visitor. He then takes on the role of son both to a father and to his God. The same beggar changes visibly before our eyes from a ragged, persecuted, pathetic figure to one of force and authority that earns even Calan's respect.

The ways of perceiving God are by no means confined to those of Noah and Calan; indeed, almost every character sooner or later is given an opportunity to show his own way. It is here that Barlach's dramatic inventiveness has fullest rein. Awah apprehends God (and the angels) most directly and most sensuously in a kind of ecstasy; we believe her when she laughs in pure joy at the presence of God or when later, at the approach of the rainstorm, she intones half-deliriously "the eternal song": "I can see it ring, I can hear it swing, the end cradles the beginning in her arms." Her adoration is a child's pure delight and an unaffected pleasure in taking delight — she sees God in an explosive beauty suddenly enveloping her. It is the "sturdy Shem" who understands her and wishes to make her his wife. He claims to have difficulty explaining his vision of God, but he actually does very well: "He hides behind everything, and everything has narrow chinks, through which he shines. . . . I see him often through the chinks, it's so strangely sudden, it opens, it's gone, not a trace of a joint to be found. . . ." And the mutilated shepherd, who has served as Calan's sacrifice, may be the humblest of them all: "The word [God] is too big for my mouth. I understand that he is not to be understood, that is all my knowledge of him." A senselessly abused victim, the shepherd nevertheless is guided by a profound optimism — "Where cheer is speaking, there I will remain," he says, even though flood waters and frenzied animals are closing in. These various views are less an attempt to define the deity than to characterize the people who hold them.

One participant in this drama remains, whose connection to the plot is more tenuous and whose view of God is by far the most negative. The hunchbacked leper seems after all to be the incarnation of a mistake: ugly and diseased in body and soul, he is a universal outcast, a purposeless existence. His sole cry is an unremitting curse of God and his injustice. More than a mistake, he screams — a demonstration of God's illwill. He is the Thersites of *The Flood*. In his blind fury he strikes God, again disguised as a beggar. The shepherd says of the leper: "He curses his God who gave him everything: leprous sores, a deformed body — and a heart," and Calan adds: "He has a right to curse." It is significant that he shares Calan's fate, indeed, is yoked to him in the last climactic scenes and partly consumed by ravening beasts. His final act is to impersonate Calan in order to deceive Noah — he meets his fate as he has lived, wholly unconverted despite his sufferings. One can see him as the underside of Calan's gigantic self-assertiveness and selfhood; like Calan, he also taunts Noah for using "God's will" to his own purposes. While he is wholly reprehensible, the magnitude of his protest, his clamorous insistence that his case too be heard and "explained," are reminders that Noah's God is guilty of inflicting pointless suffering. The sternness and aloofness of the angelic chorus, as well as their exaggerated allegiance to God, are counterbalanced by the leper as another chorus-figure with his strident, unceasing imprecations. His claims undercut all the others' more benign concepts of God, including Calan's.

Gratuitous cruelty, cruelty by neglect, and cruelty according to design — these merge into a theme that has risen to acute prominence in our time; in a German artist like Barlach, known for his kindliness and personal warmth, it is particularly revealing. In this drama of manifold cruelties, Barlach uses every means to achieve verisimilitude in his characters and setting. His portrayal of biblical life as stark, nomadic, governed by uneasy alliances, but chiefly by might, is impressive; and the attendant cruelty is no doubt meant to be, in part, an expression of that life. But Calan's maiming of the shepherd has a special quality. Ostensibly a test of Noah and Noah's God, it is really the act of a superman who takes for granted the right to dispose of others' lives, even for the sake of an experiment. Later Calan comes to realize that the shepherd's "drops of blood have swelled to seas and drowned my herds and my dominions" and that he can "taste what came from my deeds." He even rejects Noah's God because he is "a violent God, as I was violent." The play does not then sanction the experiment, but one feels that its full meaning is lost in Calan's final grand formulation of

God. For however idealistic and powerful that is, however magnificent, the selfhood he sees his God wishing on him clearly excludes any concern (compassion, pity, mercy) toward his fellow creatures. It is as though Calan had been right in theory but had merely been guilty of a tactical mistake.

Noah's refusal, on the other hand, to challenge the mutilation with anything other than words, his genial acceptance of everything as God's will, gives license to an equal, or possibly greater (because more covert, better rationalized), cruelty. His callous abandonment of Calan and the leper to the beasts is the chief evidence of this. Nevertheless, the play grudgingly admits that Noah acts "correctly"; he has at least the good sense to take all precautions to survive, however dubious a victory that is — equally dubious as would be a world peopled only by Calans. And on a somewhat lower scale, the leper's cruelty toward the shepherd, Chus's role as loyal executioner to Calan, even the thoughtless passing of Awah from man to man — all these instances of man's inhumanity to man evoke the wistful admission that cruelty is the very fabric of this life. A certain mystery envelops the maimed and martyred shepherd: his unshakable faith, his humility, his beauty (compared by Awah with God's), his uncertain fate in the flood are perhaps meant to prefigure the new teachings of Christ, a wholly unselfish, transcendent love that otherwise is not found in the events of the play.

"Was it sad or funny?" a character in *The Genuine Sedemunds* (1920) asks after a grotesque scene in front of a family mausoleum. The two Sedemund brothers have come to lay a wreath in memory of Old Sedemund's wife but are prevented by Young Sedemund's embittered denunciations and exposés. The play is both sad and funny, with perhaps a greater emphasis on the latter, as the mad, mixed-up doings in a charivari world lead to a searching treatment of what the title implies: the genuine versus the false. With the dexterity and intrepidity of a Prospero, Barlach moves from one strange and febrile locale to another while alluding to even stranger ones: fairgrounds, a beergarden, an insane asylum, a graveyard, a make-believe hell, a chapel, and a graveside encounter with the dead; and populates them with grotesques: a madman, a wheelchair cripple, a debauchee, an ascetic, a

11

pettifogger, ghosts, and bogeymen. There is much macabre humor, and there are at least eight corpses playing their grisly parts. Again, as in *The Flood*, we meet gratuitous violence, but now a horse is the victim. What begins as naturalism rises to hysteria as if one were trapped in the fair's fun-house. It is perhaps Barlach's most Expressionistic play, though with his distaste for easy categorization he would have protested strongly against such a label.

What brings these many diverse elements together is a recently deceased lion. His death is kept a secret by Grude who has been given a day off from the insane asylum to attend a funeral, and who manages to hoax everyone into trying to recapture the lion supposedly at large. The lion gains important meanings as the play progresses and as Grude's prank reveals the disparities between the genuine and the false. As a matter of fact, the play is full of paradoxes: a madman who is saner than all the officially sane citizens; Sabina, a "wheelchair-saint," who plans a seduction; Old Sedemund, a connoisseur of debaucheries, the only one recognizing a deity; Young Sedemund, the leader of a vastly ambitious program for improving man, committing himself to the asylum; the daemonic lion as an agent of good. One soon discovers that the title of the play is ironic and that there is far less of the genuine than its opposite to be found.

The lion stands for a reminder of aliveness, "a savage's conscience," a timeclock ticking away that says there is something more vital and more dangerous than the blandness of mere everyday existence. But the "good lion's" ferociousness can overpower one: "He opens wide his jaws inside you and eats you up, skin and all, and makes you a part of his majesty." In one sense, as the organ-grinder remarks, we are all equal before him, but in another, we dare not take the chance to discover, through him, where our true realities lie. Old Sedemund is determined to "defeat the lion"; it is doubtful whether, at the end of the play, he has succeeded for anyone but himself; for Young Sedemund's final accusation against his father is that the "lion's gullet howl[ing] wrath upon us" makes mockery of the genuineness of the Sedemunds. As in *The Flood* Calan sees his salvation in a transcendence of himself, and as *The Blue Boll* expounds the perilous but rewarding road to becoming, so too in this play the lion serves to exacerbate man's knowledge of himself and compels him to take a stand.

The brilliance of the play does not lie, however, in the depiction of this humanistic-theological theme, but rather in its now strident, now ironic attack against man's shams, pretensions, and self-deceptions — the not genuine in him, or, better, his disingenuousness. There is a veritable catalogue of sins: Uncle Waldemar's perjuries, the militiamen's cowardice, Greedycock's foisting off his illegitimate child on another, Grude's disregard for his wife, Old Sedemund's dissipations and his demand upon his dying wife for a false confession of an imaginary offense, a confession that led to her suicide. At one point, Old Sedemund, bristling at being taken as the arch-practitioner of vices, proves that while all the good citizens profess only the highest principles of morality, in practice they complaisantly accept in their neighbors and in themselves both heinous and petty crimes — "everyone," he cries, "shall be nailed to the cross." A more general indictment is made of official immorality that bestows a decoration on an ineffective, bedraggled person like Mankmoos and also sanctions the corruption of "our institutions," of "things as they are": cutting corners here and there, blinking at child-trade, giving preferred treatment to "our most eminent citizens."

It is less clear whether Barlach means to attack Young Sedemund's Utopian organization; his Adamism sets out to discover what in man requires improvement and finds it in man's need to sacrifice himself on the altar of an ideal — "giving makes grace." (Barlach wrote in a letter: "Give man a high ideal and he is relieved . . . of the suffering of the self. . . ."[8]) But then the ascetic puritanical Young Sedemund finds himself so much at odds with his world that he retreats to the insane asylum, as though to take Grude's place, while the latter, possibly restored and a father-to-be, dances merrily with his wife over the graves of the dead to a future that is nonetheless unlikely to be an improvement on the past. In such a compromised world no one acquits himself with honor. It may be that Young Sedemund comes closest to it, for he has at least the most optimistic vision even though he lacks the drive and the practical sense to make it actual. "I do think," he says, "in the

[8] *Ibid.*

end everything in the universe harmonizes into a delicious feast for the ears," but he quickly goes on to talk of those, like his Uncle Waldemar, who are no more than cosmic musical rests. He behaves with great tact toward Sabina and Mrs. Grude and rises to intense indignation toward his demagogic uncle and rationalizing father. But that kind of sanity, Barlach seems to maintain, is wasted on this world. And as Old Sedemund demonstrates in the scene in the abandoned chapel, this world is a literal hell: again in a prankish mood, he has no difficulty persuading the bystanders to accept the role of hell-brothers and follow him in a mock parade through that hell.

In 1921 Barlach witnessed a production of *The Genuine Sedemunds* in Berlin. He complained in a letter to his friend Reinhard Piper that only the secondary characters like the organ-grinder, Sabina, and Mankmoos succeed in holding the stage. He added that with a cinematic pace and Expressionistic techniques "I don't want to have anything to do." [9] It is not difficult to argue that the success of the play lies exactly in the bright and varied spectacle, in a wry, Till Eulenspiegel, topsy-turvy humor. That a made-up lion should act as a catalyst in revealing the more genuine motivations and values is the final irony, and a cruel one: only fear can finally unmask the latent violence and sources of scurrility, and fear hovers not far beneath the plausibly smug surface. Those who are proof against that fear (like Young Sedemund) make a pathetically heroic stand against the shams but cannot begin to vanquish them, only withdraw into the fastness of an asylum.

In *The Blue Boll* (1926) two unhappy, life-weary people meet and by a series of mistakes and seeming accidents stumble upon the fresh beginning of a better life. Each emerges from his crisis shaken by a searing experience of the human plight. Kurt Boll, a well-to-do landowner, sees his coddled, easygoing life as suddenly pointless, unsatisfying, trivial, and belabored by hollow truisms of those who surround him with love, as his wife does, or with respect, as the mayor and townspeople of Sternberg do. He is given to fits of temper in which his face turns blue — hence the blue Boll. Grete Greendale, again, is so hysterically obsessed and repelled by the physical, by "flesh," that she has left her

[9] *Ibid.*, p. 104.

husband and escaped to Sternberg. There she tries to obtain poison in order to liberate her children from that abominated flesh into pure spirit. A beautiful girl, she numbly admits that she is a witch, nor does she see anything wrong with that. Boll is attracted by her otherworldly pallor and evident despondency. Both are half-people, both find themselves caught sliding toward death, Boll toying with suicide, Grete planning the murder of her children. The drama's success lies in the gradual, hardly perceptible changes that both experience. "All kinds of things come to pass unnoticed in the dark of a person's inner life," the mayor asserts in his most important speech. These changes seem right and inevitable once they have taken place. And, though similar in effect, they are characteristically different for the two.

Boll moves from a contemptuous dismissal of all possibilities of human transcendence to a sympathy for Grete's plight. After failing to procure poison for her through a mischance or because he has second thoughts (the play does not make clear which), he must submit to her repeated taunts of being a weak, vacillating person who "does now this, now that." The self-confessed devil Elias offers to make him whole by giving him a "hellish charge," thereby accepting him in the league of those who adhere to the principle that "each is nearest to himself." Boll has chafed under that very formulation of life, one of egotistical indifference. Rather, an uncomplicated sympathy for another—Grete—takes root in him and is nurtured by the Gentleman until it reaches more and more people, like Woodfresser and Otto Pompmaster. Life to Boll is no longer a sterile, static entity but a process of becoming in which individuality may well be lost but something indefinite yet far greater gained. Barlach was well aware of the difficulties his readers might encounter with such a semi-mystical becoming. He said in one of his letters: "It is the inconceivable magnificence of the happening which I believe is forever hidden; one cannot touch it with one's finger, never understand its purpose. Sometimes experience seems to me to point to the absorption of the individual in the superindividual (but then what is that?) as a redemption and dissolution of all human creatures." [10] And Barlach wonders if an analysis of human motivation can dramatize this becoming. Nevertheless in *The Blue Boll* he shows the psycholog-

[10] *Ibid.*, p. 177.

1 5

ical effect of it by Boll's altered cast of mind after he has tied himself to something outside of, and greater than, himself. It is then that courage returns, then that he gains an effortless candor toward others, a lucidity and openness, all of which contrast sharply with his earlier vagaries, his crabbed compulsion to torment, attack, and befuddle people, his macabre imaginings. The play opens with Boll admiring the church steeple enveloped in mist — a somewhat sinister, threatening image. At the end, he understands with perfect clarity both the power and the limitations of an imposing woodcarving of an apostle he has never before noticed. He has undergone a test, namely the need to face, to deal with, to accept a parallel change in Grete. His becoming, the recognition that such becoming is not compulsion but a voluntary turning of the will, has been both subtly and convincingly demonstrated.

Grete Greendale's hallucinations are more actual than Boll's fantasies: visualizing the spirit literally choked by flesh, she is determined to set it free. Her test comes as she "witnesses" her children's treatment in hell. In two brilliantly conceived scenes in Elias's Devil's Kitchen she discovers that, since one's afterlife has been determined by the tenor of *this* life, death, far from being a simple release, can hold greater terrors and degradations than does "being in the flesh." The coals of the Devil's Kitchen "burn where needed, they destroy nothing but what is spoilt," Doris, the innkeeper's wife, assures her. What the mysterious Gentleman accomplishes in helping Boll to his becoming, Doris does for Grete. Doris is a type of stolid earth-mother, who assuages Grete's feverish obsession and turns her from her contemplated deed. She relieves her of feelings of guilt by giving her a sense of at-oneness with large and more pervasive and benign forces heretofore unsuspected. Grete, too, moves from self-induced terror to calmness and dignity as she recognizes her responsibilities toward her children.

Most material in the change is the Gentleman, in whom some characters discern God, and others Satan; he is treated with disdain and contempt by Otto Pompmaster and with comradely courtesy by Boll. When accused of clothing himself in mystifications he concedes that he is indeed "a faint and meek reflection of the infinite . . . a weak, hardly discernible adumbration of God." Yet he does have some of the best lines in the play. In an obvious reference to Goethe's *Faust* (taking an anti-Mephistophelian point of view) he says: "There isn't a spot you could spit on where something doesn't hover waiting to be thrust into existence, waiting to leave its cocoon." But again there is something Mephistophelian in his provoking Boll to undergo his last and most crucial test, that is, the temptation to achieve his becoming by suicide. It is apparent that the Gentleman is hardly meant to embody either good or evil, in the usual terms, but that he is an agency of the divine: he has a hand in those changes that lead to a fuller existence, a becoming of "shoots sprouting into blades." But the individual must have started on that path of his own will. The becoming he metes out to Otto Pompmaster is sudden death. Otto's rigidity, his tirade in favor of irresponsibility except in marriage (he takes an incredibly mechanical view of it), his refusal to step in any sense beyond his confined existence, do indeed signify virtual death.

The Gentleman is one of those strange, mythic, and yet quite plausible figures that reappear in many of Barlach's dramas. The less ceremoniously he is played the better, Barlach thought, and "the more unimportant-harmless his doings are represented the more forceful will be the presentation of the happening, the 'becoming,' which is intended as a dark force in the background controlling the action." [11] In a strange way, his mission is to tell man: submit! But the submission must be voluntary, a fully conscious commitment to becoming — "I must" changes to "I want," the wanting expressed as a total allegiance to the growing force within one. Though his is a negative commitment, Elias expresses it best: "What Elias does, he must do, and what Elias must do, he wants to do."

The secondary characters provide more than a setting and a humorous undertone to the major themes. While people like Woodfresser, the mayor, and Virgin reflect the atmosphere of small-town life — Sternberg is certainly Güstrow — they also give subtle support to the central theme. Virgin the watchmaker is a dour character, unpleasant to the point of nastiness, who provokes the antipathy not only of Boll but of the reader. Yet it turns out that he is the "local correspondent" of the Gentleman and in that capacity forces Boll into taking his first responsible step toward Grete. This stern taskmaster signifies the arduousness

[11] *Ibid.*, p. 137.

of Boll's later becoming, his very name suggesting the purity of that ideal process. The pertinacious Woodfresser who first alerts the town to a strange visitation — a shoe attached to "Satan's hindquarters" left to him for repair has disappeared — is rather easily swayed "now this way, now that": he jumps to quick conclusions. Though he readily accepts the Gentleman as God, Woodfresser's becoming is nevertheless a maudlin affair.

On the other hand, Boll's wife makes a genuine if tentative start of her own. Upon first meeting her, she impresses us as the epitome of smugness and egotism — she is dead certain that whatever she does not understand cannot possibly exist. Gradually she comes to realize that to allow her husband to carry out his immediate obligations toward Grete is a means of restoring his health and restoring him permanently to herself. In this metamorphosis the Gentleman has also played a part, but it is Boll who tells her that harder tasks are ahead: "The honey of humility can help you in your sour toil to a sweet becoming." Becoming is sour toil and tough business, by no means a pure act of grace. There are two other characters that never appear on stage but are presented as vividly as any. The pompous but goodhearted Baron Ravenclaw was the first to humble Boll, yet to no effect. The encounter between Boll and Ravenclaw, related by Virgin, is meant to give a foretaste of the changes in store for Boll. And there are only three things we know about Bertha, the wife of doomed Otto Pompmaster: that she invariably goes to bed at the same early hour, that she has extraordinarily fine teeth, and that she forbids the company assembled at the Golden Ball to drink coffee — but these details are enough to show her to us as a sister of Martha Boll, smug, obsessed with meaningless routine, but far less likely to break out of her circumscribed existence.

Bertha, together with nearly all the other characters, reminds us that the play converges upon large moral issues: the possibilities open to man in achieving self-fulfillment. This intense moral concern holds for the first two plays of Barlach, as indeed for all of them. Critics were quick to draw attention to one of the ancestors of his dramas, the miracle or mystery play, although Barlach himself rejected any such connections. The conflict between two generations in *The Genuine Sedemunds* recedes before the much larger attempt to define abstract genuineness, and in *The Flood* it is one kind of God pitted against another, signifying the choices that man must come to terms with. Even if they do not rest on traditional antitheses of good and evil, his plays nevertheless have the ring of a mystery play about them: moral forces brought to the human level, "made flesh," yet leading back, always, to the more than human.

To recapitulate, the major concerns of the plays collected here are these: the relation between a child and parent (or man and God), the limitations and reductions that are characteristic of man's physical existence, the perversions man has instituted to render that existence even more depraved, man's need for and path to self-transcendence, and the ideals by which that transcendence may be brought about. Barlach's remaining five plays touch on closely related questions. Their major themes are sketched here briefly to give an idea of his dramatic works as a whole.

In *The Dead Day* (1912), Barlach's first drama, which has the austere setting and nameless mythic figures of a Nordic saga, the fate of a son's commitment to life is explored. He is a weak son dominated by a brutal, earthbound mother, a son who fails partly through his own uncertainties and is partly prevented from riding away into sunnier worlds on a stallion provided by his spiritually freer, more positive, but blind father. On the side of the mother are enlisted malefic ghosts and gnomes who join to exploit the father's blindness. Her attempt to poison her son leads to both his death and hers. *The Poor Cousin* (1918), set in an innocuous vacation spot near Hamburg, begins with the attempted suicide of Hans Iver and ends with its consummation — nothing he or anyone else can think of saves him from his despair. This play looks forward to *The Genuine Sedemunds*, published two years later. Here too, threatened or actual violence rips the masks off innocent bystanders who would rather have left things as they were but who are now pushed into lacerating self-confrontations. In only one person is there a clear change for the better. In *The Foundling* (1922) Barlach creates even more bleakness: a devastated post-war countryside with a fleeing, suffering humanity and opportunists exploiting the disorganization. A man who is known as the red emperor is nominally in charge; cannibalism prevails. Isolated clusters of refugees appear, each more suspicious and terrified than the last. A crippled foundling, symbol of these twilight times, awakens the sympathy of one of the passing wretches and by divine grace is transformed into a beautiful child, a savior. The effect of an individual assuming wholly unselfish responsibility for another, re-enacted in more familiar surroundings in *The Blue Boll*, is to create a path, the dramatist asserts, to God. Another who purposely sets out on a search for God is the title figure of *The Baron of Ratzeburg* (1951), a quasi-historical drama posthumously discovered and never wholly finished by Barlach. Dissatisfied like Boll with the meaningless, trivial complications of life and its injustices, the baron joins a pilgrimage in search of a more human existence, in search of God. He endures great suffering and is taken into slavery. Encounters with a hermit and later with Moses reveal to him that serving God is not a command but a privilege that man torturously earns for himself. His return home causes only resentment; he becomes a source of complications. But he is able to save his illegitimate and unappreciative son's life by sacrificing his own. "I have no God, but God has me," he cries near his death. His companion in these painful journeys is Offerus, in search of the "highest master" whom he finds temporarily in Marut, a Calan-figure, but a more fiercely uncompromising, utterly ruthless destroyer than Calan. Barlach's last completed play was *The Good Time* (1929), which deals with an ideal society on a Mediterranean island in which all physical and spiritual complaints have been resolved, a society in which everyone carries "absolute insurance." The members think of themselves as god-like, but the "good time" is hollow: it cannot be had in this life. The heroine finds fulfillment in giving her life for that of a stranger.

Barlach often complained that his dramas were interpreted too "metaphysically," that critics and directors fell to subtilizing the meanings at the expense of the entertainment. And it is true that his dramatic resourcefulness results in brisk scenes full of surprises, in lyrical scenes and somber ones. He is a master of evoking many moods. As he said — and demonstrated: "I believe one is entitled to demand of the drama all or nothing, wherever it is a matter of expressing absolutely and radically a fundamental feeling." [12] But at the same time his unusual lan-

[12] *Aus Seinen Briefen*, p. 47.

guage, his metaphoric daring invariably give the impression that more is meant than said and that he invites each reader to grasp that meaning in his own way. Serious critics have come forward with substantially different interpretations of the same plays, attesting more to their vitality and richness than to their obscurity. Barlach wrote: "People want to 'know' and ask for the word, but the word is useless, at best a crutch for those who are satisfied to limp along. And nevertheless there is something in the word that presses into the innermost being when it comes from the loudest, that is, the absolute, truth. But each understands it differently, he hears that which becomes understandable to him, or rather, he becomes conscious of it according to his part in the whole." [18] This explains his unceasing innovations with language. His diction often shoots from abstract to concrete; he devises new word formations, and familiar words acquire so many and such specialized meanings that the reader feels he is in the midst of a new language. The multiplying uses of "lion" as a symbol and image in *The Genuine Sedemunds*, or of "power" in *The Flood*, or of "must" in *The Blue Boll* are examples. Now he has Calan describe God as a spark, now Old Sedemund pictures his soul as an invisible point. Along with such verbal daring goes his predilection for puns and for occasional euphuistic antitheses, and also his strategic use of several North German dialects, always assigned to characters of limited imagination but of common sense. These last are likely to have revealing names. If all these devices account for the flexibility of his style, they simultaneously invite ambiguities. Finally, one must mention his experiments with syntactic innovations: run-on sentences, purposely indefinite pronomial references, ellipses, and many others. They in turn produce the effect of a nervous breathlessness, of sudden ranges of emotional intensity, and give us the feeling of momentarily witnessing the birth of fateful issues. One is constantly amazed at the reserves available to Barlach: he appears to have said all that can be said but then pushes further — and takes the reader with him.

It is as though he dealt with language as with a block of cherrywood that he must destroy in order to create from it. Such a twofold attitude perhaps explains the fruition of his "double talent," his being driven

[18] *Leben und Werk*, p. 178.

now to the plastic arts, now to literature to convey and justify the fullness of his vision. It also explains the poetic quality of his dramas even when he chose the most ordinary small-town locales for them. (And, one may add, it explains the difficulties of his translator.) No great ingenuity is needed to show that the major theme of his plays — the striving toward a magnificent reality beyond and above the casual day-to-day existence — is beautifully exemplified by his language, his style.

All of his plays, especially the three printed here, have scenes and characters that cannot be described as other than grotesque. Instances are the leper's tirade in *The Flood* (Part V, Scenes 3 and 4), Old Sedemund's processions through hell (Scene 6), or the visitation of three cadavers in *The Blue Boll* (Scene 6). In *The Poor Cousin* there is a kind of witches' sabbath around a man called "Lady Venus" and a straw doll. These grotesque scenes usually take place toward the latter parts of the plays. With Barlach's humor at its most cutting and macabre, with the tone rising to a feverish pitch, these scenes form a kind of climax — man strutting in his material depravity, all flesh, all dross, and only remotely human. The grotesque is followed by scenes unusually sober and clear, as though catharsis has taken place, as though the attempt can *now* be made to formulate the constituents of transcendence.

It is tempting to speculate whether the grotesque is what Barlach failed to get into his sculpture and hardly into his graphic art, and whether he was therefore drawn to the stage to present it there in all its gaudiness, violence, even repulsiveness. Most of his sculptures embody individual man, ecstatic or expectant, caught in earthly forces and struggling with the here and now while longing for some supernatural event, suffused with intimations of a superhuman vision that will release him. The grotesque, which dwells on the precarious earthly entanglements, finds its visual form only in caricature, and caricature has always appeared inimical to the sculptor's art. It follows that one might regard the grotesqueries so prevalent in his dramas as a complement to the rest of his work, and, conversely, as the means of freeing him to endow his sculptures with that purity of solitude and that concentration with which they listen to a different drummer. He wrote in one of his letters: "Remember — matters being what they are — that it looks hopeless for us, so you must save yourselves, at least in spirit, to a worthier state, since after all you cannot all destroy yourselves." [14] The destructive element in his plays, to oversimplify, is embodied in the grotesque; that element must be purged before the truly human can find its grandeur in the more than human.

But it is that very shriek of grotesqueness that connects him with other Expressionist playwrights of his time. Indeed, it may be of value briefly to point out the additional links between his plays and theirs. Hand in hand with the grotesque goes the tone of the visionary, the prophet on the last verge of time exhorting man. This heightened tone that in Barlach and others frequently becomes incantatory, alternating with a falsetto, is not unusual in an Expressionistic dramatist who like Sorge attempted to "stage" a fugue-like music with strategic repetitions of themes and phrases. Furthermore, in much of the drama of the period one grows uncomfortably aware that the characters fail to communicate — as though they were just talking past one another. We find this in Barlach, and we find it in the dramas of Hans Jahnn, for example. Barlach shares the others' lack of interest in analyzing character and in justifying motives psychologically, nor is he concerned with the punctilious plotting of the well-made play. But, like those dramatists, Barlach is always aching to proclaim a dire need for reform, a new faith, with the same vigor with which Sternheim, for instance, asserted a universal nihilism.

Fundamentally, Barlach's plays are like the Expressionists' in that they are plays of ideas rather than character, but he was at great pains to delineate the *effect* of those ideas on his protagonists. Since they are apocalyptic ideas that demand nothing less than the reconstitution of man — best shown in Young Sedemund's Adamism, or at least the rediscovery of his true nature and true destiny — there is an urgency about this kind of drama that often veers toward exaggeration and in lesser playwrights to rodomontade. He partakes of the widespread desire to tear down the façade of nineteenth- and early twentieth-century optimism, behind which he too discerns a deep, despairing melancholia or else a defeated incomprehensibility of life. What Walter Sokel calls the "daemonization of everyday reality" took the form in Barlach of the

[14] *Aus Seinen Briefen*, p. 48.

grotesque, in Toller of the elevation of the machine to an archfiend, and in Kafka of the suspiciously casual manner of narration. But Barlach stands apart from the other Expressionists by adhering to a personally-conceived Christian drama of redemption, returning neither with Kokoschka to myth nor with Kaiser to clever reinterpretations of history. The movement in his plays is from a secularized, lost, misguided condition of man, encumbered by original sin, in which man often suffers unbeknown to himself, to a point at which a savior appears or salvation seems at least possible. But he demands a sacrifice. His first drama concludes with the line: "Strange that man does not want to learn that his father is God," and in his last, *The Good Time*, the heroine accepts her death with the realization that "her guilt is canceled." If Barlach's is the only truly religious attitude in the drama of the period, he shares the others' garrulous optimism in the possibilities of a new beginning. The youthfulness of the movement — some critics have called it a late flowering of romanticism — also re-echoes in his plays.

Moreover, he shares a pervasive desire to experiment with the potentialities of the stage and thus to disassociate himself from the naturalistic tradition. Herein the entire group was much influenced by Strindberg's late "dream plays." In addition to his attempt to refashion the language, Barlach paid close attention to visual presentation: lighting, long silences that call for pantomime (as in Hasenclever's dramas), quick shifts of scenes, the representation of great natural disasters on the stage, and so on. But even the more realistic settings, in, for example, *The Genuine Sedemunds* and *The Blue Boll*, afford visual shocks: the wooden figure of Christ in the first and the carved apostle in the second are meant to come briefly alive.

Barlach's prose presents the translator with a peculiar challenge — more, I think, than with any other modern author must he exercise the function of critic and interpreter while fulfilling the humbler role of translator. Barlach's attempts to push language beyond its limits create vexing problems. Uneasy compromises were necessary. As is well known, English is less hospitable than German to abstract key words like "becoming." But there was no choice. Or again, it was impossible to reproduce with any fidelity the North German dialects for which Barlach had such a sharp ear and which provide a good deal of the humor in *The Genuine Sedemunds* and *The Blue Boll*, although I have tried to come close with American idioms and colloquialisms. Perhaps the loss of some of his puns and his frequent alliterations is less serious.

I have taken a number of liberties. Whenever I could, I found English equivalents for German names, both of persons and of places; I simplified Barlach's syntax chiefly by reducing the number of run-on sentences in order to adapt them to more natural English prose rhythms; and I also simplified his punctuation, especially the exuberant use of dots, dashes, and exclamation marks. I well realize that my practice must strike the connoisseur of pure Expressionist prose with all its syntactic and typographical intoxication as somewhat adulterated wine. But I felt that a more sober presentation would allow the reader unfamiliar with Barlach to gain a clearer view of what is most essential in his plays.

THE FLOOD

A DRAMA IN FIVE PARTS

Cast of Characters

NOAH

AHIRE, HIS WIFE

SHEM, HAM, AND JAPHETH, HIS SONS

CALAN

CHUS, HIS SERVANT

A DISTINGUISHED TRAVELER

TWO ANGELS

AWAH

ZEBID

A HUNCHBACKED LEPER

THREE NEIGHBORS

A YOUNG SHEPHERD

A BEGGAR

Part I

1 ⸕ Desert. Evening.

A HUNCHBACKED LEPER: Are you still with me, my dear hump? (*Turns around to see.*) We're a devoted couple, you and I; I'm just sorry I'm not as handsome as you. But let's admit it — our third member is still the best — our beloved leprosy. If the robbers smell him, they rush away fast enough: he is our watch and ward, and he who gave him to us desires us to love and honor him. Somebody's coming dressed like a loafer. (*Turns to flee.*) Out of his sight, dear hump, so that he won't get angry and beat you in his wrath! Quick — away, away, leprosy and hump — wait, I'll go with you, good friends, all of us nicely together. (*Goes off.*)

A distinguished traveler makes his appearance. Two angels accompany him, one at each side.

FIRST ANGEL: We know you in all your shapes.

SECOND ANGEL: We find you in every place.

FIRST ANGEL: Everywhere —

SECOND ANGEL: Wherever you walk in the shape of your likeness.

FIRST ANGEL: That you made of clay.

SECOND ANGEL: Whom you love more than all of us, who were born of light and strength and fire.

FIRST ANGEL: Whatever your seeming in time's disguise, we always know your being.

SECOND ANGEL: We find you in every shape.

TRAVELER: They are not as they ought to be.

Angels are silent.

2 9

TRAVELER: They think thoughts I do not think.

Angels are silent.

TRAVELER: They want what I do not want.

Angels are silent.

TRAVELER: Speak!

FIRST ANGEL: You know!

SECOND ANGEL: They want what you do not want.

TRAVELER (*violently*): They are unlike me, and your thoughts say: who are you that they could become other than you wished? (*Quietly:*) I am sorry I made them.

FIRST ANGEL: Nevertheless, there is one who is as you willed him to be: your servant and your child.

TRAVELER: Then I am sorry for all the others.

The Angels cover their faces.

FIRST ANGEL: You — from eternity to eternity —

SECOND ANGEL: You — all beginning without end —

TRAVELER: I?

FIRST ANGEL: You — all splendor and all holiness —

SECOND ANGEL: You —greatness and goodness —

FIRST ANGEL: You the storm, you the silence —

SECOND ANGEL: You all seeming, you all being.

TRAVELER: And they — they should be different from me?

The Angels cover their faces.

TRAVELER: It must not be. Off with you in all directions — look for that man who is my servant and my child. Look for others like him, find many who can bear being called my handiwork: who are as they ought to be, who want what I want, who think as I will them to think. I am sorry for the others. (*Angels go off.*)

Bells are heard in the distance. Calan appears. He carries a rug and proceeds to spread it out.

TRAVELER: Your camels rest, your men are eating, and you are going to pray?

CALAN: I prefer to be alone, that is why I kneel apart.

TRAVELER: And pray?

CALAN: I'm talking to myself. If that is prayer, then I pray.

TRAVELER: Perhaps you have reason to thank the one who gave you the camels.

CALAN: I took the camels from one who took them from another. (*Points to his sword.*)

TRAVELER: Have you shed blood?

CALAN: Only my enemy's, his children's, his servants' — his wives are my wives now. I thank God that he gave me strength, speed, cunning, endurance, and courage — courage and the fine sense not to waver in adversity; eyes not blinded by the sight of blood, ears not invaded by horror when bleeding children cry. I thank him if he takes pleasure in my thanks.

TRAVELER: Do you suppose God takes pleasure in the cries of bleeding children?

CALAN: Why does he give them voices, if he is afraid of their crying? And how should he be afraid when I am not?

TRAVELER: You are a flaw: your wickedness is not *his* work, your wrath not *his* will, your deeds are not of *his* thoughts.

CALAN: Where was my evil conceived, if not in his evil? No, my wickedness also comes from him. He who laid me down in my wickedness, hatched me in wild blood, did no better than I who have beaten the children with my sword's edge until they bled.

TRAVELER: You have turned to evil. He will put his hand on your camels.

CALAN: Then he treats me as I treat my servants — afterwards he will be sorry he indulged himself, just as I am.

TRAVELER: If you loved him you would speak differently.

CALAN: Love — does he love me? I trust that he doesn't need my love and my prayer, nor does he let me prosper just because I do his will. Can I lift myself up to him, who is above all, when I am not? If he exists he knows nothing about me. I gladly allow him his provinces, but he must let me live in my way in my desert and in my tents. If he were like the one my pious neighbor talks about, if he needed praise and service and thanks and bondage, wanted obedience in return for mercy and fatherliness . . .

TRAVELER: What then?

CALAN: Then I would need to question and explore. My thanks and bondage might be a useless and bad bargain. A wretch would pity his poverty. Gifts and graces? And he milks me as I milk the stolen camels, makes cheese of my slavery, a cordial of my praise, butter of my thanksgiving . . . this is the question I would have to explore: is it crude to believe that the son is of the same breed as the father — free like him, master like him — just and good like him — growing strong and powerful from the strength of his majesty —— if it were not so, I would have to believe myself the stolen child of an unknown God, and badly cared for, unworthy of his father.

Chus comes running.

CHUS: Master . . .

CALAN: Why don't you speak?

CHUS: I am afraid, I am afraid —

CALAN: Speak without fear, Chus. Speak.

CHUS: An angry swarm of huge hornets attacked the camels, stung their eyes and nostrils, legs and bellies, drilled poison into their ears and rumps, and . . .

CALAN: And?

CHUS: Don't kill me, Master. We struggled with the fleeing herds but we ourselves were stung . . .

CALAN: So they are scattered?

CHUS: All scattered in the desert, and most of the men ran away in fear. Only I alone, Master, dared to stay. Don't kill me.

CALAN: I will act like Noah's invisible master: if you serve me well, count on my goodwill. Be faithful, fool, for faith is your advantage.

CHUS: I don't know what you mean. When the opportunity came I could have taken a horse like most of the others, could have stolen cattle and women. I did not, and I serve you in friendship. Truly, Master, I stayed of my own free will. (*Goes off.*)

TRAVELER: Did you hear? He stayed for love, although you are a hard master.

CALAN: I wonder why. Maybe it suits him here with me. I am fond of him, he is not like the others. Yes, if he were not my servant he might be my son. They stole the women? But surely not Awah, the one who shared my tent from one full moon to the next? (*Starts to go.*)

TRAVELER: Don't forget to give thanks if God should put your property back into your hands; make an offering; give Noah, who is God's

friend and God's servant, a part of your goods. And say to him: behold, thus God rewards his children.

CALAN (*laughing*): If I get the camels back he shall have the woman. He
really shall!

2 ⸏ Open space between Noah's tents. A grove in the background. The
Leper sneaks by and looks around idly. Noah and his three sons enter and
drive him away.

NOAH: The morning is like a man saying his prayers, friendly and thankful,
and we — we are in it and it is around us. Bring me a kid, one of the
youngest.

JAPHETH: I suppose we won't need the whole animal? The entrails are fine
for a daily burnt offering.

SHEM: Use one of the many piglets. They smell as good and burn as readily
as a kid.

HAM: I kept the wolves from the pasture last night. I'm tired and want to
sleep. (*He goes off into the next tent.*)

NOAH: Just when my heart is full of thankfulness, when I really feel a great
joy in the freshness of the morning — as if the fat of the land were puls-
ing up from my feet through all my limbs into my heart and head and
then dissolved into gentle, quiet well-being — then you pull long faces
and cool my kindling thanks with artful contradictions. Who wants to
make offering for blessings in a sour spirit? At least wash your hands,
children, to offer up your meager thanks.

SHEM: You gave Ham a wife, but you let the two of us run around the
neighborhood, to be beaten up by furious fathers.

JAPHETH: We are supposed to work and give thanks besides! I feel a kind
of thankfulness myself when I can lie around and be lazy with all my
heart. That's my kind of offering.

NOAH: You shall have wives and wives will drive out your laziness. Believe
me, I love you — and oh, I too lived lightly along until the worries came,
and the blessings with them. It worries me to see you dissatisfied.

SHEM: Oh yes, it worries him! I heard him tell our mother: I will have no
intermarriage with the godless. He wants daughters who are pleasing
to God, as if it didn't matter much more what kind of wives *we* want.

3 3

JAPHETH: I worry about his worries. But our children mustn't be born pitiful because of them. I want a woman with firm flesh, or all the trouble is for nothing — pleasing to God, no — there on the other side of the river they are certainly not pleasing to God, but it's enough for me if they please me.

NOAH: You are godless boys indeed. But courage, God has powerful scythes for your sins.

Ahire enters with a pitcher on her shoulder. She is elderly and fat.

AHIRE (*stops in passing and puts her hand on her head*): The full moon shone on my head last night. When I opened my eyes it was as bright as day and I couldn't go back to sleep — there is war somewhere in the north. I saw creeping smoke and I smelled burning. May God preserve us from our enemies.

NOAH: May God preserve us. Our servants are in the mountains with the herds. Defenseless as we are, may God preserve us.

SHEM: Weren't we going to slaughter and offer up a kid?

JAPHETH: Let's go, Shem. We'll find a handsome animal for the offering. (*Both go off.*)

NOAH: Even so, they are good children. Sometimes choosy and difficult the way children are, after all. Dear God, Japheth, the poor thing, was born with a queer look, one has to love him twice as much because of it. God willed it, let God be praised. (*He picks up the pitcher and carries it a few steps.*)

AHIRE: But because of it he has it harder than the handsome Ham and sturdy Shem.

NOAH (*putting pitcher down*): Well, do you think so? (*Wipes off sweat.*) The sun really burns. In what way is he less favored, do you think?

AHIRE: With women, for instance.

NOAH: Oh, with women! Many a man took a wife with a wandering look, and in the end cross-eyed Japheth's wife may be as beautiful as another man's, and good besides — what more does he want? So it will be better, when he is tormented by her great loveliness, for *him* to have the queer look than for her. There, there — neighbors are coming to call on me, let me receive them. I would gladly carry the pitcher farther. (*He helps her pick it up. She goes and he looks after her, shaking his head.*) Have my eyes stayed so young? That they would gladly be entangled in a fresh web of loveliness and lightness and pleasure? She is not light, not fresh, not pleasurable, but a good pious woman, a very good woman. *Three neighbors come. There are greetings.*

FIRST NEIGHBOR: Noah — (*He spits, nudges the second.*) You go on.

SECOND NEIGHBOR: It was good enough, you know it better than I.

THIRD NEIGHBOR: You overreached yourselves in being wise before — now your wisdom has fallen on its face.

NOAH: Step into the shade under the canopy. Take these rugs and allow me to draw cool water and bring you a refreshing drink.

FIRST NEIGHBOR: Nothing to drink, but we'll sit down. (*They sit.*) Listen, Noah!

SECOND NEIGHBOR: That's the way, no drink but we'll sit. And now, listen Noah!

NOAH: I am listening, dear friends, but I wish you would allow me to refresh you. But as you like . .

FIRST NEIGHBOR: Listen, Noah. Your herds are getting big, your herds are growing very big.

SECOND NEIGHBOR: Very big, that's right, listen, very big.

NOAH: God gave them to me. I took the riches that blossomed around me, I held the cup and let the great mercy fill it.

THIRD NEIGHBOR: Now then, about your herds, Noah.

FIRST NEIGHBOR: Very big. The pasture here in the river valley is becoming too scant for all of us. Who ought to give way, Noah, I put it to you — which of us should give way?

NOAH: Which of us should give way?

FIRST NEIGHBOR: Should or will, who will give way? The three of us have considered it. We don't want to. But who wants to? One must.

SECOND NEIGHBOR: Only one.

THIRD NEIGHBOR: Because of the size of the herds that God's mercy gave him. Nobody else — he himself says it — and so he must yield because of God's great mercy. There is going to be a drought this summer — it has been dry much too long now. The big herds will find no fodder.

NOAH (*half to himself*): My servants are in the mountains with the cattle — I am alone with my sons.

Silence. The three neighbors look at each other. The First Neighbor nudges the Second.

THIRD NEIGHBOR: Your men won't be back.

FIRST NEIGHBOR: He's right. They're going to stay up there.

SECOND NEIGHBOR: God allowed it, he willed that they should die. It was pleasing to him.

NOAH: Even so, let God be praised.

FIRST NEIGHBOR: But the animals are alive, heavy animals, goldmines of blood and fat, but . . .

SECOND NEIGHBOR: But the mercy ran into our cup. We took what ran over out of plenty.

Noah rises. The three others remain seated.

FIRST NEIGHBOR: He will give way. You see, he yields.

SECOND NEIGHBOR: I could have foretold it.

THIRD NEIGHBOR: He trembles in his great haste, his knees are shaking with concealed hurry. He gives way.

NOAH (*short of breath, addressing the Second*): You are right, he allows it. Therefore what you do to me pleases him — all dead? Peleg too and Put, Put also?

THIRD NEIGHBOR (*to the First*): Is that the fat one who screamed so mercilessly? It still hurts my ears. (*To Noah:*) I must say, Put was no credit to you — a lout, a noisemaker — they're all dead, but he had very little talent for dying.

Japheth appears and stands quietly, surprised. The three look at each other, questioning and considering.

JAPHETH: The kid is in its place, Father. We were wondering where you were.

NOAH: Oh my dear Japheth — yes, we will offer up a sacrifice, we will offer a kid and praise God — (*weeping*) — praise God and give thanks. (*He goes off with Japheth.*)

THIRD NEIGHBOR: You blockheads! You have swords under your clothes and still give him a chance to come to his senses?

FIRST NEIGHBOR: I thought you were supposed to do it — don't you have one?

THIRD NEIGHBOR: It's too hot for me — and before he bled to death one of his sons might have come around. About Ham now, I want you to understand, I don't want to finish off Ham with the others. My daughter Zebid arranged it. Ham must live. No, today it would require too great a hurry.

FIRST NEIGHBOR: Too great a hurry, you're quite right. By the time we could get home the sun would be high in the heavens, and I already had a bad time on the way over. The longer we sit here in the shade the more we'll have to sweat outside. (*They stand up slowly.*)

SECOND NEIGHBOR: They say there are countries where it rains for whole days together, but I don't believe it. (*All go off.*)

HAM (*looks after them from the tent*): No, they're not in a hurry, but stand still and turn their heads. Are there three? It's not three any more, how did that happen? Are they meeting others and holding a council? That could be evil counsel for us. Well . . . well . . . Now I see the sky between them: three are getting shorter, disappearing behind the hill, the other two — a man and a woman — are coming closer. A young woman, a very young woman — the burden of the sun's fire dances around her shoulders. Calan, Calan is the man. Is he coming with a sword under his clothes too?

Noah enters with Shem and Japheth.

NOAH: Both of you stay back. Ham, you go with them too — tell your mother as I told you that whatever God allows to happen must be his own doing and shows his power. Tell her that, and she will teach you how light the burdens grow if — oh, how much I have to talk, while you stand there with your mouths open, hear nothing of the resounding voice which penetrates through skin and bone into the heart — go — I want to receive him alone.

Shem, Ham, Japheth go off.
Calan and Awah enter. She is veiled.

NOAH: Welcome Calan! You are stopping with a poor man. I walk with invisible crutches, and oh — how easily they too could break!

CALAN: You are as rich, and richer, than you were, friend Noah. As rich as you were before, because when I came home yesterday and heard what had happened, I went at daybreak and took everything from your three good neighbors — their own and their stolen herds. I, who am great and strong and powerful, took the herds and shut them up away from them. All you need do is go and count out your property to the last hoof. My servant Chus stands with his legs spread wide to guard your goods. I was lucky, Noah.

NOAH (*breathless*): Oh how hard it is to bear God's wrath, and then almost harder to bear his mercy.

CALAN: Wait. I was saying, you are richer than you were before. I promised to make God an offering in return for his help when I was threatened with the loss of much property, and look — I am offering up my sacrifice. Take this treasure from distant lands — where the earth lifts up to touch the sky. (*Points to Awah:*) She is good, Noah, and it is good to live with her. Be content, God's mercy deals out gifts with a magnificent hand. You have deserved it. (*To Awah:*) Go to your master and kiss his feet.

Awah unveils and bows down before Noah.

NOAH: All the cattle, Calan, all the fat strong cattle and the beautiful young bulls too?

CALAN: Every horn and hoof! Awah is her name.

NOAH: Come Awah, come Calan. Step into the shade, lie down and rest. You shall be refreshed. Rest.

Awah rises. They sit down. Noah remains standing and rubs his hands.

CALAN: Take good care of her, friend Noah, she is of distinguished family. If she cries, think your own thoughts and walk around her with a light step.

NOAH (*sighing*): All my men — Jebel, Put, and Peleg with them — those who were my friends, are murdered. I must weep in the midst of this great good fortune. Kir, who never did anything but laugh, hardly more than a child and already wise and so willing — all gone!

CALAN: Not all, Noah: they lied to you like dogs. Well, it's true Put and Peleg are dead — they were cut down fast. A few others got away wounded, and a good number were camped in a neighboring valley. At the first noise they drove the cattle up higher and hid in caves and craters. No, on the whole, Noah, your luck has held up well.

NOAH: My wife and sons sit together in unhappiness . . . (*He hesitates.*)

CALAN: Why do you hesitate? Call them and let them rejoice too.

NOAH (*looking at Awah*): You have brought me great good fortune, and great restlessness, Calan. — He allows it, and thus it is pleasing to him — does he allow it?

CALAN: She is your property, and you must take care of it. I am as good to you — if not better — than your invisible friend. How would it be if you gave me a place beside him, let me, instead of him, take care of things for you? Don't be afraid, you will have no burdens added to your old ones: no services, no sacrifice, no thanksgiving. Although I am only an unimportant god, you have ears to hear my word and — best of all — eyes to bear witness that I am. Look here, Noah, for the kind of demands you're likely to make I am as good as he is. He permitted what was contrary to your best interest — fortunately for you I was able to prevent it.

NOAH: Oh oh oh, Calan — (*choking:*) I owe him thanks for my existence. Gratitude, Calan, is my best fortune. I don't breathe if I can't give thanks.

CALAN: Fine. You shall go on thanking and offering, Noah. I am not jealous, as he is, of other gods beside me. I will let you be idolatrous, and will not call you godless if you don't serve and praise me. No services, no bondage, Noah, and not even obedience. I want you to be free before me — not servile, as you are before him.

NOAH: My heart stops beating in horror. Calan, if leprosy eats me, can you heal me?

CALAN: But I will not strike you with pain, sorrow, or sickness. You will not be called my creation to suffer from the faults of your master. He formed you with the gift of yourself, but how often you have to curb your own will when it wants to lead you to your own pleasure — if you want, those three others, your murderous neighbors, shall yield to you. Do you want it?

NOAH: If God doesn't want it, I don't either.

CALAN: After you've asked him, tell me if you are allowed to want. He put you into their hands, I put them in your hands — I see you have only a pitiful knowledge of God, and no trust in him at all. Why don't you say: yes, I want it? If he doesn't agree, and if he is stronger than I am, he can always put you back into their power. Perhaps your will doesn't come from him at all, if you can doubt whether your will is his; or didn't he himself know what he wanted when he gave you your will? But there's no hurry, I am more patient than he, if he punishes his own creation for its shortcomings. You can sleep on it — but pick up your animals and make use of my servants until yours have found their way back to you. (*He goes off.*)

NOAH (*slumps, burying his head in his hands*): O God, how difficult you are to understand — you made me and made Calan, my sons, my wife, and — (*He looks up and looks at Awah:*) And this one?
Ahire comes.

NOAH (*embracing her*): Let your heart leap up, Ahire, as it did in our best days. Don't speak, don't ask, but feel only how good it is to breathe freely. Everything is ours again, our want is over, we are as great as we were before — let the burdens fall from your heart, let joy gently touch your soul.

AHIRE: Our sons are cowering together in a little band, but I — oh, I would gladly have died with you, Noah. Calan was here with you, what did he bring you?

NOAH: He took everything from them and gave it back to us, every horn and every hoof. We need only take.

AHIRE: I must weep to wash away my fear. Let me sit down, and sit down with me and let me weep, weep a long time — weep and in between ask questions and smile at you. It pleases me so, to recover slowly from sorrow, Noah: to take small steps to the great joy. Come sit with me and take my arm. (*She sees Awah.*) Who is she?

NOAH: Awah is her name. She is Calan's sacrifice, offered up in return for God's help.

AHIRE: To me? As a maidservant, as a child — as a child, Noah? (*She puts her arms around Awah.*)

NOAH: No — to me, Ahire. Given to me and for my own.

AHIRE: To you — not to me? (*She looks from one to the other.*) Give her to me, Noah. Look, my weeping, my happy weeping, is lost in expectancy. Yes, Noah, you must give her to me as my own.
She has released Awah, stands a little apart, and studies her. Awah is frightened, rushes to Noah and embraces his knees.

NOAH: I know, you don't want to let me enjoy her, Ahire. Why do you desire her?

AHIRE: Japheth shall have her. Japheth holds tight to what he has. She is the right one for Japheth.

NOAH: Japheth? Japheth? Poor child!

4 0

AHIRE: There are little boys running around the neighborhood — father-less children and maids' bastards — Japheth's boys, let me tell you, an evil brood is in the making, and the less one wants to hear about it, the more violent one's anger. All that has to come to an end, Noah. And if now there should be children playing and rolling around, chil-dren born of you and her — why, if God wants to permit it, I will not. She shall be Japheth's wife, and Japheth knows how to increase his property, better than you do. (*She shakes herself.*) I don't want to weep any more at all.

NOAH: Poor child!

AHIRE: When your herds and men were stolen, you said: God willed it. Is this foreign thing dearer to you than herds and men?

NOAH: If God would strike me blind, this could be solved, but God left me my eyes. Be gentle with me, because my good eyes make me as pitiable as Japheth with his squinting ones. We both deserve your forbear-ance — I don't want to see Japheth's brood — neither out there, nor inside with me.

AHIRE: I don't suppose your poor eyes alone will make this poor child rich. Give her to Japheth — Japheth's eyes need her more than yours. — They are coming, Noah, our sons are coming; say yes, will you say yes? I would curse God if he let you say no — I'll curse him with my next word unless you say yes.

NOAH: Don't curse, Ahire. God does not wish to be cursed, he doesn't want it to come to that. (*To Awah:*) Go — go to her. You are her child.
Ahire clutches her. She screams once softly.
Shem, Ham, and Japheth come.

Part II

1 ꜰ Desert.

THE HUNCHBACKED LEPER: Are you still with us, dear hump, and our beloved leprosy too? Come on, come on, before somebody hits us. (*Sneaks away.*)

THE FLOOD

A Beggar on crutches goes by with dragging steps. Two Angels meet him, stand at right and left.

FIRST ANGEL: We know you in all your shapes.

SECOND ANGEL: We find you everywhere.

FIRST ANGEL: Wherever you stay.

SECOND ANGEL: In the likeness of your image . . .

FIRST ANGEL: Of man, whom you love more than all of us, who were born of light and strength and fire.

SECOND ANGEL: Of the earth-clod, whose misery you have flung around your shoulders.

BEGGAR: Your talk is silence. You veil your will in words.

FIRST ANGEL: We will as you will.

SECOND ANGEL: And cannot want, except as you will. But they can want otherwise.

FIRST ANGEL: Men can want otherwise.

Beggar gestures humbly.

FIRST ANGEL: Earth is bad material for your work — there is wolfseed in her. Earth permeates man with her being, nourishes him with wolf's milk.

SECOND ANGEL: What the children suck from the mothers starts from their eyes like fiery wrath.

FIRST ANGEL: It tangles them together in packs so that they run wild through the world like beasts.

SECOND ANGEL: Fathers beget their wives, mothers bear their husbands.

FIRST ANGEL: They build houses for animals and clay images, they give their own deformed gods your majesty and grandeur.

SECOND ANGEL: Your image has become an abomination.

FIRST ANGEL: Your world has fallen into madness.

BEGGAR (*shaking his head*): And what about Noah?

FIRST ANGEL: Your child and servant Noah?

SECOND ANGEL: Noah is the only one among them all.

BEGGAR: I want to see him. Go and announce me to him.

Angels silent; the Beggar makes a pleading motion.

FIRST ANGEL: You, all splendor and all holiness?

SECOND ANGEL: You, greatness and goodness?

FIRST ANGEL: You the storm, you the silence?

SECOND ANGEL: You, all seeming, you all being?

BEGGAR: Tell him he shall see me with his eyes, touch me with his hands. No more, nothing about my appearance, nothing about my dress. Go. *Angels go off. He limps on, talking to himself pitifully.*
I'm sorry, I'm sorry I did it. They shall rot. I will root them out and drown them, sink them — forget them, forget, forget! Spawned from a false seed, they are not my children, not mine. They were poured out in overflowing love, but born as shameless hate. Bastards, bastards, bastards! (*With his crutch he threatens the expanse about him.*)

2 ⸕ Near Noah's tents. The Leper darts past. Japheth and Shem.

JAPHETH: Strange, how different she is from all the others. Almost mute, she's the humble servant of your whims, but high and mighty in a way that makes you think she washes herself all the time just because you've touched her. It's no comfort being with her, I'd much rather have that fat Zebid for my wife.

SHEM: I'd try it with her though, if worst comes to worst, Japheth.

JAPHETH: What, with your clumsy messing around? Ha — I know how to handle her better than that! That's a laugh — Shem.

SHEM: It just slipped out like that. I'm as serious about Awah as you are about Zebid.

JAPHETH: That's an uplifting piece of seriousness, at least in words and thoughts!

SHEM: And that's just how I meant it — but Ham makes a quite different face, one that means more than words and thoughts. How often he takes her in to his wife, where she's nursing her little doll, as if the world needed her example. And in between laughing and rejoicing all kinds of unintentional things happen — you get absent-minded and easily put things that belong in someone else's pocket into your own. I know all about that.

JAPHETH: You know about that?

SHEM: I'm no worse than the rest of you characters — I just don't fool myself. And Father Noah himself, by day no zest and at night no rest — always staring straight ahead: he sees her even with his eyes closed.

JAPHETH: The old ones are the worst. I've known that a long time.

4 3

SHEM: Idolatry, nothing else! No matter how he scratches, he's still got the itch. Doesn't he look quite affable when she laughs at the way he runs on about God, which happens often enough? Then she looks up and around, and feels behind the walls to see if he's standing there. She thinks God is his father or cousin or fourth son, hiding in a corner somewhere, but maybe he'll yawn or sneeze sometime — that there may be something not quite right about his looks, that he's lost his shape. God haunts her soul, it's no more than that, but still he's in it, in her and with her — it's something she has, and holds onto. Come on, we have to dig holes and set traps before the wolves and wild children outnumber us. (*Both off.*)

Ahire enters.

AHIRE: They all talk only about Awah, and the things I don't hear, I see. All these new expressions and looks, this unfamiliar stopping and going and turning around, waiting and waving — Awah — nothing but Awah!

Awah enters, carrying a lamb in her arms.

AHIRE: Are you coming from the pasture outside, Awah?

AWAH (*nodding*): Father gave it to me. I'm just afraid God will eat it. I'm going to take it to bed with me, if he comes I'll scratch.

AHIRE: And what will Japheth say to that, as both young and old sheep always have lice?

Awah puts the lamb down, begins to undress and shake her clothes out.

AHIRE: But look, Awah, Shem is still standing behind those trees — and how you've uncovered yourself! You should be more afraid of Shem's glances than of lice, Awah — run into the tent, finish your business behind skins and blankets. (*Shakes finger at Shem.*)

Noah, with gestures of humility, leads in the two Angels.

NOAH: Rest under my roof, delight my soul with your stay. No other place would serve you with its life and its all, as this one will, between my tents and near this grove. It all comes from God, it is all yours. Ahire, don't stand there, get busy, pour water into your best dishes. I'll help you carry if none of the children come. Awah — oh Awah!

AWAH: Who are they, Father?

NOAH: God's messengers, Awah, messengers with God's words on their tongues. (*He embraces Awah impulsively.*) Child, oh Awah, please

44

rejoice. Ahire, what are you waiting for, we have to butcher — let's get busy — but quietly, children, move quietly, honor our guests with actions as soundless as silent prayers.

Ahire steals away, frightened. The Angels smile, Awah claps her hands in delight, Shem watches fearfully from the distance.

FIRST ANGEL: We will rest and wash the dust from our feet.

SECOND ANGEL: Make whatever arrangements you wish for us.

NOAH: The lamb I gave to Awah — Shem, come quickly, kill the lamb and give it to your mother to roast.

Shem realizes he is discovered and fearfully withdraws further. In the background Ahire motions to Awah. Awah goes out, returns carrying a heavy jug of water.

NOAH: Ahire, Shem, what are you waiting for, what are you afraid of? They're afraid, Awah — how can they be afraid?

Awah kneels to wash the Angels' feet. Noah carries the lamb off. The Angels smile and Awah smiles back. She dries their feet with her hair, caresses their knees and thighs.

AWAH: Tell me where I can find God.

FIRST ANGEL: He will come and you shall see him.

SECOND ANGEL: You shall see him and not know him.

AWAH: See him and not know — no, if he is as beautiful as you I will recognize him.

FIRST ANGEL: I will kiss your eyes and you will recognize him. (*Does so.*)

SECOND ANGEL: I will touch your ears and you will feel his voice. (*Does so.*)

AWAH: Will he come soon?

FIRST ANGEL: He is near.

SECOND ANGEL: He will eat of your lamb.

FIRST ANGEL (*rising*): The day carries us away.

SECOND ANGEL (*rising*): Time pulls at our feet.

FIRST ANGEL: Tell Noah he will see him.

SECOND ANGEL: Promise him, he will touch him.

They go. Awah throws herself to the ground crying. Noah enters.

NOAH: They wouldn't let me go — (*upset*) — are you alone, Awah? Where — where — angels of the Lord, God's messengers, holy ground where your feet walked! (*Stumbles, falls down beside Awah, kisses her hands.*) Your hands touched them, your soul weeps for them — give me some of your weeping, give me of your pain — share with me, Awah.

AWAH: He is coming, they announced that he is near. You shall touch him and you shall see him. You shall see God. He is coming, God is coming.

NOAH: See — see God? With my own eyes? (*Terrified:*) He who gave me sight to judge cows and calves would cast the power of his eternal light on my eyes? Two mouseholes to harbor the image of the highest on high? They will crack open, burn up, they will be blinded. (*Stands up.*) Ahire is right, Shem is right — it was an apparition, a mockery, it was illusion and lies. Up, Awah, get out of my sight, hide in the dark of your house, go on crying in the corner — but watch out, my grief may break out in anger. Up — out. Bah, bah, nothing but idol-worship and madness. (*He pushes her away and crouches down, sullen and despairing, in the shady corner under the canopy.*)

JAPHETH (*running*): Something flew past me like hot wind — as if clothed in a liquid web of sunbeams — two talking giants with rushing and panting and swarming and slipping of wings of air on their heels — over me, passing through me, they ground me between their words like millstones — Father, Father, how frightened I was.

NOAH: You too, all of you were afraid. You are joyless, without freedom, without peace — only Awah and I are different — oh God, oh God, give me back my joy — intelligence is anxiety, caution is fear.

Ahire and Shem come back.

NOAH: Talk together, but I am deaf. I will not and cannot hear, covered by grief and buried in bitterness. (*They surround him and all look at him.*) Oh fool, fool, fool, to let myself be duped by your prudence, oh the torture of lost bliss. (*He is enraged.*) Go somewhere — don't stand and look at me — I let myself get confused by your windy words, held back by your resinous hands, while joy, peace, and freedom departed. Suffering, dear suffering, is all I have left — leave me my suffering, leave me that little bit of lost pleasure. Go — all of you, go!

Ahire looks at him fearfully, Shem shrugs his shoulders, Japheth turns and goes. Ahire and Shem follow. Noah plucks some grass and chews on it. Calan saunters in.

CALAN (*listening*): You can hear it all the way up here: the cattle are bellowing for water. (*Noah ignores him.*)

CALAN: Yes, Noah, it's settled. A lot of cattle are going to die.
Noah chews.

CALAN (*sitting down with him*): Pray for rain, but for a lot of rain, more than a handful. How do you do it anyway? I've already tried it, but it didn't work. I'd like to learn the trick — if it helps, prayer is a fine thing.

NOAH: Your prayer has nothing in common with mine.

CALAN: I think it does. Noah, let us both organize a sacrifice. Everything is ready, the sacrifice and the suppliants. You make the sacrifice and I'll watch and learn from you. Just lately I got my hands on a young, handsome, spotlessly healthy, curly-haired shepherd from across the ravine, and my man, Chus, is bringing him now. He's made to be sacrificed — a showpiece of a sacrifice. Look, that's why I came — your putting Awah to bed with your sweaty-skinned Japheth won't offend me. Her first son is mine, anyway, and once he's born I don't care what happens.

NOAH (*staring straight ahead*): — as if dressed in a liquid web of sunbeams, that's how they go by —

CALAN: What are you whimpering about?

NOAH: Joy, peace, and freedom pass over and through him —

CALAN: Noah!

NOAH: He was ground by their words as if between millstones! (*Defensively:*) Calan, Calan, what do I care whether Awah's first son is Japheth's or yours — two speaking giants like hot wind! Why don't you listen, two talking giants and panting and rushing and slipping of wings — (*He sobs.*)
Chus comes with the young Shepherd.

CALAN: The sacrifice, Noah, wake up!

NOAH: God takes no pleasure in human sacrifice. It is an abomination to him.

CALAN: My dear Noah, God will take what we offer him. He doesn't sniff at the meat, but judges according to the giver's heart. If you give gladly, he'll take gladly.

NOAH: He alone is master of this man's death or life, Calan.

CALAN: Not he, but I. And I make you the judge.

NOAH: Take him back. A man is not a thing, like an animal.

47

CALAN: But you did take Awah and offered her up to Japheth. Evasions, Noah, — we must have a sacrifice!

NOAH: I will not cut into a man's flesh, I will not butcher God's child, I shed no blood, God will not let himself be mocked. Thou shalt not kill.

CALAN: If you could sacrifice Awah to Japheth, God will allow me my sacrifice too. I am determined to try out your God, Noah. I have friendly intentions toward him and he will recognize my good faith.

NOAH: I don't want to be your accomplice, Calan.

CALAN: But God let him fall into my hands. God sent the drought and makes the country poor. Apparently he needs a sacrifice, Noah — and just look at him, isn't this a gift worthy of God?

NOAH (to Shepherd): Don't be afraid. Your life is in God's hands.

CALAN: Have you decided what to do about my proposal? Shall I stand next to God before you? I am strong and powerful and gracious. If *he* is master of life and death, *I* am not behind him in that.

NOAH: Calan, your power is great, but God's is greater. You are a man, and he does not want idolatry. Take pity on me and don't torture me with such desires. You are going to be poor too, Calan, poor because of the drought and according to God's will.

CALAN (grinning): Oh no, Noah, not poor, that's not the point. For whatever God takes from me in the drought, I will reimburse myself with from the full treasuries of distant lands. And reimburse you Noah, you too — don't be afraid of God and his drought. God's drought is my servant and helper, and yours too, Noah, yours as well.

NOAH: I serve him also in drought.

CALAN: I'll have to show you that I am as mighty as God. (*To Chus:*) Take him behind the trees of the grove and cut off both his hands, then bring both hands back here. (*To Noah:*) If he lets it happen, I will take it as a sign that the sacrifice pleases him, or else that his wrath is powerless against even my inferior godhead. In that case he would be lower than I — I would not even call him master of this drought. (*Chus off with Shepherd.*) We'll see, Noah, we'll see — *he* or *I*, *he* or *I*!
Noah wrings his hands.

CALAN: Are you afraid his power won't be great enough? My word can cut off hands — hear whether his word saves them. (*Screams are heard.*) Who do you say, Noah — who is master, if not I?

NOAH: Say another word, Calan. (*Screams continue.*) Kill him outright and stop the screams reverberating in my bowels. Speak, Calan, speak.

CALAN: What, just to soothe your insides? Ask the other one that, Noah. The sacrifice is done. Let him get his fill of screaming, because there are many who cry out, yet their cries are not drowned in his mercy. Let him trouble to say the word, if he likes quiet. I gave the offering. Now it belongs to him, let him do with it as he pleases. (*Chus enters, carrying two bloody hands.*) That's fine, Chus, you can nail them to the post here. Let him see that Calan does not take back a gift. *Chus does as he is told.*

CALAN (*to Noah, who covers his ears*): Take your hands away, hear what your God grants you to hear. Anyway, if he lets him scream he must enjoy the noise, it must tickle his bowels. Or could it be that even if he wanted quiet, his word would be powerless?

NOAH: I spit on you, Calan, I spit on you. (*Spits.*)

CALAN: On me, Noah? That comes as a great surprise — on me?

NOAH: On your act, Calan, on your abominable action. (*Spits.*) Butcher — murderer — sadist!

CALAN: I am more and more surprised, Noah.

NOAH: Shame on you, monster, raving tempter of God!

CALAN: Why, Noah, it's you who are raving. I don't begrudge God more beauty than mine, but are his actions really less shameful than mine — that is, if what happened really was shameful — if it was, Noah, if it was? If it was shameful, then it was shameful to watch, to allow, to listen, the way this pretty God and this pious Noah did — shameful, shameful.

NOAH: Do you think that I, a peaceful old man who puts his great trust in God, should stay your hand?

CALAN: Do you *not* think so? When you put your trust in God, perhaps God put his trust in Noah. And in the midst of so much trust and confidence, I became a butcher and torturer. Will you promise me to spit on God if it turns out that he let the sacrifice take place, although he despised it? That would make me a murderer only because of my longing for God's heart and because of God's omission. Look here, Noah, that makes God the murderer of my innocence — don't you see that?

NOAH: Poor, horrible Calan, where can we find peace and joy and freedom for you?

CALAN: Don't worry about that — I'm not a man of your kind. I am the child of a greater God than yours, a child of God, Noah, a child dethroned, lost, stolen, abused, and neglected, but a God! Who was that looking around the corner?

NOAH: Around the corner? I saw nothing.

CALAN: I did. Look, here it comes skipping across the path again — a pretty bowlegged gnome, a queer little old man — take the sack from that fence, Chus, run after him and catch him. (*Chus hesitates, confused, but then understands Calan's stern look and a secret signal and goes.*) Really, I think you're ashamed of him — but it was certainly he, Noah. Be a man, Noah, and admit it — it was he, God himself jumped across the path.

NOAH: He? A little old man, a gnome — enough blasphemy, Calan, I am ashamed for you.

Chus returns, bringing the sack, but is still uncertain whether he has understood Calan's whim correctly.

CALAN: Well done, Chus, tie him up and let's have him. There! I know it must be he — he couldn't look any different — and I can certainly understand why you'd want to lie to get a God like this off your neck. If it's all right with you, I'll take him along and have some fun with him — maybe he's smart enough to train. (*Shakes the sack.*) What a catch, Noah's God in a straw sack! But let me tell you, if he bites I'll beat him. Now I am sorry I cut that poor fellow's hands off for nothing — he's much too good for a God like this.

NOAH: You blaspheme, Calan, you blaspheme, blaspheme. (*Buries his face in his hands.*)

The old Beggar on crutches appears and stands beseechingly in front of him. Noah looks up.

BEGGAR: The wolfchildren attacked me. I am torn, ragged, and bleeding. Take pity on me! (*Shows his wounds.*)

CALAN: They did right to rough you up a little. Better for you to be food than eat it.

Noah stands up slowly, approaches, deeply shaken.

BEGGAR (*awkward and trustful*): Look, a stone hit my chin, and I have scratchmarks all over — beatings, so many beatings. I'm hungry, too. (*He looks at Noah, smiling.*)

NOAH: Beatings? And you're hungry too?

BEGGAR: I'm so thin and old, I'm helpless and don't need much. (*He smiles.*) And still I have to go hungry.

NOAH: And you come to *me* for food?

BEGGAR (*quietly*): Yes, to you, Noah, to you.

NOAH (*shyly*): Oh the time — what a lot of time has passed since then —

BEGGAR (*quietly*): And you have grown old and almost a stranger — how this long time has changed you! (*They look at each other, trying harder and harder to recognize one another.*)

NOAH: Won't you come closer?

BEGGAR: You won't drive me from your door, will you? Won't set your dogs on me? I am very lonely in the world, and I only dared come from so far because I thought you would take me in. I had a lot of trouble on the way. And still — you look so different.

NOAH: Oh Father — from what far distance have you come to me?

BEGGAR: I can't stay long, either. I just wanted to see you and be refreshed.

NOAH: So you're still in this life after all, poor old Father. But why must you drag yourself so painfully through the world?

BEGGAR: The former time has forgotten me, Noah, and I have lost touch with it, I am confused and have lost my way. But now I am with you, my son, Noah.

NOAH (*falls at his feet, embraces his knees, rises again and looks at him searchingly*): Is it you, Father?

BEGGAR: Yes, Noah, it is. Have you forgotten me?

NOAH (*shaking head*): I'm confused, but still, you have been my father. Father, the children are men and we have become big people — and you, a stranger far away?

BEGGAR: Yes, we've moved far apart from each other — my concerns are no longer your concerns — and yet, Noah, and yet you were once my son.

NOAH: Come to the house and take what I can offer you.

He draws the Beggar closer, motions him to sit.

BEGGAR (*pointing to nailed-up hands*): Yes, times have changed. In my day they didn't cut men's hands off.

CALAN: In our day, you old fraud, you scrounger, fathers don't reproach their sons, but the sons their fathers. But I had the hands cut off and nailed up — I, Calan, child of the God who gives me strength not to be a slave. (*He shakes the sack.*) Neither Noah nor his God could stop me.

BEGGAR: Perhaps God will requite you in your children.

CALAN: My God won't revenge himself on my children — that's typical of Noah's God. And I stuck Noah's God in this sack, just in case, to keep him from taking liberties with me. Get yourself washed, get the dust and blood washed off.

Noah bathes the feet, washes the face, arms, and hands of the Beggar.

CALAN: Do you know that water has become expensive, you dirt-trap? Those two bloody hands pray for the return of every drop wasted on you, and if your ears weren't too lazy, you'd hear the man whose dumb hands pray for drops, groaning and yelling for water. (*Screaming is heard.*) Do you hear? He's praying in our place, we showed him where. That's how they pray in our day.

BEGGAR: Out of the wells of the deep an ocean shall rise for every drop of blood. From the gates of heaven a flood shall pour down for each fearful breath this lamenting man draws.

CALAN: Oho — what an overflowing fulfillment!

BEGGAR: You would do well to drown out the man's sighs in mercy, because the stomachs of heaven shall vomit in answer to them.

CALAN: What are you whining about drowning? How did my word get in your mouth?

BEGGAR: My ears are not as lazy as you thought.

Enter Ham, annoyed.

HAM: The river's drying up, the animals are dying, and the wild wolf-toothed children drink their blood. Every day the herds get smaller, Father.

NOAH: That's Ham, our second one — look Ham, don't be startled — this old man once rocked you on his knee — can you still recognize him? You ought to recognize him.

HAM: I've got more important things to think about — what about that bloody man in the woods? Who cut him up so shamefully?

NOAH (*to Beggar*): He's got children already, Father — that's how everything changes and is marked by time. You shall see them.

BEGGAR: Did they turn out well — and your sons too?

NOAH: They're all good children, Shem, Ham, and Japheth, all good people, thankful, god-fearing, and obedient.

HAM: To be exact, we never bothered much with obedience and god-fearing. Where is my mother, and my brothers? Or don't I get an answer to that either?

NOAH: Look for yourself, Ham, and tell your mother to prepare the tenderest cut from the lamb's loin, gently roasted, and to bring it — for him — (*hesitates*) for a hungry, old, tired —

CALAN: Bum — for an old bum and liar, Ham, who should have been rotting in his grave long ago. Tell her that, Ham.

HAM: I know what I'll say. If he's got to eat, a tougher piece will do. (*Off.*)

NOAH (*hurrying after him*): The loin, Ham, the loin — please, I beg you, let it be the loin, make sure it's the loin. Do it for me, Ham. I'd go myself, but to leave him even for a minute makes me tremble.

HAM: It'll be all right, Father. (*Off.*)

NOAH (*back*): They don't understand the grace of beholding you, old Father. Don't hold it against them — time — oh, time went ahead on nimble feet, and I, how gladly I fly back to the lost old days.

BEGGAR: I came for you, Noah — come, child, come — you obeyed me even unto the last hour — I beg you as you begged Ham, grant me obedience.

NOAH: Speak, Father, deny yourself no wish, ask, command.

BEGGAR: Leave the peace of this valley, Noah —

NOAH: Leave the land, give up my holdings?

BEGGAR: Go to the mountains and build.

NOAH: To the mountains, with all my herds?

BEGGAR: Without the herds, Noah, only with your sons, your wife, and your sons' wives. Build in the mountains.

NOAH: But why should I retreat to the mountains and leave all I have?

BEGGAR: There's going to be a flood, Noah — listen, you must build a house, a strong house of wooden beams. Look, like this — three hundred ells long, fifty ells wide, and thirty ells high — a house to live in while the flood is rising. And let it rest loosely on its foundation so that the flood can lift it up, and you will live upon the flood while the world disappears before your eyes. Let it be thus.

CALAN: Build, Noah. Build strong and long and high and wide — a floating house — and you can watch from the roof as your herds drown.

53

NOAH: A flood, Father? Why must there be a flood?

BEGGAR: God is sorry he made man. You alone are worth saving, you and your sons and your sons' wives and children.

NOAH: But you, Father, what are you worthy of?

BEGGAR: I will find my way back to *my* time, I will find the past days again.

CALAN: But you'll have to give him camels to ride and cattle, to drive away his sorrow, Noah — otherwise he won't get on his way.

BEGGAR: And then, Noah, consider your herds closely, take your best breeding animals of all kinds and food for them and your family with you into the floating house. But you must give all your other goods and accumulated property to your neighbor Calan, because he helped you once in adversity. (*To Calan:*) For if your God is stronger than Noah's he will save you and your property from the flood. (*To Noah:*) Give it to him, give him everything today — say the word now so that he becomes master of everything by it. (*Ahire comes with dishes in both hands.*) I will not eat until you promise to do as I say.

CALAN: Say the word, Noah — say it to Chus, he'll cut this clever adviser into little pieces for you. (*To Beggar:*) You think I'd reward you? You can be sure, if we find you outside, you're dead — Chus, look at him closely, wherever you see him again let him die by the sword.

Noah has gone to meet Ahire; he has taken the dishes and has spoken softly with her. She looks at the Beggar and shakes her head.

AHIRE: He is *like* him. He has his eyes, Noah, and his beard, and almost his voice. Let him eat and rest and then give him something for the road. You have strange visions, poor man — be charitable but don't be foolish — no, no, the dead stay dead, Noah. (*Off.*)

Noah offers Beggar the dishes, but Beggar refuses, smiling.

NOAH (*calling after Ahire*): Send Awah with a cool drink!

He kneels in front of Beggar and holds up dishes. Beggar refuses again.

BEGGAR: Your word, Noah, my beloved son.

NOAH (*dejected*): Oh Father — to give away all my herds and go to the mountains, a poor man — how could anyone promise that?

CALAN: Nevertheless, promise, Noah — listen, you know I'm your friend — look here. (*He gives Chus the sack. To Chus:*) Take it out and let him escape. (*Chus goes off with the sack.*) Let him set the flood in motion if he can. Go to the mountains and build, then if my God calmly blows the flood away, as I know he will, you can come back and claim your herds — hoof by hoof and horn by horn — take them back from my hands as once before. But then we'll sacrifice together to that God whose child I am.

BEGGAR (*to Noah*): If you obey my word, the effect of the blessing I gave you when I died will be increased a hundredfold. Grant me obedience, Noah. Have you forgotten who I am?

CALAN: On the other hand, you're right, Noah — why should you want to live when everyone else is going to die — especially since they will die guiltless, since their guilt is God's guilt. That too has to be taken into account. Die with us if the flood can't do anything but come. You're not even to blame for your piety, you aren't guilty of that either.

BEGGAR: Your obedience will bear fruit a hundredfold, Noah.

Awah enters with the pitcher, stops near Calan. She drops the pitcher as she throws her hands up to her face.

NOAH (*picking up pitcher*): It's all right, Awah, only a few drops spilled. (*Awah looks around.*)

NOAH: What do you see, child?

AWAH: The world is less than nothing, and God is everything — I see nothing but God.

BEGGAR: Believe her, Noah, she saw God.

AWAH (*covering her ears*): God is the enormous silence. I hear God.

BEGGAR: Believe her, Noah, she heard God.

CALAN (*touching Awah*): Here I am, Awah, look at me.

AWAH: Don't disturb me. (*Looks around her.*) Everything God, everything God!

CALAN: Do you see me, don't you hear me? It is I, Calan, Awah.

AWAH: Yes, Lord, I hear how your flood will destroy all flesh. Yes, Lord, I see: we will live, the raven flies, the dove flies, the mountain of salvation, Ararat, towers above the flood!

BEGGAR: Listen to her, Noah, God speaks with her.

CALAN: Speak to me, Awah, it's Calan.

Awah bends down for the dropped pitcher, looks around astonished, laughs, and takes it from Noah.

AWAH: You caught it when I dropped it, Father? Just listen what Japheth told me — when I was sitting in the tent, scolded and crying, he said

5 5

people don't catch lice from sheep and lambs. Then he kissed the tears away and let me take a little water to wash. (*To Calan:*) I had a vision of many clouds in the sky, and water rising all around over everything — it was cool the way it is at home in the mountains. Oh Calan, why did you bring me here, into this drought?

NOAH: Wait just a little while, Awah, we'll leave this drought for the cool mountains. Even today, or tomorrow, we'll travel fast and not look back. (*To Calan:*) Take all my herds, Calan, hold them tight in your hands. I will never ask to have them back.

AWAH: Is God in the mountains too? The messengers promised that I would see and hear him.

NOAH (*cheerfully*): God is great and the mountains too rest in God, Awah. God is everything, the world is less than nothing, remember what I tell you.

AWAH (*shaking her head*): How can he come to us, if we're so tiny in him? (*She laughs.*) How eager I am for the mountains!

BEGGAR (*piteously*): I'm hungry, Noah — I need a bite. Your obedience will bear fruit a hundredfold.

NOAH: Take and eat from my hands, Father. Look, it's the loin, and tender fat moistens the tissue through and through.

CALAN: If God is everything, how do you account for the wicked?
He follows Awah with his eyes, walks around Noah and the Beggar, shakes his head, shrugs his shoulders, and walks off slowly.

Part III

1 ⸝ Desert. The Beggar. A pack of savage children, gesturing like animals and howling like wolves, swarm around him. While he stands patiently, they snap and strike at him. The Angels come and post themselves at his side, whereupon the pack scatters.

FIRST ANGEL: We know you in all your shapes.
SECOND ANGEL: We find you everywhere.

BEGGAR: There is no virtue among men.

Angels are silent.

BEGGAR: My work mocks me.

Angels are silent. There is howling in the distance.

BEGGAR: It is no longer my voice. They slaver at me, they rage against my will — speak.

FIRST ANGEL: They do not know your will.

SECOND ANGEL: They do not see, they do not hear.

FIRST ANGEL: Their soul knows nothing of you.

BEGGAR: But whom does their soul know, whom do they see and hear?

Angels are silent.

BEGGAR: I sink under the burden of my wrath, I rage against my work, I rage against myself.

Angels cover their faces.

BEGGAR: Away with mankind, that I may find peace! Off with you, back to the lands of giants born of light, shake off earth's dust and bathe in the might of divine fire. Let me take charge of my work without you.

Angels go off. Hunchbacked Leper appears.

LEPER: There is frenzied howling behind me; in front of me, no hope — I curse him who brought me into this raging world. (*He desperately thrashes about with his fists, and gives the Beggar, who steps back, a glancing blow.*) Why don't you strike back! (*He strikes himself in the face.*) Shame on you for being, shame on you for existing to need beating. If I did not exist, the world would not be cursed.

BEGGAR: Because of *you* the world is cursed?

LEPER: Because of me! Yes, because of me! What good is the world if it has even one single being damned and rotting! They hound me with howls and curse me and call me evil — and I am evil because they hound me and curse me — and they laugh and they mock. And before me, what kind of future is there before me? I breathe air without hope and will continue to breathe hopeless air until my very last breath. Then the jackals who devour me will grin and say: what a magnificent hump, that; without it, what a worthless creature! Ha, what a tasty tidbit my hump will be for them. Scum even for jackals, that's me. — You, you wretched beggar, you can at least look back and wish you had your youth back. Well then: don't you want to be young as you once were, or does the world hold two of my kind? You say nothing: are you like me? Come, let's curse, the two of us. Shake your fists like this: cursed be the God who made the good beings good and the evil ones evil! Oho, still silent? Afraid he'll get angry? Then you do after all have something to lose for which you tremble? Now what could that be — and what is it that could still frighten me in the end and make me flatter him? Ha, I have it, yes: I also have something to lose. (*Stands, legs apart.*) I — I am sick of him — not of myself as I used to think — but of him who is to blame for me. I spit on him, why, I puke on him! (*To the Beggar:*) And as I don't want to strike the empty air, you stand for him, take his place, and now you take that for him, and that. (*He strikes Beggar.*) Let me beat him like this, and kick him in the rump like that, and maul him so. And finally permit me to smear a little scrofulous leprosy right into your face, like this, so that *he* may realize how I feel about him.

2 ◢ Wild mountain woods. There are felled trees, the wind whistles through the leaves. Shem swings his axe at the tree trunks. Whenever his blows cease, there are nearby sounds from a second and third axe. Awah enters.

AWAH (*standing in front of him and letting the wind flutter her garment*):
How lovely, Shem, to have this freshness cool the body. All of you, with your red noses and blue fingers — why, leave off your chopping, Shem, and listen how the wind blows through the woods.

SHEM: The minute this chopper ceases to bark, it bites Noah's ears: lazy sons! And right away he comes running. — If it were not for you, Awah, I'd warm myself in the sun far away, and my eyes would search out the way to recover my white nose. But because you are here, my eyes are content, Awah. (*He sits and looks at her.*)

AWAH: But the beautiful angels, *their* noses were not red. Feel, Shem, how warm my hands are. (*She takes his hands.*) The angels were like smooth ivory to the touch; you and Japheth and Ham have hairy skin. How lovely it must be to touch God; perhaps I could even caress him, Shem, do you think he would permit it?

SHEM: Why not, Awah — put your hands on my cold cheeks and pass them over my forehead and eyes. Pretend I am God and I gave you permission.

AWAH (*does so*): Your cheeks are soft, and your forehead smooth, Shem.

SHEM: Think of God, Awah, pretend he sat here where I am sitting, and let you fondle him just as much as you wanted.

AWAH: I love God very much.

SHEM: So do I, Awah, we both love him very much. I know more about him than my father and all the rest. Listen, I'll tell you something. But for now it's enough that your hands are so kind to me, enough for today. If I were God you'd have to thank me, but because I am Shem I thank you. Now listen.

Awah sits next to him.

SHEM: God is not everywhere, and God is not everything, as Father Noah claims. He hides behind everything, and everything has narrow chinks, through which he shines, shines and flashes. Such thin, delicate chinks that you never find them again if you turn your head even once.

AWAH: Have you seen him, Shem?

Shem nods.

AWAH: What did he look like, Shem, what did he look like?

SHEM: He looks like nothing that is. How then can I tell you, Awah? But, if you want me to, I will try to remember; only give me a little time until I can put it in words; ask me again another time. I see him often through the chinks, it's so strangely sudden, it opens, it's gone, not a trace of a joint to be found — very strange, Awah.

Noah, wielding a stick, drives the hunchbacked Leper and maimed Shepherd before him.

NOAH: Good-for-nothings! Sluggards! Off with you to your own cursed places!

Shepherd raises his stumps imploringly. Noah recognizes him.

NOAH: You — is it you, without those sacrificed hands? Calan struck you, not I. God let it happen, not I. Why do you persecute me?

SHEPHERD (*looking at his arms*): They have stopped bleeding, but I drag myself to my brothers in pain and terror. (*Pointing to the slopes.*) I must cross the mountains. (*Points to Leper.*) I found him on the road; he shall remain with me and find food and friendship.

NOAH: Your brothers will drive him away. It's no good, I'll have nothing

5 9

to do with you. Away! Calan did it, and God allowed it to happen, not I.

LEPER: If one day a Greater God defiles noses and ears, you'd better prevent it, Noah, don't let it happen. Give up your own noses and ears and do it willingly, as long as God remains entire. (*Pointing to Shepherd.*) He is a child of God, and you have not prevented Calan from striking him. He will accuse you before God, he will say: he did not prevent it — Noah is the man's name, Noah, who is the servant of God.

NOAH: Not so loud — and away with you! I'll have nothing more to do with you.

SHEPHERD: Oh the wounds and the pain. I am ashamed of my wounds and my pain, I am ashamed to be mutilated.

NOAH: Away with you! They are the works of God that you assail with your words.

AWAH: These are God's works?

NOAH: God's own works, Awah. Don't look.

AWAH: God's works are horrible, if these are God's works.

SHEM: Take a look, Awah. Myself, I would not like to have done such deeds.

NOAH: Away with you to your cursed places! (*He drives them off. To Shem and Awah:*) Pray to God and you will not be infected with leprosy, serve him and you will keep your hands, fear him and you will be spared. Love him.

AWAH: I cannot love him, if these are his works.

SHEM: Nor I, Awah; he is a harsh master.

NOAH: We shall build, Shem. Ham and his oxen are bringing the trimmed beams — no, they have seen nothing and understood nothing, these two. When the flood rises and the multitudes flee to the mountains where we are building, we will have no room to spare for anyone except us and our animals. (*To Awah:*) They do not deserve to live, Awah; we alone deserve it, and you along with us.

AWAH: He was beautiful and had no hands — Japheth is ugly and *has* hands.

NOAH: Had he prayed he would have kept his hands.

AWAH: But I did not pray either, and I still have mine.

NOAH: Love Japheth, Awah, for that is God's will.

AWAH: Japheth no — not Japheth. None of you is as beautiful as he without his hands — and God doesn't love him?

SHEM: He is a harsh master, Awah, who does not return hands.

AWAH: I do not want to be Japheth's wife; I do not want Japheth to lay his grimy hands on me again — help me, Shem, I would much rather be your wife.

SHEM: Do you hear, Father? She would much rather be my wife.

NOAH: Oh children, we shall all be swallowed by the flood if we don't build.

SHEM: I will build on one condition only: give me Awah. If not, I'll take her beyond the mountains and wait and see if the flood does reach that far, or whatever it does. And Japheth is not going to deliberate long but find himself a spot among fat Zebid's people — he isn't going to build for sure. It would be best if you gave him Zebid. I guarantee you'll marvel at the way his hands will stir during the day all for the floating house, as long as they can rest at night on Zebid.

NOAH: That big heathen woman who dances with her father's men before wooden idols? Who violates her younger brothers before their time?

SHEM: Then Awah will stay with us in our tents. Anyway, after the flood Zebid would find little joy in her drowned manservants and stinking brothers.

NOAH: Where could Ham be — Ham will tell you what sort of fellows you are, you and Japheth — Ham, Ham!

SHEM: And look, Father, since the fat Zebid is not going to stop her dancing and carryings-on on account of Japheth, Calan could, if you were to ask him . . .

NOAH (*moving restlessly back and forth*): Ham, Ham!

SHEM: Ham, Ham!

HAM (*from the back*): Wait, I'm coming.

Ham appears. Shem speaks to him.

NOAH: Calan? Calan? (*Wringing his hands.*) I should beg Calan to drive that heathen woman to us, that abominable idolatress with her raging debaucheries! She who will choke our peace and devotion with carnal corruption! What have you to say, Ham — Ham, what do you think?

HAM: Zebid, I must tell you, Father, has but one fault — not that she is such a big heathen — why, we could cure her of that soon enough because she has often told me that her God was essentially no better than any other.

NOAH: She told you that? What have *you* had to do with her?

HAM: Oh well, that's all long ago, so long ago I've practically forgotten it. Makes no difference either way. She was always a little short of breath and needed someone to make her laugh because then she'd recover right away — and in those days I was a regular wit, you see.

NOAH: But what was her fault, in your eyes?

HAM: A marvelous build — that's beyond dispute — what thighs!

NOAH: But her fault, Ham, tell her fault!

HAM (*rubbing his forehead*): Her fault? Did I say anything about a fault? No, she has no faults, not the smallest, none at all — oh yes, now I remember, but after all it's none of my business what faults she has; if Japheth wants her, he'll find out. Why should I scare him off?

NOAH (*in despair*): The flood, the flood, and you stand there talking back and forth about Zebid's build.

HAM: I can't help it — a truly magnificent build. What does bother me though is that there may be no flood, and we've become paupers only because we're scared of water. And Calan is far and wide the mightiest in the land — —

Japheth has been standing in the background for some time.

NOAH: At times I lose all hope that you are worth saving. Awah, child, the world is less than nothing, and God is everything. Come along, come, talk to your mother, arrange it with her, but don't forsake me in this job. We must build!

SHEM: I build only for Awah.

HAM: And I will also do my part. If the flood comes, it will be more cheerful where we are — with fat Zebid along — than squatting on dry land. If the flood doesn't come, we'll all be Calan's slaves. Therefore we should not let his interest in us grow deaf. Let's keep reminding him by asking him for favors. The occasion is right. A good wedge, I maintain. Calan has a bag full of ideas, and needs a wedge.

NOAH: A wedge?

HAM: Yes, precisely a wedge. He may bring us Zebid with good intentions or bad — with her lot comes friendship or enmity, or a little of both —

but Calan's fingers crave this chance. Calan will think he can further his schemes through her.

JAPHETH (*stepping forward and jumping with joy*): And I will do my part too, I will, and Zebid will witness that I keep my word. (*Embracing Awah.*) Oh Awah, how happy I am that I shall have Zebid!

Part IV

1 ⌁ Desert. The Distinguished Traveler, dressed as in Part I, and Noah meet.

TRAVELER (*in passing*): Hurry — hurry, Noah, hurry — have you no camels?

NOAH (*stopping*): I am a poor man — no, I don't own one animal that would serve me — I go my way as my breathing permits. Your feet too are sinking into the dust. But since you urge me to hurry, I wish to ask only if the road continues through drought and dust to the lower valleys — are there more parched pastures, more animals perishing of thirst?

TRAVELER (*nods, turns back, puts his hand on Noah's shoulder, and pushes him gently down; they sit*): Yes, more; but you must hurry, hurry, after we have rested a little while together.

NOAH: Calan, they say, is far and wide the mightiest in the land — have you heard of Calan?

TRAVELER (*nods*): What do you want with him? He is indeed mighty and powerful.

NOAH: I must ask his help. I must plead for the daughter of my neighbor and enemy, for my son — if Calan helps me, and helps at once, Japheth's suffering will cease before it is too late.

TRAVELER: They are bad people, Noah, I know them — is it Japheth then whose life has turned to grief without Zebid? But he already has a wife, lovely and of gentle blood. — Zebid? No, I tell you, Noah, Zebid will

6 3

ruin your children and your children's children. She is godless and has forgotten God and dares to thrive without God.

NOAH: Maybe it wasn't her fault she grew bad — is she to blame if her food was offal and made the oozing rot set in? Japheth cannot help himself, and he cannot help himself because he is so good-natured.

TRAVELER: Turn back, Noah, turn back at once and leave the godless to their own devices. Go back to the mountains and exhort Japheth to obedience and honor.

NOAH: Japheth without a wife? How can I exhort him! Why blame Japheth's good nature if it demands a godless woman? God gave him that nature.

TRAVELER: Take him in hand, and he will respond.

NOAH: I have three sons but only two wives among them, bad prospects for decent conduct at home, good sir. We have need of the country's godless daughters. They will perish if I don't hurry. (*He rises.*) God can change their hearts, if he so wishes, since he has made it impossible for my sons to live without wives.

TRAVELER: Hurry home, Noah, do not be obstinate. Your eyes see only the stony drought across the land, your ears know nothing of the drunken turmoil in its cloven depths. You are parched with hot breath, but you do not feel the trembling and raging of oceans in the breaking breast of the earth — already the winds of heaven have abated their fiery blasts, are slackening into smoldering, moldering sparks, expiring in terror of the roaring blackness that has been imposed over the world. Hurry home, Noah; give your thanks by obedience to God, and do not mingle with the godless. The tents of him who dwells among the wicked bloat with evil like pregnant wombs.

NOAH: Sir, I say no: God is also lord over wickedness; he can shackle it, he can turn defiance to obedience.

TRAVELER: Can he, Noah?

NOAH: God, who wills the good, should not be able to master evil? No, one must not think so godlessly, sir. I must hurry.

TRAVELER: What does God have to do with evil? It is not *he* who is the maker of evil — if life is to become better, let them see whence they got it.

NOAH: You sound much like Calan, who is godless — God can destroy evil, he can also better it.

TRAVELER: Do *you* mean to master *him* — do you mean to press your measures into his hands? Go home, go home, Noah, go home!

NOAH: If he were not to subdue evil and turn it into good, oh sir —

TRAVELER: What then, Noah, what then?

NOAH: Oh sir, it would sound as though Calan were saying it, Calan, God's enemy — no, I cannot say it.

TRAVELER: What does Calan, God's enemy, say?

NOAH: He says, the good comes from God's goodness, and evil from God's malice — if God were wholly good and nothing but good, then God's malice could not be evil, and all that is evil would be good.

TRAVELER: Can you hear the wolfchildren howling in the desert? That is evil snarling at good. It slumbers as yet in Zebid's voice, but one day it will wake and howl horribly out of the mouths of your children's children — go home, Noah.

NOAH: If God lets children grow up as wolves, they have a right to bark and snarl and howl. (*He glances about alarmed and strikes his mouth.*) Who said that — words that stung my ears like hornets? (*He strikes his ears and rushes off.*)

TRAVELER: You too, Noah, are *you* beginning to rot too? — Blunder! Failure! the world shouts at me. Look how you have miscreated me! it howls at me. I fear I shall find little joy in you and your children.

2 ⸗ Mountain woods. The Ark looms in the background. Noah and Japheth are working.

NOAH: The deer and the fox, the lion and lynx, and all the other four-footed animals are trotting about our building so at peace with each other. Look, Japheth, they are surely fleeing the flood, and God's spirit drives them to us so that we may preserve them.

JAPHETH: True, Father, and now the birds come flying around and about, ravens and doves, and all the dwellers of the sky, and they are settling modestly — each in his little nook. No one pushes, no screaming or chirping or cackling: they build where we build, rooms within our rooms, and suspend lofts beneath our loft, clean feed everywhere piled high. One can see they plan to stay with us a long time, Father.

NOAH: They shall, Japheth — they shall stay. God gives them the measure for what they needs must do. The signs are multiplying, the time is growing ripe.

JAPHETH: The time is growing ripe — yesterday I walked down into the valley, and walked farther than I had planned, looking for Calan, and I trembled in anticipation of Zebid. There I overheard two fellows on the run, one of them panting so hard the other could hardly find a chance to speak. Still I heard that in the lands lower down moles and hamsters and all creeping things are rooting and scrambling up, by thousands, to daylight; every thing wiggles and squirms moistly; bodies devour each other for every dry finger of land above the mud. Yes, the time is growing ripe. Is Zebid really coming, Father?

NOAH (*sighing*): She is coming, Japheth — alas, that there was no other choice! Calan agreed, and Japheth, how Calan smirked, when he promised to persuade her, with force if need be.

JAPHETH: She will be quite content when she realizes the flood is rising, and the flood is going to make her forget all that happened before.

NOAH: What a pity, what a pity!

Awah and Ahire come, the latter scolding.

AHIRE: Speak to her, Noah — she won't listen to me, she laughs when I scold her and shakes herself in an abandon of joy — look, she walks as though swaying on heaving ground.

AWAH: I awoke at night and my heart was delirious. More beautiful than all angels is the weaving ringing, the unchanging new, the eternal song.

Her hands imitate the movement of waves.

I can see it ring, I can hear it swing, the end cradles the beginning in her arms.

Heaviness creeps on silent feet, hears a word and casts the surge of a glory forever light upon the heart — the word and the wave are at play, they lift holy powers up and down — everlasting glory arises and dies, eternal holiness roars and soars into being. It swells — threatens, thunders, now is silent — swelling and is silent — threatens and thunders . . .

The rush of heavy winds is heard.

NOAH: The time is ripe, winds are pushing the flood nearer.

Ham and Shem come running.

JAPHETH: The storm has calved and hurled screams at the mountains.

SHEM: Rocks whimper and whine.

They cling to one another while the storm rages.

NOAH: Commend yourselves to God's care, take heart, children, trust in God.

Silence.

SHEM: Our building stands fast, look how it stands. The winds passed it by, not a joint creaked — and yet listen to the outcry of trees falling in the forest.

NOAH: God built it — go into the house, children, and look after the women.

HAM: The storm has jammed my voice into my guts, my feet want to creep into the ground.

SHEM: Hold on to me, Awah, try to stand — now a step at a time. The heavens have burst and their tatters flap about our ears. Things spin in my head.

HAM: Walk ahead, Shem, and keep quiet. Who knows what ideas such blind, frenzied winds get — don't spit while the heavens cough. Go on, they have taken on too much and now try with less force.

Ham and Shem go off with Awah and Ahire.

NOAH (*looks about, takes a deep breath*): Lord, your judgment is a terrible one. Listen to it traveling in the distance, Japheth. Hold me up, Japheth, my knees buckle.

JAPHETH: It was like a trumpet, and the old time fell over.

CALAN'S VOICE: Look, there is the house, Zebid, a building like a castle.

Calan and Zebid enter.

NOAH: God commanded the trees to become beams and break into boards under our hands, Calan; yes, and he bade the belly of the house to stretch according to his will and our need, and the walls to thicken in order to accommodate the herds of the Lord. — Welcome, Calan, and thank you, Calan. (*To Zebid:*) Child, here you shall live with us in God's shelter and shadow. (*Reaches for Japheth's and Zebid's hands.*) So be it, take hands and love each other.

6 7

ZEBID (*drawing back*): Calan told me that Ham had turned out his wife and wanted me in her place. He said nothing about Japheth.

CALAN (*laughing*): Japheth, Japheth, Japheth, that's whom I meant, a mere slip. Of course Japheth.

NOAH: It was entirely a question of Japheth. Japheth turned away his wife. He has deserved you on account of his longing and the pangs of his heart.

ZEBID: A man has to be more than a Japheth to deserve me! Look at the way he's standing there — hey, Japheth!

JAPHETH: Don't you remember, Zebid, what you said the night of the full moon when I met you on the road? We held hands and let go, many times: if I wanted you, you said, I'd have to do it in spite of you, only then could it ever be. This has happened. Now accept it, because this is the way it happened.

ZEBID: Oh, how you've trapped me. (*To Japheth:*) If you know how to hold me, well and good. Try it, Japheth, but remember I have my eyes on Ham.

CALAN: Try it, Japheth.

NOAH: Don't try it, Japheth — say no, Japheth. Such laws as Zebid obeys bring no peace, no freedom, no joy.

CALAN: She obeys laws that bring her joy and bring her *her* kind of peace and freedom too. I procured you no other dowry, no other legacy, than Zebid as she is, with her own laws and all. Try it, Japheth.

JAPHETH: One day you will thank me, Zebid; you already owe me your life. And if you will not thank me today, you will thank me tomorrow. I have saved you from the flood and stepped between you and the destruction that follows you. You will breathe, Zebid; when all other breathing on the wide earth has ceased, you will breathe freely, cheerfully and in peace. By this you see who I am. If you don't know it today, you will know it tomorrow and weep for joy. Come along to Mother. (*Takes hold of her and leads her off.*)

CALAN: How do you think she's going to thank him, Noah?

NOAH (*shaking head*): It is now time, Calan, the time is ripe — today we will put the roof on the house, and, Calan, you well know that the time is ripe.

CALAN: You mean because the mice and moles are drowning in their holes? We are not mice, Noah: I am not.

NOAH: You think your God will ward off the flood, or have you also prepared beams and boards? Don't forget, Calan, it was Awah, bereft of her wits, Awah who without warning or instruction saw the flood. The animals of the woods are gathering near the house; the birds are settling in by twos, as God directed them, in my rooms. The time has come, the land below has sucked its fill and is ready to disgorge from its lap. God's work proceeds.

CALAN: And you and your sons and their wives are the only ones deserving to live — how is that, can it be believed?

NOAH: God wants to save us as we are, Calan — I think we are as good as God wills us to be, no better no worse.

CALAN: And I too, I was created the way I am. And now tell me, Noah, who commanded my nature to be incurably mine, like leprosy, who if not God? If not your God, then some other God. It was a God, Noah, and I remain his son.

NOAH: Let us not judge, Calan, since you are my guest today. Your God or mine, we shall see.

CALAN: Not a guest, Noah. I am the one who said he wanted to be stronger than *he*, and I have proved to you that I am stronger.

NOAH: Let us not judge, Calan, we shall see who the strong one is, you or he.

CALAN: My men obey me; when the flood rises, they will gather about your building as I ordered them to — just as he commanded the animals to gather. If *he* is about his work, I am no less about mine, if there is water in *his* hand, I have fire in mine. Your house will burn, Noah, my work will overcome his. There will be a God who rules, but not yours; if we die, we die because of the one, not because of *him*.

Chus stumbles in exhausted and falls.

CHUS: Do not kill me, Master; I am dying, there is no need for the sword.

CALAN: Don't be afraid, Chus, speak.

CHUS (*breathlessly*): When you rode off at night, the river reversed its course. In the morning, as we awoke, the ground cracked northwards and severed the valley up to the mountains. A wall of water rose from the depths and fell and broke, divided as if by a stroke of sword. I am dying, Master, not of toil, nor of wasted strength, I am dying of terror, my heart has been clubbed to death, my ears are full of nothing but (*covering his ears*) — they are shrieking, shrieking, and water clogs their breathing souls. Kill me, Master, that I may suffer it no longer.

CALAN (*pulling his hands from his ears*): Where are my servants, Chus?

CHUS: They've had it, all dead: hear nothing, see nothing; their bodies wheeling in whirlpools, rising and falling.

CALAN: The herds, Chus, what happened to the herds?

CHUS: All in motion, as though grazing with bloated bellies in the water, their legs wobbling, their heads hang downward, jaws agape. All voices are stilled, and yet they will not quit my ears — kill me, Master, kill!

CALAN: Where did my neighbors flee?

CHUS: All flesh, man and beast, all without feeling, without sound — my ears alone carry within them the wailing of the valley, all flesh is spoiled. Ask me no more, Master, kill me!

CALAN: You are lying, Chus, nothing is lost, many are saved and await help. Up, Chus, live, obey!

CHUS (*kicking at him*): I have obeyed long enough — now it's for *you* to obey: kill me, beggar, pauper, kill me, bankrupt, bum!

CALAN (*shouting*): What do you say I am, you slave you, who — Chus?

CHUS (*rising*): Don't kill me, Master, your voice is loud and lovely, your voice will drive their shrieking from my ears. You are Calan, the master, and I am Chus, your servant. But, Master, I am the last thing remaining of all the things you ever possessed. You are a poor man, but I am Chus, your servant.

Shem and Ham and Japheth approach hesitantly; farther back are Ahire, Zebid, Awah.

NOAH: The time is ripe, the time is ripe.

CALAN (*turning violently on him*): The time is *ripe*? The time is rotten when a God must labor to turn the breath of his world to water. Nice doings for a master! Awah, you are in their midst like a grain of seed wafted from the lands of bliss to the lands of damnation. Seed of freedom, seed of joy: damned be Noah's and all slaves' peace! (*To Chus:*) Come, Chus, my child, show me what my ears will not believe, I must see, see. (*Makes as if to go.*)

CHUS (*shuddering and pointing slowly with his finger*): Look! To the very edges of the sky, painless, soundless, lifeless, moving sluggish in slimy flood, bloating carcasses arching to the light, belly crushed on paunch, dead human-kind is floating and dead beasts, camels, cows, sheep, bulls, and calves, a fleshy carpet of stinking corruption spanning the depths.

CALAN: I have to see, come, child, come Chus.

CHUS (*shakes himself*): There is terror in my ears and eyes.

CALAN: It may be bad to look back, let us look ahead. (*To Noah:*) Why do you stand there, lazy dogs! To work! God will command a roof to his structure. Use your hands, work, you; sweat and get it done, so that we shall live to see you swim when the flood finds its way up here.

Part V

1 ⸍ The same place by night. Rain and storm. Calan and Chus.

CALAN: They put some food out when it got dark. Eat, child.

CHUS: I can't — eating is like a shriek in my ears, breathing is a shriek in my ears, all life is a shriek, which dies only at the sound of your voice — speak!

CALAN: I cannot go on, Chus; live, child, while you can.

CHUS: Have pity. Death crouches in my ears and roars at my soul. Take out your sword and kill this death, so that I become like all others — no sound, no pain — use it.

CALAN: Take hold of its point and guide it to where your heart rises. Now.

CHUS: I thank you for your compassion — there's the spot — now push.

He falls.

CALAN (*listening intently over him*): Still a whisper of life, a faint breath, another, the weave of warmth above his heart, so faint, and now a silent nothing — finished. (*Sits down.*) I'll keep watch and wait until the body is cold.

71

The Leper and the Shepherd grope their way near; in the dark Calan remains unnoticed.

SHEPHERD: Your cursing has tired you out, it has made you hoarse. Here's Noah's settlement, whence he drove us off. Everything sleeps — go to sleep too; I'll watch over you.

LEPER: If we go on in this grimy blackness, we'll topple to our deaths. Give me some covering and let me sleep. I'm starved, but God and Noah need it all for themselves. Hoarse? Yes, but once more: life be damned! (*He lies down; Shepherd sits near him.*)
Silence.

CALAN: Where are you going?

SHEPHERD: We were looking for the pass over the mountains. But the clouds hung dense everywhere and then sank down heavy on us, pushed us to the ground. We are fleeing them into the valley.

CALAN: The time is ripe.

SHEPHERD: What do you mean?

CALAN: If you want to earn yourselves something to eat, help me dig a grave here for my dead child. Let us wait, he's still warm.

SHEPHERD: I cannot dig, sir, I have no hands. Calan ordered them cut off, and Chus, his servant, did it.

CALAN: I am Calan, and Chus, my child, otherwise known as my servant, lies here by me. He died. Your drops of blood have swelled to seas and drowned my herds and my dominions. Your moans compelled all the world's clouds, drew them above our heads — the time is ripe.
Silence.

CALAN: Why are you weeping? I can hear you well enough.

SHEPHERD: I do not know why.

CALAN: Why does he keep cursing, your hunchbacked friend?

SHEPHERD: He curses his God who gave him everything: leprous sores, a deformed body — and a heart.

CALAN: He has a right to curse.

SHEPHERD: I would weep for God, who caused it all.

CALAN: But you do curse Calan who took your hands?
Silence.

CALAN: You must tell me — here I am, Calan, whose powers and substance God took in return for your hands. Then curse me, go ahead, for I have done worse to you than God did to that one with his sores and his deformities.

SHEPHERD: Curses rise from blindness, but I can see.

CALAN: What do you see?

SHEPHERD: I am ashamed to speak of God and have never spoken of him. The word is too big for my mouth. I understand that he is not to be understood, that is all my knowledge of him.

CALAN: You're right, it's because of Noah that I got to prattling about God. It's as though the maggots in my guts had said: Calan must eat meat, if he doesn't he's unjust to us, and Calan be damned.

LEPER (*awaking*): Whom are you talking to?

SHEPHERD: Calan.

LEPER (*starting up*): To Calan? The great Calan?

CALAN: Calan has shrunk, he's poor, cold, hungry, and soaking wet — but it's Calan, brother.

LEPER: Poor and soaking and cold? And still you love life, Calan, and so you're in luck. Who is that sleeping near you?

CALAN: One who preferred dying to eating. You must help me dig a grave for him. Over there is a jug; hearten yourself, have some wine and food, for you are one who prefers eating to dying.

Leper eats and drinks greedily.

CALAN: Eat and drink, no one begrudges you, but don't begrudge it your brother.

LEPER: He's not my brother.

CALAN: Then give him his share as a friend.

LEPER: He has no hands, can't lift the jug, no fingers to hold it.

CALAN: Hold it for him, then; let your hands carry it to his mouth.

LEPER: Too late; all gone.

CALAN: Now help me dig.

LEPER: Jackals too want a feed; it's a pity to deprive them of this fine meal. Calan, Calan, how you've sunk, sitting there in wretchedness among wretches, reduced to listening politely to jeers and gibes. Too bad about your fine pride of yesterday — I am sorry for you, my dear Calan.

CALAN: Do you value your life?

LEPER: Mine?

CALAN: Yours, which out of brotherly wretchedness and friendship I shall take from you with this sword. Too bad about this lovely sword, but if it can impress on you the meaning of brotherhood —

LEPER (*shaking Shepherd*): Get up, brother; is this a time for loafing when the frost and wet are our only shelter? We are headed for warmer, drier parts.

SHEPHERD (*rising*): I'll go with you, provided there's an end to cursing.

LEPER: Oh well — if you hadn't let them knock your hands off, you could cover your ears with them now. I didn't do it, thank Calan for it. (*Both leave.*)

2 ⸗ The same. A grey day. Calan is digging a grave. Zebid watches.

CALAN: You threw away those wooden idols, Zebid, while we were on the road — idols you stole from your father when we left. They got too heavy for you when we began to climb the mountains. That was bad, Zebid. Those wooden gods are the best after all. They don't hold off suffering, but at least they don't bring it on — now you're stuck with Noah's God.

ZEBID (*crying*): Is it true what they say, the whole land is under water?

Calan nods casually.

ZEBID: You're lying. (*But she continues to cry.*)

Calan nods.

ZEBID: What about the water, is it true or isn't it?

CALAN: Please yourself: no one believes but what is convenient to believe. You don't want the water, so you don't believe the water is there. You'd sooner have me lie than know it is flooding the land — and so you believe that I lie.

ZEBID: Everyone lies here, everyone except Ham.

CALAN: That's more convenient for you, so go ahead and believe it.

ZEBID: If I cannot trust myself, whom can I trust?

CALAN: Trust your opinion of Ham as you trust the firm earth. Have you fallen in love with Japheth yet?

ZEBID: I don't want to owe my life to him, but he keeps reminding me and expects me to love him. (*Weeps loudly.*) If they're all dead, then Mes is dead, Sin is dead, and Asad is dead, and so many many are dead.

Abbir too! Have you really become a beggar, Calan? They're saying it, but they say it very quietly.

Calan nods.

ZEBID: You're lying.

CALAN (*nodding*): You're right again, Zebid — look, I still have Chus. Help me bury him. Then I shall truly be a beggar, if they want to call it that. (*They place him in the grave.*)

CALAN (*throwing earth on the grave*): He shall not drift in the water; whirlpools shall not rock him, as they rock all my wives and children. Rest, Chus, my child.

ZEBID: Your child? Your servant!

CALAN: A master has servants, a beggar doesn't.

ZEBID: Are you going to be begging from us, Calan?

CALAN: Beg? What have you servants got to give! I want to see how servants swim. Now he's safely under ground, Zebid, and now the flood may come.

ZEBID: If we swim, you won't drown either. Ram too is dead, I almost forgot — oh Calan, not him dead too! Once he baited Japheth so, that Japheth blushed and stammered and stood there furious and still didn't dare strike. For all of us who saw it — a joy to behold, Calan, believe me.

CALAN: I believe you. But now Ram has his mouth full of water and Japheth mocks them one by one without blushing. He makes up for the fun you had with Ram, and with Mes, and the many others. — There comes Noah bent double leaning into the wind — oh, how unnaturally he walks. I can tell that he wants to drive me off.

Noah enters.

NOAH (*to Zebid*): You must be freezing here in the wind, child — go inside, warm yourself, you're getting too wet. (*Zebid goes.*)

CALAN: I am cold and wet, Noah.

NOAH (*rubbing his hands*): I too am freezing, Calan.

CALAN: What have you decided, you and your sons?

NOAH (*looking around*): Have you eaten, Calan? Was there enough wine in the jar? There's more if you want it.

CALAN: The time is ripe, Noah, what good is food and drink. The animals of the forest have taken refuge in your house and found compassion.

I'll be satisfied with a little space in their midst — and Calan is by himself — a pair of wildcats for Calan!

NOAH (*embarrassed*): Where is your sword?

CALAN: I have helped you many times — you know it, and don't forget it — many times and willingly. Do the wild animals give you trouble? Why, I'll help you once again — let's go inside, all will be taken care of in no time. (*Makes as though to move.*)

NOAH (*stops him aghast*): Not inside, don't go inside, Calan. There's no danger from the animals, they are tame and quiet and gentle with one another. No, Calan, not the house.

CALAN: But I am freezing and wet. I want to get warm and dry my clothes.

NOAH (*weeping*): You'll make yourself master over us, Calan. You will float in God's house and make slaves of me and my sons. You know that, Calan.

CALAN: If God permits it, it will have proved to be God's will. That you know, Noah.

NOAH: Where is your sword?

CALAN: Here, there, somewhere — don't be afraid, Noah, your life is in God's hands. Those were Noah's words of comfort for the one who lost his hands. (*Japheth comes running.*)

JAPHETH: Come into the house, Calan, warm and dry yourself. (*To Noah:*) Even if none of you want it, it cannot be otherwise; he belongs to us. (*To Calan:*) They deliberate and argue back and forth how to deal with you, but they are agreed on just this: you're a robber and will find your just reward in the flood. (*He pulls him away.*) Oh Calan, how good Zebid is to me, believe me, believe me, good and obedient, and — Calan — she has but to touch me, and I'm consumed, yes, deliciously gnawed to my very guts, believe me, Calan. Then I am like one transformed, no longer Japheth but almost like her, Zebid herself, as though I really were Zebid, and there's nothing like it in the world. Come into the house, come! (*They go off.*)

3 ⌐ The same. Storm. Shem and Ham.

_____

HAM: Our women are going crazy — Calan here, Calan there. What do you think, Shem?

SHEM: You signaled me to come out, Ham — I'm waiting for your word.

HAM: We're already Calan's servants and nothing more — you, myself, all of us. You must be aware of that, Shem?

SHEM: Ham . . .

HAM: Wait! Father knows best what Calan is about — he's traveling with us, and we are traveling with him, and if it should chance that the storm eases, he'll take our women and shear the wool off our sheep and tear the fat from our ribs. Father has a point.

SHEM: Ham . . .

HAM: Wait, let me finish — well, what do you think, Shem?

SHEM: I agree — Father understands. You understand. I do too.

HAM: That all you know? It's not much.

SHEM: No less than all of you know.

HAM: If we can slaughter cattle and kill wolves, surely we can also finish off Calan.

SHEM: I've thought about it all last night, Ham, and you know I have a cool head; but my heart is sick at the thought of murder. Until there's a good opportunity and the moment is just right and as long as we can count on keeping our eyes open — oh, Ham —

HAM: But, Shem, just think of Awah. Isn't that comfort and encouragement enough for what we have in mind?

SHEM: That's what you think. I'm more worried over Awah on your account than Calan's. There, that stopped you, Ham. I've noticed what I'd just as soon not have noticed.

HAM: What have I done?

Shem is about to answer.

HAM: I take it we are discussing Calan.

SHEM: But the discussion turned on you, Ham.

HAM: Well, now, I'm eager to hear it, Shem, very eager.

SHEM: You've taken a fancy to her, and that in itself is more than enough. And then these little liberties, so little they are seen and overlooked the same instant. But your desire keeps circling around her, Ham, and your longing for her has long lustful fingers.

HAM: Lust and longing and desire? I need time to consider that one. Lust and desire and longing, eh? But Shem, shouldn't we rather be exploring a convenient way to dispatch Calan, whatever way, no matter where?

7 7

Lust and longing and desire — well, well. Who's pitched into the ground here, Shem, looks like a grave.

SHEM: Like earth piled on someone. Who could it be?

HAM: You're not going to get any answer from him. Help me, Shem, let's question him with our nails — lust and longing and desire indeed! Too much is too much. (*They dig.*)

SHEM: Here's a hand sticking out, Ham; lift the arm high and the head will follow.

HAM: Chus! — Chus it is, and, as a matter of fact, a dead Chus. That much may be freely stated — let him be, Shem. It is Chus, Calan's right hand, Calan the Second had he lived — we're rid of this one. God permitted, as Father would phrase it, Calan's right hand to wither — good to know there's one hand less raised against our freedom. Close the vault and let him lie as long as he wants to. Let him desire, Shem, grant him his lust and longing for rest. (*They throw earth back on the grave.*)
Calan and Noah approach. Ham and Shem stand off to the side, listening.

CALAN: You did build with blessed hands. God helped you and God loves the beasts as he loves you — yet for me he has provided no shelter. Admit it, Noah, the animals' type of existence does not smell exactly like God's praise and glory. I have seen, if I'm not mistaken, your sons' bastards down in the valleys amid wolves: they yelped and snapped their jaws and fangs like any godless beast and they perished as everything did, whereupon God waxed angry — wait, Noah, something else —

NOAH: Oh Calan, speak, but speak in kindness. Why have you brought me here?

CALAN: Listen. See there — that's the grave of Chus, and Chus lies safely anchored in the earth. I don't want to toss about in the waters amid stinking beasts either, who knows where, chewed by who knows what fish. Promise me, Noah, you will put me here beside him, bury me next to him. Well?

NOAH: I, Calan?

CALAN: You, Noah.

NOAH: You in the grave, Calan? Does one bury the living?

CALAN: Not the living — the dead, Noah — I shall be dead when I have reached my destination.

NOAH (*wringing his hands*): Calan, Calan, you are living and you speak of dying?

CALAN: You must do that for me, you or one of you — Chus, who would have done it, demanded it of me and now I demand it of you. You or one of you. Why not, Noah, if God permits it — and me, after all, who scorned God and am his foe — well?

NOAH: God will deal with you according to his will — don't torture me so, Calan: how can you still joke!

CALAN: He whose son I am, Noah, he who put me into this life free and without fear — has forgotten me. Or, rather, he is done with caring for me, because he gave me much — and I thank him for all he did give. But I don't want Noah's God to drown me with cattle and camels. I am stronger than he, don't forget it, and want to die as befits a son who is no slave to his father. Now then.

NOAH: I shudder, for God commands "thou shalt not kill."

CALAN: Well, in that case I'll ride out the flood and mock your God. You will all be my servants — then your house will be my house, your wives my wives, and your hands will stir at the command of one whom I shall appoint. God is done with, God lets me hew his hands — is that how it is to be? (*To Ham and Shem:*) Come here, both of you, and ask a blessing of your father for this business.

Ham and Shem stand undecided.

HAM: You are armed, Calan, a sword and two hands — throw it down and turn your face away.

CALAN (*laughing*): My sword? Shall I let myself be slaughtered like a beast! No, Ham, my sword was born with me, my sword is part of me — if you want to get at me, you must dare my sword. God, if he is stronger than I, will put swords into your hands and command them, as he commanded the building of the Ark, to do his will. But if God gives you no swords, you are my slaves — look, just look what an inch-long faith you have in him — declare your faith and you'll have swords in your hands.

THE VOICE OF THE LEPER: Mother, Father, Noah, Noah, Calan, brothers, friends — Mother, Mother!

7 9

LEPER (*comes tottering with fear*): Oh oh oh, they're coming, oh, they're climbing.

CALAN (*shaking him*): Where's your handless guide, wretch, where have you left your friend?

LEPER: Calan? Am I with Calan? Noah, O Noah, help me, Noah!

CALAN (*striking him*): Speak — where is he?

LEPER (*looking over his back*): They're coming, they're climbing after me, thousands of bloated carcasses on the tide, hanging from trees and slapping against the mountain and heaving their bellies and rolling over each other and shoving themselves forward with the rising flood.

CALAN (*striking him again*): Where did you leave him?

LEPER: Oh Calan, all my stinking curses are at my heels, mountains and mountains of curses, gagging and dumb, want to crush me between them, knock out my breath. (*Embraces Calan convulsively.*) Calan, Calan, help me, hold me, don't let them kill me!

In the meanwhile Ham and Shem have approached. As the Leper embraces Calan, they suddenly loop ropes around both, tie them up, and throw them upon the ground. Japheth joins them.

HAM: The hands, Shem, the hands — tighter, tighter, hold the arms, round again, once more — a knot till their bones crack, pull, Shem, pull!

JAPHETH: Where's Calan — Calan, where are you?

HAM: Calan has hidden himself under a net; where are you, Calan? (*He pulls out Calan's sword.*)

JAPHETH: Bound — you've bound him? What has he done to you?

HAM (*pushing him aside*): My hands are shaking, Shem, you take it and finish it, just plunge it in!

SHEM: My hands are not shaking, but my heart cannot do it. I don't understand this kind of business. You do it, Ham.

HAM (*coming close*): Get away, all of you, and don't look — why should your eyes slash at my hands? (*The sword falls to the ground.*)

CALAN: You do it, Japheth, pick it up and run it through both of us — do it, dear Japheth!

JAPHETH: I can't, Calan, there's blood in your body, and your sword is so terribly sharp. (*Runs off.*)

CALAN: Noah, Noah, remember all I've done for you — now do this for me, Noah, strike!

NOAH: Your life is in God's hands, Calan; place your heart at his feet, and he will loosen your fetters. Neither I nor my sons shall be your judges. (*To Shem and Ham:*) Come, children, the time is ripe for God's vengeance. (*Takes the sword and goes off.*)

HAM (*clapping Shem on the shoulder*): You're free, Shem; time has seasoned our freedom.

LEPER: Must I rot here with Calan, oh you marvels, you heroes, you kings, oh you divinities you! (*They are about to go; he screams louder.*) Your hands, oh your clever, quick hands, you benefactors — Calan is your enemy, only he; but I, I am your friend, a pitiable, miserable particle of goodwill for your welfare. Turn us over, shove me on top so I can breathe when he drowns — what harm have I ever done you, O you ornaments, O princes, O you paragons, you butchers, you rotters?

SHEM: He's right, Ham; why does he deserve this?

HAM: He? Well, let's give him his wish, let him lie on top, and let him look forward to a ripe old age. (*He rolls them over.*)

LEPER: Shem, O Shem, how the ropes cut into my freezing flesh, O Shem, how I would lick your feet, Shem, what have I done to deserve this?

CALAN: Go on, untie the poor fool.

LEPER: Untie me, good friends, I'll do anything for you and from my heart — but he must remain slung in ropes coiled around and over — I despise him. I'll do it gladly, gladly.

HAM: And spoil our sweet freedom — he's got hands, Shem, and Calan will promise him half the world. We, Shem, are the lords of the earth. (*Pulls him away with him.*) Take a firm hold on your heart, and generation upon generation will give you their blessings. (*Both leave.*)

4 ╱ The same. Darkness. Calan and Leper.

LEPER: God is getting even with you for your crimes, Calan; God is doing it, and whatever he does, he does to abundance. For this execrable existence he wished on me *I* should get even with *him*, but it seems to me justice always strikes the wrong party, even now. God helps himself to my right to vengeance, and in his eagerness avenges himself on me. Do you think God is only deaf? I suspect he's also blind; at least he can't see in the dark, or else he'd be uneasy to find us obviously being treated with unreasonable equality, as though equally guilty. What about it, Calan? Do you think God might get fed up with the misery of this world? Do you think just for once he'd throw up because bitter, burning human wretchedness took a bite out of his majestic paunch, while claws of prayers scratched his belly sore? Is it possible he has a heart? I doubt it.

CALAN: Shut up, tormentor!

LEPER: What did you call me? Tormentor? Why then I'd be like God — God forbid that I should think *that*. No, tormenting he understands beyond all understanding and comprehension.

CALAN: The slaver drips from your mouth into my eyes and runs over my lips. Be quiet, as I am.

LEPER: Gnashing your teeth, Calan?

Calan is silent.

LEPER: Calan — hey, Calan! Too proud to talk to me? I want to cure you of your sin; see, I'll slobber the juice from my rotting mouth all over you. That will take care of your pride, and your groans will merge harmoniously with mine. So we are lovers, lovingly coupled. We may not gambol in high spirits, but then we're nice and cozy, nice and cheerful. What do you say, humble brother Calan?

Calan is silent.

The Shepherd approaches crawling.

SHEPHERD: Who speaks of humility and cheer? Where cheer is speaking, there will I remain.

LEPER: Here, here, brother, here, in this slimy spot — here where we are rocking in wanton rapture — it's me, brother, me and Calan, tightly coiled in bands of true brotherhood.

CALAN: What path do you choose when all lead to ruin?

SHEPHERD: The rising waters pointed the way as I lay exhausted on the ground — the flood is filling up all lower depths and hounds every living thing upwards. I am wandering with the four-legged tribes who left their caves and dugouts and holes in the mountains. Do not lie there. Get up, and let us join the flight of moving creatures.

LEPER: What — get up? Save us from our present glory: undo the knot-tings of skin and hemp and we shall wander together in cozy cheer.

SHEPHERD: I have no hands to help you.

CALAN: No, he has no hands, he has none, he cannot help, and the flood waters are hounding every living thing upwards.

LEPER: Serves you right; smack your lips, Calan, with the taste of God's just reward. But why should I, just because you chopped off his hands, lie here in slimy cheer? You got what you deserved; why me?

CALAN: I can taste what came from my deeds; I'm getting what I deserve. But this avenging God is still not the true one. Noah's God is a violent God, as I was violent, and I shudder before such divinity. Here I lie in this slime and take pity on his puny grandeur.

The shepherd drops to the ground and thrashes about.

LEPER: What are you doing there? Why whimper — want to kill the world with your blows before it finishes you?

SHEPHERD: The snapping, starving vermin, throngs of a thousand ravenous beasts — they are upon me. (*He pulls himself up and disappears.*)

LEPER: Upon you? Upon me too, biting everywhere at my body — have pity, God, have pity, God — speak, God, say but one word in your defense, and I will listen. Speak, shout — just clear your throat!

For a moment one hears nothing but the rustle of rain, then low thunder in the distance.

LEPER: Oho, is that it? No: a half-answer, a damned evasion, a pitiful defense; your distant growling dodges the question. Maybe you have a heart after all and wouldn't want to drive your beloved beasts from their meal? Yes, maybe, maybe a heart after all, a pretty gentle heart, as is proper and fitting for a gracious God toward his hungry guests. Fodder, that's what you are, Calan, fodder for ravaging beasts; listen to them wheeze and wail, feel the blaze of their fangs singeing your flesh; now you taste in your fingers what you once did to others — Calan —

5 ⨍ The same. Mist and a grey light. Two shapeless figures roll on the ground. His garments drawn tight about him, Noah comes wading frightened through the mud. He puts a jar on the ground.

NOAH: I heard whimpering all night long, all of us heard it, but my sons kept the door barred. Where are you — Calan, where are you? I have come to still your thirst.

FIRST FIGURE: Here, Noah. Give me, give me.

NOAH: That was not Calan's voice — who are you, wretches?

FIRST FIGURE: I was Calan, but the animals have chewed my tongue, I cannot speak in my former voice — give me to drink.

NOAH (*drawing back*): Take what I leave here for you — I know you no longer.

FIRST FIGURE: The beasts sucked out our eyes, peeled the flesh off our fingers — we cannot see, we cannot reach — give us, Noah, give us.

THE OTHER FIGURE: Now speak of God's wrath or speak of God's justice, if you dare.

NOAH: *That* was Calan — Calan, is it you? — poor Calan!

CALAN: *Now* speak of a just God, speak of God's vengeance, dare!

NOAH (*drawing back farther, his hands covering his eyes*): God's ways are just, but his might surpasses the strength of my eyes. They cannot bear the sight of his work.

CALAN: When the rats tore my eyes from their sockets, Noah, I began to see. I can bear the sight of God; I see God.
Noah moves still farther away.

CALAN: Are you listening, Noah?

NOAH: Oh Calan, what do you see — God is my shepherd, I shall not want. He will guide me through the flood and save me from destruction.

CALAN: That is the God of floods and of flesh, that is the God who has it that the world is less than nothing and God is all. But I can see the other God who will have it that the world is big and God smaller than nothing, a point, a spark, and all things have their beginning in him and all their end. He has no form, no voice.

NOAH: Poor Calan!

CALAN: You poor Noah! Ah Noah, how glorious it is that God has no form and cannot make words — words that issue from flesh — God is pure flame, a glimmering spark, and all things tumble from him, and all things return to the abyss of his flame. He creates and his creation creates him anew.

NOAH: Oh Calan — God who passes immutable from eternity to eternity?

CALAN: I, too, will journey to that place from which I was tumbled and also through me does God grow and with me change into the new — how glorious it is, Noah, that I too have no longer a form but am finally only flame and abyss in God — now I sink toward him — God becomes Calan, and Calan God — he in my lowliness, I in his splendor — one indivisible.

HAM: (*rushing in*): Where — where — where are you, Father, what keeps you? There were jolts and tremors in the depths of the earth and the desert of the flood is rising to mountains, and its walls are rolling down on us — live, Father, live lest God's wrath bury you with the lost! *He pulls Noah away as one hears the roar of approaching tidal waves.*

THE GENUINE SEDEMUNDS

Cast of Characters

OLD SEDEMUND

YOUNG SEDEMUND

UNCLE WALDEMAR SEDEMUND

GRUDE

MRS. GRUDE

SABINA

MANKMOOS, A TAILOR

CANDIDO FRANCHI

RING

GREEDYCOCK

GLORYLANE

SWINGCORD

SERGEANT LAMBKIN

BROMANN, A SCULPTOR

COACHMAN KARL

GRAVEYARD CUSTODIAN

GRETE MANKMOOS

MILITIAMEN

CITIZENS

CARPENTER'S APPRENTICE

GARDENER'S BOY

SANATORIUM ATTENDANT

SUSEMIHL, A BOY SCOUT

Scene 1

A row of booths at a militiamen's fair. In the center is Candido Franchi's Animal Circus, the front of which is papered with hunting scenes of a ferociously romantic nature. The most shattering scene is at the top: a lion, apparently jumping from the skies, attacks some chocolate-colored men. It is the early afternoon of the third day of the fair. There is little activity as the place is still asleep after the preceding day's surfeit. Sitting in a wheelchair and followed by two or three boy scouts, one plucking a guitar, Sabina slowly rolls past. A Carpenter's Apprentice with a child's coffin on his shoulder arrives and stares at the picture of the lion. He is joined by a Gardener's Boy carrying a wreath.

CARPENTER'S APPRENTICE: Where the devil d'you think you're going with that bouquet?

GARDENER'S BOY: Somebody ordered it for a funeral in the old graveyard. I'll get rid of it there.

CARPENTER'S APPRENTICE: Can't say it's that easy with my coffin. My boss started boozing early in the morning. He said: take it there on time — but he forgot to tell me where — so how am I supposed to know! Maybe you saw him?

GARDENER'S BOY (*shakes his head and spits*): Who cares about your boss! There won't be no shooting before three, 'cause someone is going to be buried with music. If you make it in time to the beergarden you'll meet him there, maybe.

They stroll off. Grude, dressed for a funeral, appears and enters the animal tent after looking around hurriedly. Mrs. Grude comes a second later. Clearly on the track of her husband, she is about to follow him in. She hesitates, then stops, quite unable to decide. At the same

time, Young Sedemund has come from the other direction. He is in
the company of Mankmoos, a tailor. He halts in order to speak but
she ignores him. Mankmoos is a creature of distress, with the face of
an alcoholic and a white patriarchial beard. Suspended by a colorful
ribbon, a medal dangles on his chest.

YOUNG SEDEMUND: So you rushed bright and early to my father — and did your business with him turn out good or bad?

MANKMOOS: Last night my wife died on me, Mr. Sedemund, and so I thought. . . . You see, Mr. Sedemund, I have five little children at home. My wife weighed a solid 180 pounds, and knew how to get things done — —. Well, I thought to myself, go to Mr. Sedemund, and so I went to your esteemed daddy. But your Uncle Waldemar stopped me. Up to that point he was quite nice and friendly. He told me to wait a minute because your father was lying in bed sick. At last he sent down this note. (*Pulls out a note.*)

YOUNG SEDEMUND (*takes it and reads*): "Upon careful inspection of my financial resources I do not find myself in a position to come to your aid with any sum worthy of mention"— — well. So that's what he sent down. Then what?

MANKMOOS (*who has in the meanwhile been staring at the picture of the lion*): Then I went upstairs and right into the sickroom.

YOUNG SEDEMUND: And?

MANKMOOS: And heard your uncle, Mr. Waldemar, finish the story and heard them laugh. They laughed about my wife weighing 180 pounds. So I got mad, you know, and was about to turn to your father, and in fact went up to his bed where he was having his breakfast, stretched out so comfortably. Alas, Mr. Sedemund, I should be so sick and eat so well.

YOUNG SEDEMUND: And what happened in the end?

MANKMOOS: The end? Shouldn't I say first what I told him?

YOUNG SEDEMUND: No, I can imagine.

MANKMOOS: In the end — Mr. Waldemar opened the door for me and said very kindly if I wouldn't be so good as to — but he didn't mean it.

YOUNG SEDEMUND: Why not?

MANKMOOS: It wasn't at all kind, it was two-faced.

YOUNG SEDEMUND: So, that's when you took to your heels, Mankmoos?

He sees Mrs. Grude and approaches her. Mankmoos remains standing.
Mrs. Grude? Good afternoon, Mrs. Grude. (*They greet each other.*)
Tell me, for heaven's sake, Mrs. Grude, where is Grude? I was just
now in the — — institution and was told he got leave for the day to
attend the funeral, the one that's to take place in the churchyard near
the new shooting range. So I came to see him.

MRS. GRUDE (*confused*): Yes, that's right. They're burying old Gimpel.
At two.

YOUNG SEDEMUND: Where is our Grude now?

Mrs. Grude points to the entrance of the booth.
Young Sedemund looks at it in surprise.

MRS. GRUDE (*drying her tears*): I was also at the institution and got the
same information, Mr. Sedemund. And now he's run into that tent as
though frightened and hiding from me.

YOUNG SEDEMUND (*taking her hand for a second*): Oh God, Mrs. Grude.
(*To Mankmoos:*) All right, Mankmoos, there anything else? But no,
I guess I have a number of questions to ask *you*. Wait for me in the
beergarden. Or do you have to get home to your children?

MANKMOOS: I'd rather wait for you a minute, Mr. Sedemund. Here I know
what I'm supposed to do, so to say. At home it's always: Mankmoos
here, Mankmoos there, as if there's anything I could do about my
wife's death. I'd like it better if she was still alive.

YOUNG SEDEMUND: All right, then wait for me in the beergarden. (*Mank-*
moos goes off.) Mrs. Grude, how did it actually happen that Grude
entered the asylum? As you know, I haven't been here for years.

MRS. GRUDE: Really, it wasn't my doing, Mr. Sedemund, his being committed. If one can put it that way, he committed himself on his own
and entirely against my wishes — went to the doctor and demanded
admission. He always used to say: either all of you are mad or else
I am.

YOUNG SEDEMUND: Yes, yes, that was his way of clowning. He always did
express himself strangely.

MRS. GRUDE: But he isn't insane either, he's only — peculiar, you know.

YOUNG SEDEMUND: Do you think *he* thinks he's mad?

MRS. GRUDE: Ah, Mr. Sedemund, since you went away his good angel has
left him.

YOUNG SEDEMUND: Why, I thought, Mrs. Grude, you'd have it in you to take my place as a guardian angel. At least you had the opportunity, didn't you?

MRS. GRUDE: Oh — I — that's the whole point — who am I, what can I do? I could only love him.

YOUNG SEDEMUND: And probably that wasn't enough?

MRS. GRUDE (*weeping*): Should I have put on a show of sharing his fictions? If a man grows up in the backwoods, brought up by a grandfather who sees ghosts, you can't really expect him to be quite right in the mind.

YOUNG SEDEMUND: I know — but this is an old story.

MRS. GRUDE: Wait! Grude still believes, maybe not in the phantom who inhabits the house, but still in — oh, what do I know — in something — ask him yourself. It went so far that I ordered him not to see his invisible ghostly visitor. Whatever lives, he maintained, must always have some kind of contact with the hidden. Everyone is a double, and is never totally by and of himself — you're a waxflower, he told me, a thing and nothing more, you are not secretly carrying on with sunlight as each buttercup is. And so it went, on and on, and he grew wilder and more furious with his recriminations. When at last he went into that institution he did it largely for my sake, because I assume I was sicker than he from all the arguments.

YOUNG SEDEMUND: The genuine Grude.

MRS. GRUDE: And look, Mr. Sedemund, I am going to confess something to you as a good old friend of my husband, something I was going to tell him myself today. I am *not* a thing, am *not* alone, at least not any longer. (*She smiles through her tears.*) He is always with me, but not as bogeyman or phantom. In his own form, almost, and yet different and quite real. That's why I went to that place today and why the doctor sent me quickly to the graveyard after him. As I saw him walk in front of me in the distance, I am positive he saw me too. So he turned and slipped into this tent, and here I am, outside.

YOUNG SEDEMUND: Do you want me to go after him and tell him you have to speak to him alone?

MRS. GRUDE (*shakes her head, and touches his arm*): How can I shout at him what has to be said quietly? No, Mr. Sedemund, wait here for him, but don't tell him anything. Let him find out for himself what it is his business to know about me. Just be patient with him.

YOUNG SEDEMUND: As you like, Mrs. Grude. People have to treat each other with patience — and warmth. Let me walk you to the corner.
Both go off.
Grude emerges from the tent with Candido Franchi.

FRANCHI: Maybe you know a dottore? Poor Caesar he make me feel so sad, very sad — hang down his head left, hang his head right, very unhappy — and it very bad sign that he sit like he want to lay a egg. It look very, very bad for him.

GRUDE: Poor fellow, that Caesar. Yesterday he still howled with such a hunger of the desert that the air in the garden behind the institution came alive. Yes, my dear Mr. Franchi, we have all an inaudibly roaring lion in back of us. That's what's best about us: someone in full majesty is out to catch us and gulp us down — that we should deserve it, eh?

FRANCHI: Oh, I gotta your meaning.

GRUDE: All day yesterday while he was roaring I thought: what am I, after all, if not the spirit of his stomach, his body-soul — not mentioning of course his actual jaws and belly. That's why I am not — myself, you see, until his majesty takes pleasure in devouring me.

FRANCHI: Oh, I understand . . .

GRUDE: There's always two of us. The lion behind me is also a part of me, a kind of my true self — is that more or less what you mean too?

FRANCHI: Exact, very exact so!

GRUDE: You really acquire a proper self-respect if you know there is such a splendid roarer from the vast desert behind you, who is out to swallow our bones and that little soul of ours and who roars with delight in anticipation — doesn't that make a person want to roar with delight himself?

FRANCHI: I understand very good.

GRUDE: Well, you run off to the vet. How do you expect to prolong your own bodily existence if his time runs out? Dr. Brownrider, No. 7 Ocean Grove. Turn right and then straight ahead: No. 7 Ocean Grove.

FRANCHI: Capisco, I whiz like mad for the poor Caesar. (*Goes off.*)

GRUDE: Yes, go. I wish you all the best, you and your Caesar.
In the meantime Sedemund has returned.

9 3

YOUNG SEDEMUND: Look who's here, Grude, old friend . . .

GRUDE: Hello! How marvelous that you should come today. (*They shake hands.*)

YOUNG SEDEMUND: Why just today?

GRUDE (*pointing to the picture of the lion*): Look, how he overwhelms them, the savages' conscience overwhelming us savages! And now that the poor fellow is suffering in his guts and cannot roar, much less jump, you arrive with your paws and can wash my head.

Shakes his hands once again.

I'll tell you everything: the doctor decides in no uncertain terms that my case is Greek to him. He doesn't want to hear of madness. He wants to drive out the Greek element, you see, and that's why everything remains as it is. (*Laughs.*) My wife told you everything of course; did she cry too?

YOUNG SEDEMUND: Yes, Grude, she cried. And as she is kind, she wishes the best for you and herself.

GRUDE: Wait! (*Takes hold of him and turns him round and round.*) Are you then the cause of all this hullabaloo? (*Reconsiders.*) Adamist, political babe in the woods, etc. etc.? With such publicity what are you doing in this quiet neck of the woods?

Young Sedemund takes a telegram from his pocket and gives it to Grude.

GRUDE (*reading*): "Father critically ill. Your presence absolutely imperative — Uncle Waldemar." Is he dead?

YOUNG SEDEMUND (*folding the telegram*): He isn't even sick.

GRUDE: That shows good sense, but how sensible was Uncle Waldemar's summons?

YOUNG SEDEMUND (*shrugging*): Please, no playacting! Your mind is as sound as it ever was, but with something extra which needs time to clarify itself. But as someone with a bogeyman in his conscience you shouldn't have taken a wife who has hardly left childhood herself.

Grude looks at him narrowly.

YOUNG SEDEMUND: I am not supposed to tell, since she told me not to. Well, what do you want to know? I received the telegram, came, went in the morning still unwashed to my father's house, met a crazy character of a tailor-patcher, who bumped into me and served me up an incoherent breakfast bulletin of my healthy, deadsick Papa consuming a royal breakfast on his deathbed. What do you think of that? More: this tailor has better ears than one would suspect because somehow he got wind of the name of the doctor who takes care of my father: Professor Doorknob of Rostock. I knew right away: Professor Latchbolt is the one; and then I remembered this . . .

GRUDE: Yes, of course — I know what you're going to tell me: when your mother's time was running out, one evening at sundown, she took hold of your head, and turned your face to the wall so you couldn't watch her as she spoke: my son, if one day your father lies on his deathbed and Professor Latchbolt directs his cure via long distance, and if Uncle Waldemar is there running the show, then, son, keep your ears pointed and commit yourself to nothing that you can't carry through.

YOUNG SEDEMUND: Professor Latchbolt was again and again my father's last court of appeal, whenever he wanted to go against my mother's wishes. By his say-so my father's good fortune expanded despite my mother's authority. My father was and is under the spell of numerous dissipations. So he found or invented in Professor Latchbolt a kind of medical pack animal that carried him over the desert to distant pleasure grounds where he lived it up magnificently — all thanks to Professor Latchbolt's ready compliance.

GRUDE: This Professor Latchbolt must have been a kind of bogeyman to you and your mother.

YOUNG SEDEMUND: Exactly. A phantom power supporting the paternal view of things, insofar as he saw them in terms of his own well-being, put perhaps like this: "What must I do to be happy in my own way? . . ."

Again Sabina wheels past. They gaze after her.

GRUDE (*putting his arm on Sedemund's shoulder*): Wait! Take a look at that crippled girl. Though I met her only this morning, I have sneaked into this maze of booths merely to follow her. She does something to me, you know — eyes full of deceit and, at the same time, of piety, and then such a piggish mouth — a witch!

YOUNG SEDEMUND: It is also possible to think of her as a saint.

GRUDE (*absent-minded*): And — Uncle Waldemar, Sedemund?

9 5

YOUNG SEDEMUND: Uncle Waldemar (*shrugging*) still trumpets his hosannas out backwards, just as he did then.

GRUDE: Then? When was that?

YOUNG SEDEMUND: When a certain something befell my mother, about which I was not told, but which I believe broke her heart. She pined away while I was mostly kept away from the house, ostensibly to help her recover. I remember only that her grievance resounded within me when she sat at the piano. I came to realize I was made of that despair. It must have been that dusky evening you spoke of earlier. Now I keep my chin up and think of my mother — because Father (*showing the telegram*) occupies that equivocal deathbed.

GRUDE (*thoughtfully*): But, Sedemund, what about those rumors about you, or rather, you and your entourage?

YOUNG SEDEMUND: It isn't much of anything.

GRUDE: But still . . . what about that Adamism of yours that everybody laughs at?

YOUNG SEDEMUND: Adamism is a poor tag. They hung it on us; now we are trying to defend it, we Adamists. The Bible has it that Adam set to tilling the earth, which is to say, he stopped philosophizing. As you know, Adam too had no daddy, no traditional moral creed, but could entrust himself to his own open, live good sense. In this vein, we are publishing our letters and don't care what the public says about us as long as they continue to read us.

GRUDE: I can picture your father's reactions to all this, good friend Adam. But what do these political babes in the woods have to say for themselves?

YOUNG SEDEMUND: A one-time friend called us that. By ridiculing our platform as brainless baby-cries he succeeded in attaching an image of baby-smells to our project.

GRUDE: Your father must regard himself highly honored to have such an honorable son! Is it possible he was so hurt that for appearance's sake he had to take to this deathbed? You did want to hear, didn't you, what I thought of his indisposition?

YOUNG SEDEMUND: You may have a point. If you're interested, by the way, I'll tell you what makes these babes in the woods tick. Our plans are the simplest. (*They slowly walk off.*) We take an inventory of ourselves and our fellow men. If there is going to be a new order, we first want to know what the nature is of that which should be enhanced. So that when at last the worthy bride and groom are enjoined to be fruitful and multiply it won't seem quite so cynical — we . . .

GRUDE (*points to the animal tent*): You'll have to inject them by state law with a savage's conscience — if not in shape then in quality like a lion. *Both go off. Candido Franchi comes running and meets Ring, the owner of the flea circus.*

RING: Candido! Candido!

FRANCHI: No, Mr. Flea Circus, nothing!

RING: Why isn't Caesar making no racket no more? Say, is that nothing? It sounds terrible I tell you, rumbles all through me, his being so quiet.

FRANCHI: You know already?

RING: What's louder than silence? You can't do his hollering. Have you found a doctor?

FRANCHI: He come right 'way, he say, right 'way. But first he ask have I got plenty insurance. I got very scared.

RING: You up-to-date on his funeral premiums, eh?

FRANCHI: Si, si, he got *that*!

RING: He's old, eh? Moth-eaten fur, no teeth!

FRANCHI: Could still swallow you up just like you are, but whether he could shit you out, fishbones and ever't'ing, that I don't know. Dear collegio, what you feed your fleas? Cost you much?

RING (*pointing to his armpit*): Eat their fill, twice a week.

FRANCHI: If one break his leg, there are doctors for bugs, maybe?
He grows calmer, pulls out his tobacco pouch and fills his pipe.
I tell you, maybe when I finish tobacco, Caesar he a corpse. Look here, you donkey, maybe got six, seven pipefuls in here. (*Puts his hands on Ring's shoulder.*) Say nothing to nobody, dear collegio. Caesar is O.K., he take rest.

RING: If you give him a enema, he might last a few more weeks.

FRANCHI: I don't like jokes no more. Poor Caesar, dottore come right 'way. You want to take one more look? Come.
They go into the tent. Greedycock and Glorylane in the short green coats of the militia enter.

GREEDYCOCK: Did you tell him, brother Glorylane, that it's *my* brat?

9 7

GLORYLANE: Named no names, except that the kid's father is ready with a generous payoff. By the way, his name is Swingcord.

GREEDYCOCK: What? Swingcord!

GLORYLANE: That's right, and he wants it down in writing.

GREEDYCOCK: That crook! Is *he* afraid I'm going to double-cross him?

GLORYLANE: Be glad he takes the child. He doesn't ask who the father is, makes no disgusting difference to him. But he's a stickler for form. We'll see him in the beergarden.

Both go off. The Carpenter's Apprentice runs past with the coffin. The Gardener's Boy, still carrying the wreath, meanders in.

Scene 2

The beergarden. A shooting contest is in progress. To the right are the service quarters. To the left the open area merges with bushes and trees. In that direction lies the shooting range, from which shots can be heard. Militiamen in their green uniforms walk up and down or sit on wooden benches drinking beer. Toward the rear, the view of the road is obstructed by a dense hedge and pretty high trees, but through chinks one can still see people passing by. There is an open entrance to the street. Mankmoos slinks from one spot to another. At the same time the Carpenter's Apprentice, carrying the coffin, enters the beergarden from the street and goes searching among the trees. While passing Mankmoos, he speaks.

CARPENTER'S APPRENTICE: Where is Tessmer, the carpenter?

MANKMOOS: If he isn't here, he must be somewhere else . . . I have no use for that coffin.

CARPENTER'S APPRENTICE (*putting coffin down*): But I'll let you take a look at it, for free — a beaut, eh?

Mankmoos turns away, dignified.
The Gardener's Boy comes.

GARDENER'S BOY: Well, Jackie, if you're going to cool that box off a moment, I can do the same with this here wreath. Yeah, as they say, no master falls from the sky — yours is so punch-happy where he is, it don't occur to him the coffin needs a child.

He puts down the wreath, and they sit. On the street a hearse can be seen rolling past; it is heavily decorated with tassels, funerary emblems, and black drapes. In front of it above the hedge are visible the nodding heads of horses, covered by hoods reminiscent of medieval tournaments, and topped by tufts of horsehair. The carriage stops at a point at which the rear wheels and part of the carriage can be seen through the entrance. The coachman of the hearse and undertaker's assistants enter and sit at a table in the foreground.

COACHMAN KARL: That's what my wife told me, and now I am telling you, so now you're in the picture. Don't anyone have a drop left in his bottle?

FIRST UNDERTAKER'S ASSISTANT: You with your bottle, friend, you're on the brink of the grave yourself. You ought to try figuring out a little detour, but no: you gallop down a shortcut every time.

COACHMAN KARL: The wife told me — so that's that.

SECOND UNDERTAKER'S ASSISTANT: Pay-raise here, pay-raise there — this is something has to be considered carefully. Your wife isn't my wife, for your information.

COACHMAN KARL (*grabs the waiter by the coat-tail. and pushes the empty bottle into his hand*): Fill 'er up — hear? (*To the undertaker's assistants:*) Listen to what I have to say. (*They put their heads together, whispering.*)

Franchi and Ring appear and sit at a table next to them.

RING: Well, my esteemed colleague, is the pipe all out?

FRANCHI (*protesting with a sad shaking of his head*): I am poor devil, friend, you please say good t'ings about Caesar.

RING: How would that help you, Candido? Your Caesar up and went his way. Light up your pipe again, friend, and get yourself a new Caesar.

FRANCHI: Easy for you to say. You catch fleas from your pajamas, but my Caesar, he was not jus' anybody.

Grude and Sedemund appear and walk up and down.
Mankmoos hovers nearby, waiting to be noticed.

GRUDE: I see. Then you were innocent: your movement has nothing to do with politics. You were smeared, as far as that goes.

YOUNG SEDEMUND: Not entirely, my good friend. Shunning the highways,

99

we take side roads. Our ideas will penetrate, as it were, through people's noses — you can close your eyes, plug your ears all you want —
it won't work, you'll have to take a breath, and then you'll smell how
it stands with you people.

The waiter has brought Coachman Karl a bottle. He drinks and passes
it around. Mankmoos watches them.

COACHMAN KARL: Well, take a look at that one. Where did you get your
medal, you old crony?

MANKMOOS (*approaching*): The Grand Duke decorated me for twenty-
five years' membership in the Society for the Promotion of Common
Welfare.

COACHMAN KARL: Did I hear you say commotion is the common fare?
For that you can have a drink.

MANKMOOS (*drinking*): As a matter of fact, I haven't had breakfast yet.

COACHMAN KARL: But you had your lunch?

MANKMOOS: Who is there to fix my lunch? My wife just died.

COACHMAN KARL: She gone, eh? Well, I'd sooner be dead than in her shoes.
Here's some straight advice: let Greedycock and Glorylane bury her.
You have to be able to pay though — through the nose. Ask these fine
gents in black.

FIRST UNDERTAKER'S ASSISTANT: My wife fried me some tripe for lunch,
and that, any way you look at it, Karl, is Greedycock's and Glorylane's
tripe. If your wife doesn't serve you anything good, that's more her
business than Greedycock's and Glorylane's.

COACHMAN KARL (*giving Mankmoos the empty bottle*): If it's all right
with you, let's have another slug of this Greedycock-Glorylane brew.
Go and have it filled. (*Mankmoos goes off.*)

YOUNG SEDEMUND (*stopping in front of Grude*): People put their faith in
securing their own happiness, but they have to learn to put it in giving happiness to others. Giving makes grace. To give oneself — the
highest grace. This is man's nature: he yearns for something good, a
belief, an altar upon which to sacrifice himself. Therefore: give him
a goal, a meaning, and man casts himself headlong trustingly into happiness and grace. As it is now, without meaning, without a purpose
beyond oneself, the entire effort passes merely into one's belly and
pocketbook.

100

GRUDE: For heaven's sake, remember we're celebrating a shooting contest. If you keep talking like that, they're going to put you too in an institution. (*He notices Franchi.*) Look, my lion's daddy, suffering on account of his scion of the wilderness. I must speak to him. (*Shakes Franchi's hand.*) How is our indisposed Caesar?

Sedemund sees Mankmoos as he approaches with a full bottle and follows him. Mankmoos absent-mindedly sips again and again.

RING (*answering in Franchi's place*): Sir, he escaped, and now we are all confabulating together and counterplanning how to catch him.

FRANCHI (*looking sadly at Ring*): Dear God, how I like it to be just dat. I swear he should be happy at home in his cage tonight, joyfully gulping the fresh meat. (*Quietly to Grude:*) But, alas, he don't jump no more. I skinned him already and hung it up to dry. It look at me so awful real I get a pain in my heart, and so I went out with Ring.

GRUDE: And closed your show?

FRANCHI: Closed, complete, basta, and Ring even give day off to his bugs.

GRUDE: But if he had really escaped, wouldn't we all scurry off like bugs?

FRANCHI (*contemptuously*): No, sir, I not! You must be awful ignorant. He know my voice, he know I mean business. Like this, sir: Caesar, nice Caesar, nice, good Caesar — then he get dumb and stupid and he think to himself: do he mean it: then he don't know which; the whip or horsemeat? Then he act good — yes, yes.

Sedemund and Mankmoos approach.

GRUDE (*to Mankmoos*): Keeping your ears open? Hear how it's done? A reward is waiting if you can do it. (*Winks at Franchi.*)

FRANCHI (*agreeable*): Much much money, yes, si.

MANKMOOS: Is he far? If there is no particular hurry, I ought to have a bite first. (*Drinks.*)

GRUDE: We are talking about a lion, good man, whom you must grab by the ear and deliver to us.

MANKMOOS: What does the lion look like?

GRUDE: Haven't you ever seen one? When he creeps through the bushes he's like a big yellow dog. You *have* seen a big yellow dog?

MANKMOOS: Oh, maybe one has whisked past me one time or another. But how do I do it then? Simply put him in my pocket?

101

RING: Listen when he comes running, you yell: Hey, Caesar, nice Caesar, nice, nice. (*To Franchi:*) Right?

FRANCHI (*nods and laughs*): You try and yell.

MANKMOOS: Hey, shitter, nice, make nice, nice!

RING: And then — then you grab him by the tail.

MANKMOOS: But how do I get past his muzzle?

RING: He'll turn and walk away. He'll think: here comes a whipping, you see, that's what he'll think. But you mustn't whip him; pinch his tail till you feel the pulse right under his bushy tip, then his breath goes swoosh out his mouth, and then all you do is lead him gently home. (*To Franchi:*) Right?

FRANCHI: Jus' so. Ring, he a expert like me.

RING: Without technical know-how, there's no way of getting hold of a lion.

MANKMOOS (*looking about bewildered*): Can't I first have a little bit something to eat?

GRUDE: Let him eat.

MANKMOOS: Scrambled eggs?

GRUDE: Scrambled eggs make one scamper and scramble — perfect. Old King Frederick gorged himself on scrambled eggs into a state of majestic biliousness; you know about that.

MANKMOOS: Ah yes, I know. Eggs scrambled, then. It's a deal.

GRUDE (*takes Mankmoos to the undertaker's men and orders food. In the meantime, quietly to Franchi*): Will you sell me that hide, Mr. Franchi?

FRANCHI: Maybe yes, maybe no.

GRUDE: I'll come around tonight or in the morning.

An attendant from the insane asylum appears.

ATTENDANT: The doctor sends his compliments and says to remember not to forget to return. But if Mr. Grude has not yet spoken to Mrs. Grude . . .

GRUDE: Of course, I have to speak to my wife, and then I have to make a little purchase.

ATTENDANT: Very well, sir. (*Goes off.*)

YOUNG SEDEMUND: Oh Grude, my uncle, Mr. Waldemar, passed by outside. There's no danger he'll see me here in this crowd, but you'll understand if I look for a more shaded spot.

They move to the side among the trees. Uncle Waldemar enters looking for someone and stops at the table of Greedycock's people.

UNCLE WALDEMAR: Didn't Mr. Gweedycock go to the shooting contest? I went to his wesidence — they diwected me heah.

COACHMAN KARL: Sir, we're only the Greedycock and Glorylane men. If he was around we wouldn't be sitting. Greedycock and Glorylane don't go for sharing a table with their men.

Uncle Waldemar looks around.

Grude returns looking intentionally unsuspecting; he is about to pass, then in disbelief catches sight of Uncle Waldemar.

UNCLE WALDEMAR: Mistah Gwude, if I am not mistaken.

GRUDE: So it is, Mr. Sedemund; what can I do for you?

UNCLE WALDEMAR: What a sahpwise — a wholly unfohseen coincidence, Mistah Gwude.

GRUDE: Indeed, Mr. Sedemund. But foolish people like myself can sometimes be found unexpectedly, you see.

As they converse Grude leads him forward and places him so that Uncle Waldemar turns his back to the restaurant. He himself glances over Uncle Waldemar's shoulder as Sedemund leaves the beergarden unnoticed. While slipping through the entrance of the restaurant, he seems to disappear behind the hangings of the hearse. Grude strikes his forehead.

GRUDE: God, Mr. Sedemund, are you dressed for a funeral? Please excuse the question.

UNCLE WALDEMAR: What's the mattah, Mistah Gwude? I mahvel they ah letting you stwoll about fwee at this fair.

GRUDE (*solemnly*): I've been given a day off for the funeral — but you, Mr. Sedemund, — and how does it happen that your brother isn't here?

UNCLE WALDEMAR (*smiling in an astonished and pitying manner as though he recalled he had to do with an invalid*): My bwothah, Mistah Gwude, is vewy vewy sick.

GRUDE: And can't come?

UNCLE WALDEMAR: Natuwally not, Mistah Gwude; why, if I may ask, should or ought he to come?

GRUDE: Oh God, Mr. Sedemund, how can you ask such a question!

1 0 3

UNCLE WALDEMAR: I do not understand at all, Mistah Gwude, what yoah wohds ah meant to convey.

GRUDE: Then you have no idea — your nephew — Mr. Sedemund, tell me, where is your nephew?

UNCLE WALDEMAR: My nephew Gewahd? He'll be heah tomowwow if he isn't heah aweddy. We were expecting him last night because his fathah fell sick but — but —

GRUDE (*allowing his folded hands to drop devoutly*): What a mix-up! (*Pulling himself together:*) Is your brother *very* sick?

UNCLE WALDEMAR (*hesitating*): He is in bed on ohdahs of Pwofessor Latchbolt — still, he is —

GRUDE: And you haven't received a telegram? Good Lord, how fast, how shockingly fast, it must all have happened. His political friends, of course, refused to let anybody else —

UNCLE WALDEMAR: Mistah Gwude, for God's sake what happened?

GRUDE (*stares in deep thought at his feet*): Do you see that hearse, Mr. Sedemund?

UNCLE WALDEMAR: No, no, no, that isn't possible, my poor bwothah, Mistah Gwude, that, that . . .

GRUDE: It's almost too much for a father, and for an uncle like you, Mr. Sedemund. Take hold of yourself, please — be resolute.

UNCLE WALDEMAR: Gwacious God, Oh God — how couldst thou have let it happen — and I loved him so much, that mahvelous boy. So early to leave your fathah, and me too, you gwand, gwand boy. You see, Mistah Gwude, I can find only the homeliest wohds — —

GRUDE: Take comfort in a loving God, Mr. Sedemund. But what will the father say when he has to face the loss of his dear departed?

UNCLE WALDEMAR: I must wush to him without wasting anothah second.

Sabina rolls past, her retinue behind her; she looks back at the two. They turn to gaze after her, then look at each other searchingly.

GRUDE: Mr. Sedemund, the burial will certainly take place in an hour. What do you think — should I pass a message to the speaker about Father Sedemund's sickness, which, as you say, must perforce keep him away? A minor point: what does Professor Latchbolt call the perilous condition of your brother? Your name, Mr. Sedemund, will take on a mighty resonance in the mouth of the speaker. Where is the father, and why isn't he at the side of the grave of such a son? You must realize, that's what the people will want to know, they who have complied with all the particulars that grief for a friend exacts.

UNCLE WALDEMAR: Deah Mistah Gwude, since mattahs have come to such a sad end, and you take such a pehsonal intewest, I can confide in you: we agweed that the son became notowious in a mannah so embawwassing that my bwothah's object in sending that telegwam was above all to wecall the son home. We had heard how likely your wecovewy in Doctah Gwabbold's sanatowium appeared, and hoped to pehsuade the doctah to accept poor Gewahd's case with identical patience. All this is stwictly between you and me, Mistah Gwude, agweed?

GRUDE: Absolutely, Mr. Sedemund.

UNCLE WALDEMAR: Yoah example might have convinced Gewahd to submit weadily, whereas othahwise it could hahdly have happened without painful but well-meant intahfewence on our paht.

The Carpenter's Apprentice and Gardener's Boy stand up and pass by with their respective objects.

GRUDE: With the help of Professor Latchbolt, of course — ah, there's the wreath. (*To the Gardener's Boy:*) I am glad you came; let me have it.

GARDENER'S BOY: Good to get rid of it after all. I was afraid it'd end up as goat feed.

GRUDE (*paying him*): Very, very sad, Mr. Sedemund, but who is there to assert we ought not to consider him lucky it wasn't worse!

UNCLE WALDEMAR: Between you and me, my nephew nevah acted vewy nice toward me. How could I . . .

Gardener's and Carpenter's Boys go off.

GRUDE: Shh, Mr. Sedemund! Aren't you worried that he might hear?

Uncle Waldemar looks fearfully at Grude.

GRUDE: He always did have a sharp ear. How would the two of us look if he were to join the conversation? I have this wreath to hide my face behind in an emergency — shouldn't you consider similar precautions? Not much time left till the burial, good sir.

UNCLE WALDEMAR: Yes, yes, I must huwwy. Good Lohd, what will my bwothah say?

GRUDE: Yours is a rocky path. Go with God. (*He walks him to the exit.*)
In the distance one hears gay barrel-organ music. Grude hums a few

105

bars, as they stop next to the hearse. Uncle Waldemar looks at him sideways.

GRUDE: You are puzzled that I feel like singing, Mr. Sedemund. It has nothing to do with my disorder, rather I dreamt last night I was swimming with the blessed sense of health and invincible cheerfulness you find in mountain streams. I dreamt I swam in one that was swirling rapidly. And I was singing. That's what I remembered when I heard that ting-a-ling. Upon my word, I tell you, night hasn't fallen yet on mankind. Now, farewell till we happily meet again.

Uncle Waldemar goes off. Grude walks up and down, smiling and whistling. As he steps forward again, Mrs. Grude, who has slipped into the beergarden, stops before him just as he turns.

GRUDE: So there you are!

MRS. GRUDE: Sedemund sent me.

GRUDE: Sedemund? And you — haven't you come for yourself?

MRS. GRUDE: Yes, for myself too. But first I have to tell Sedemund that he can come out of hiding.

Sabina rolls past.

GRUDE: Has he told you about that little perambulating Sabina? If not, ask him.

MRS. GRUDE: How can I ask him about what is his business? He has to tell me himself.

GRUDE: He speaks of her as though he tended her soul like a gentle turtledove at his breast. What do you think of her?

MRS. GRUDE: Poor thing.

GRUDE: Why poor? Because she's crippled?

Mrs. Grude shakes her head.

GRUDE: Because she won't find a husband?

Mrs. Grude as before.

GRUDE: Because she will fade soon?

Mrs. Grude as before.

GRUDE: Because she's a little witch entangled with a devil?

Mrs. Grude as before.

GRUDE: Well, why?

MRS. GRUDE: Because she'll always be alone, I think.

GRUDE: Now will she? There you are mistaken: she can take her pick from a large choice. Look: men surround her, care for her, follow her.

MRS. GRUDE: But I meant she won't be a mother.

GRUDE: No one can tell yet, though I admit it wouldn't be a great good fortune for her.

MRS. GRUDE: And she would hardly dare tell anyone else about it, as I did.

GRUDE: You?

MRS. GRUDE: Yes, I told Sedemund, before I could tell you. I wanted him to see that I am not a thing, not an object; that's not what a person is, when one is so strangely in the company of another.

GRUDE (*taking a deep breath*): And what did he say to that?

MRS. GRUDE: What should he say to that — who cares! At this point words are useless. Now you know, and that's good. If you men are set on talking so big about it, talk among yourselves — I'm not going to stay. I'll send him here.

Goes off. Grude starts to follow her, but turns around and resumes his pacing back and forth, while smiling and whistling. A poorly dressed twelve-year-old girl, Grete Mankmoos, shyly enters and glances about looking for someone. Upon catching sight of her father sitting with the funeral party, she stops.

GRUDE: Are you looking for someone?

GRETE: My father.

GRUDE: What's your father's name?

GRETE: Mr. Tailormaster Mankmoos. Mother is dead and Father hasn't come home yet. I fixed his lunch a while back and he hasn't had anything to eat all day.

GRUDE: He had something here. But it would be best if he went home anyway. Have you any brothers or sisters?

GRETE (*smiling*): Fritz, Walter, Little Max, and Alice.

GRUDE: Who takes care of them?

GRETE: Me. But Auntie is going to look in on us tonight.

GRUDE: Come along, we're going to surprise your daddy. (*They cross over.*)

MANKMOOS (*turning around and staring at them*): What? Grete? Is that you?

1 0 7

GRETE: Come home to eat, Father. I looked for you in so many places.

MANKMOOS: Should've let me enjoy my little bite here, Grete. Keep an eye on Little Max. Don't you know how easily he gets in trouble?

GRETE: Yes, Father, he had another fit; but he's sleeping nice now, and Alice is watching him.

FIRST UNDERTAKER'S ASSISTANT: Man, to let your children sit and watch!

COACHMAN KARL: Listen, stupid, let her sit and watch her father dig in — it'll do her good.

GRUDE (*again pacing up and down, shakes his head thoughtfully, half laughing, half angry*): Some fathers, we!

Scene 3

Still the beergarden, but somewhat later. The undertaker's men have stayed in a group. Mankmoos, sitting apart, puts on important airs while writing busily on scraps of paper. Grete sits next to him. The sanatorium attendant is looking for Grude.

COACHMAN KARL (*to Mankmoos*): Watch out, you're dribbling snot all over those begging letters — you trying to make it look like you did some touching up with tears?

MANKMOOS: Begging letters? I don't want any presents, I am just asking for a little contribution from my customers for the funeral costs. They can deduct it from the bill later — let them get after me!
Coachman Karl stands behind him and tries to read.

MANKMOOS: You want to read something funny, read this. (*Produces the note from Uncle Waldemar.*) Mr. Sedemund sent me this letter, after he promised me a contribution to the funeral. You see?

COACHMAN KARL (*reads and bangs his fist on the note*): What holy crap of hoity-toity manners! Even bugs in dirty underwear could get mad at this. (*Gives Grete something to drink.*) Go on, drink, your father's had enough. He needs all his five fingers to fiddle with the pen.
Grete takes a sip and coughs.

108

COACHMAN KARL: Taste all right?

Grete nods through tears.

COACHMAN KARL (*patting her*): You don't belong with such a worm-eaten holdup man of a father.

Grude and Sedemund appear from the background.

GRUDE: Come, here's a table. We used to have such carefree times sitting together. See if they have something decent to drink.

Young Sedemund goes into the building.

GRUDE (*to Mankmoos*): You are going to do the proper thing by that lion, aren't you? Better dead than an ass, right? What's holding you back?

MANKMOOS: Just one more letter, to Mrs. Nicely, for a contribution to the funeral.

GRUDE: Good enough, Mankmoos; but then ready for action! A little coffee and cake? Your daughter can get it, and also something for herself. A big platter of cake, Grete. (*Gives her money.*) And a big pot of coffee. (*Grete goes off.*)

MANKMOOS: I can eat as I write. That way it won't take so long.

GRUDE: You know, you'd be smart not to say too much about that story with the lion; if you do, some punk will grab that lovely reward money from in front of your nose. As long as we and a few others know about it, all right; but, as I say, don't be palsy-walsy with everyone, Mankmoos.

The Attendant comes.

GRUDE (*to the Attendant*): Our compliments to the doctor, and tell him Mr. Sedemund and I met and, in order to enjoy this fine evening, we plan to get drunk.

ATTENDANT: Very well, Mr. Grude. You always brood too much. You don't seem able to get away from yourself — that's chiefly why you are with us. Have fun at this celebration. I very much want to see the kind of face you bring home.

Old Sedemund and Uncle Waldemar, dressed in black and carrying wreaths, enter from the street. At the same instant Young Sedemund enters from the doorway at the right, a bottle of brandy under his arm and glasses in his hand. They recognize each other despite the distance and stop without speaking. Grude is roughly in the center.

UNCLE WALDEMAR: Good Lohd, Mistah Gwude, what's that?

GRUDE: Sincerely hope it's a pleasant surprise for everyone!

YOUNG SEDEMUND: Grude, you scoundrel!

GRUDE: Why, it really did look as though you'd dived head first into the hearse; my shattered mind is powerless against such illusion. (*To the left and to the right:*) The more one marvels, the more do marvels become manifest to the multitudes. So let everybody make himself cozy at one table!

OLD SEDEMUND (*to Uncle Waldemar*): With all due respect, Waldemar, how we've aged! (*To his son:*) My dear boy, we raced here for your sake to participate in your burial. Well, the Lord be praised and praise to the Lord. You know I hate funerals on sunny days like this. Every last louse lives it up, is as chipper as its nature permits. Is that a time for putting a man below?

YOUNG SEDEMUND: You can see, here in the shade we are permitting ourselves a little lousy fun, the Lord be praised — if we stretch it there may be enough for four: a doubtful pleasure, alas, but still — the Lord be praised, praise to the Lord — a stale wine, a shabby welcome.

OLD SEDEMUND: Gerhard, you couldn't put it a little more simply, could you? I said: the Lord be praised that I see you alive before me.

YOUNG SEDEMUND: "The Lord be praised" is also what the old spinster said when her pussy's bowels loosened at last. Nevertheless, Father, I am happy to be with you. Just like the woman in the Bible who lost her penny and found it again, you've found your son in one piece and are saving yourself whole piles of pennies on the funeral. At the same time you see how accurately I read your telegram. Without hemming or hawing I said to myself: the old man has an unbeatable sense of humor and fools his shrouded alter ego.

OLD SEDEMUND: I know, Gerhard, I understand: you've paid me back in kind: you're a genuine Sedemund who can't be hoaxed. Come and find a chair; this standing around is too much for me — the shock has hit my legs.

Grude draws chairs to the table. They sit down putting the wreaths on an adjoining table.

GRETE (*to Grude*): There's only fifty cents left; he gave me that much cake.

GRUDE: Keep the money, Grete, if it's all right with your father, Tailor-master Mankmoos. Ask him first. But, Grete, please get us two more glasses. We have company.

Grete goes off.

UNCLE WALDEMAR: This joke can land you in jail, Mistah Gwude!

GRUDE: I'm already serving time — then you are not of the opinion that I am as sane as you once thought, Mr. Sedemund? The treatment hasn't quite taken?

Grete returns with the glasses, curtsies, and goes off.

GRUDE (*pouring, to Uncle Waldemar*): Congratulate your healthy nephew on failing to become one of Dr. Grabbold's patients, as I am one. (*To Old Sedemund:*) A stroke of fortune for which we cannot be sufficiently grateful. (*To Young Sedemund:*) Because you were elected, if possible by your own choice, if not, by force, to join me in the cure at my institution.

YOUNG SEDEMUND (*pulling at the wreaths*): So that was the point of it! And these wreaths of mourning were meant for me. And now I can hang them on me, one per arm. That, please note, is Father's grief at my death: he stands ready with wreaths, his sickness fell at his feet, and he rose and went forth, not to his grave but mine . . . Shall we not dedicate them to Mother? She lies so chilly in her mausoleum — yes, these wreaths are Mother's and you are the one to take them to her — from me? Do we, our family, I mean the genuine Sedemunds, die easy or hard?

OLD SEDEMUND: They die easy, my boy, easy, tender and so very gentle and considerate of others and ourselves — and furthermore we bury nobly, that's us.

YOUNG SEDEMUND: Mother died hard, you see. I don't like this easy dying, even though it is bitter to die like mother; her death was noble — do you know why? She inched across; everything burned up in her. While she was still here she meant to make her soul transparent so that it would be new in the other world. By preparing herself in such a manner that nothing of herself would remain, she committed suicide. Why did she do that?

Uneasy silence.

*Franchi and Ring stand up and slowly make their way to the entrance,
past the undertaker's crew.*

COACHMAN KARL (*to Franchi*) : Hey, if your runaway tiger fancies horse-
meat, set him on the horses outside, those pulling the hearse — they're
Greedycock's and Glorylane's nags — let him tear a good hunk from
their flanks — hey, you, circus clown, I mean you!
Franchi turns aside and leaves with Ring.
Coachman Karl jumps up furious.

UNDERTAKER'S ASSISTANT: He's all wound up in grief, Karl, let him go.
(*To Mankmoos:*) You're not trying to make me believe you saw the
lion stalk about.

MANKMOOS: I didn't maintain I saw him close up, but a little ways off,
saw him slipping through the bushes, like a big yellow dog, yes, exactly
like a giant yellow dog.

COACHMAN KARL (*who has run to the entrance and now returns*) : Listen,
everybody, listen! Greedycock and Glorylane are heading straight for
this place. (*Drinks.*) They must be turning in now.
*Greedycock and Glorylane pass close to the funeral party, with
Greedycock looking the other way, and seat themselves at Franchi's
table. Swingcord appears from the other side.*

GLORYLANE: There's Swingcord, brother Greedycock. He's come to sign
it.

GREEDYCOCK: Also that he is the child's father?

GLORYLANE: Our institutions revere their masters — he'll sign anything.

GREEDYCOCK: Is that Swingcord, brother? Have you taken a good look at
him? And then take a look at me — me and him!
Swingcord sits.

GLORYLANE (*with the document*) : Then you met the child's mother at
a dance?

SWINGCORD: Well, that happens.

GLORYLANE: And the date, to make everything fit — September — Octo-
ber — please, Mr. Swingcord, listen.

SWINGCORD: No, I refuse. This business is getting too complicated, much
too complicated. More work than pleasure.

GREEDYCOCK (*putting down money*) : Is it?

SWINGCORD (*pockets the money and scratches himself*): But pleasure is short, and work starts all over.

GREEDYCOCK (*hitting the table*): Sign, you bastard, or I'll horsewhip you! Finished, brother Glorylane?

GLORYLANE: Finished. Now sign, Swingcord.

SWINGCORD: Well, the Lord be praised. (*Rubs his hands.*)

GREEDYCOCK: Look at those filthy paws, man. Go and wash them so you don't mess up the document when you sign it. (*Swingcord goes off.*)

GREEDYCOCK: Has it occurred to you, brother, what the kid is going to say to this someday? You look stupid, I can't help remarking. After all, he is *my* boy. All you did was roll up your sleeves and deposit this boy of mine squarely on a dungheap.

GLORYLANE: To your advantage, brother.

GREEDYCOCK: Brother this, brother that; still and all, you did it!

Swingcord returns, signs, and gives Greedycock his hand.

SWINGCORD: Now you're all set: what I sign I've signed. Are you really the father of the child?

GREEDYCOCK: Guardian, not father.

SWINGCORD: I've never heard of anyone paying so much money to get rid of a ward. Oh well, don't make no difference to me *whose* child I've become papa of.

Looking at it with seething anger, Greedycock folds the document, puts it in the inside pocket of his militiaman's coat, then buttons the coat tightly.

UNCLE WALDEMAR (*to Old Sedemund*): Deah bwothah, don't bothah with a weply. Yoah son's hand lies heavy on you. I must have a few wohds on business with Mistah Gweedycock. Then we'll go.

Crosses over to Greedycock.

Old Sedemund rises. His son follows him up and down as a mute companion, staying on his left. Grude remains seated.

GREEDYCOCK (*to Uncle Waldemar*): Those are *my* men sitting there boozing, and *my* horses standing thirsty in the sun, and *my* carriage that won't get washed today. I'm not going to look; I don't want to see them.

COACHMAN KARL: The old man turns up his damn nose like he wouldn't even consider spitting on us. (*Spits, stands up, and pushes back his three-cornered hat.*) Find something to do! I have to get a breath of fresh air.

Goes out on the street.

FIRST UNDERTAKER'S ASSISTANT: I wonder what kind of fresh air that could be?

He gets up and follows. Suddenly one hears distant shouts and a general clamor. While the other men of the undertaker's crew grow restless, the First Assistant returns with the coachman, whom he half pushes forward. The coachman resists; he is without his hat and reaches with bloody hands for the knife his companion holds at arm's length.

FIRST UNDERTAKER'S ASSISTANT (*reassuringly*): It's nothing, friends, nothing. Just stay quietly at your table. (*To Coachman:*) What did the poor creature do to you, you beast? Pull yourself together: the old man's sitting right here.

COACHMAN KARL: Shit on you, you old ass with your old men! Gimme the knife! (*He lunges for it.*)

FIRST UNDERTAKER'S ASSISTANT: Someone come take the knife and shut it!

He throws the blood-smeared knife to the ground. The men surround both and one hears in a voice that is low but clear enough:

He tried to cut off the horses' ears, that savage. They're bleeding all over the black sheets.

People come running.

GREEDYCOCK (*approaching with cramped hauteur, half-choking*): Is this your gratitude, you bully, for forgiving you a dozen times? For looking after you? Haven't I told you a hundred times this is the end? Do I have to string you up myself to keep you from corroding my life?

Grabs him as though he would strangle him. Uproar and confusion. Both Sedemunds remain standing on the side.

OLD SEDEMUND: Did you hear what Uncle Waldemar said, as inspired, thank heaven, as ever: your hand lies heavy on me, the hand of my son?

YOUNG SEDEMUND (*showing him the tip of his little finger*): This much — just this much real truth, one little word of truth, no more! Why did my mother have to commit suicide?

OLD SEDEMUND: What suicide? Incidentally, don't you find your way of speaking has something of Uncle Waldemar's unspeakable rhetoric —

no? Well — no offense. All right then: she inched across in order to become quite pure? (*Half to himself:*) Couldn't it be said she died a willing death by fire, crossed a purgatory to the beyond — a purgatory she herself had kindled?

YOUNG SEDEMUND: While I was boarded out, it happened that you suddenly fell dangerously ill and were treated by the out-of-town specialist Professor Latchbolt. Uncle Waldemar was what he proved himself today, brother and support. Whatever it was that happened then affected Mother, hurt her, pained her, and finally grieved her into her grave.

OLD SEDEMUND (*half-begging*): She died of her disease, Gerhard! Certainly hers was a hard and painful dying, and she bore her suffering with more dignity than I could have. You find in all this the genuine Sedemund formula: it can't be done away with, I'm afraid, keeps glowing like tinder.

YOUNG SEDEMUND: Just as Uncle Waldemar might put it — is that, then, the truth?

Old Sedemund shrugs.

YOUNG SEDEMUND: True enough for you to place the wreath on the grave? Still you have nothing to say?

OLD SEDEMUND: Dammit — yes! Go there yourself and watch me come.

The commotion around the coachman continues. Greedycock is in the midst.

GRUDE (*rising, to one of the militia*): Have you any idea why that man is in such a rage?

MILITIAMAN: Anyway, a fine, friggin' free-for-all.

GRUDE: That all? I thought someone had run into the lion.

MILITIAMAN: What lion?

GRUDE: Didn't you know that a lion had escaped? Yesterday he could be heard roaring all the way here. Today everyone has been asking: why doesn't he roar? Tell me, can *you* hear him? But perhaps it's wiser to keep mum, or the celebration might end before it's over.

Militiaman goes off quickly. Mankmoos comes with a number of letters.

GRUDE: Tough luck, man! You busted your seams and the entire secret

115

has leaked out. Might as well have blown a trumpet or shot off a cannon.

People gather around.

MANKMOOS: Nobody was willing to believe it anyway, so I didn't care any more about keeping the secret.

GRUDE: The whole shooting match could fizzle — did you think of *that?* Please yell as loud as you can that you haven't seen the tail, much less the whole lion!

MANKMOOS (*loud*): I haven't even looked for the lion. Far too risky for me to try and catch him. With my legs — what kind of a lion-hunter would I make!

A VOICE (*from the background*): What's up?

GRUDE: A lion is supposed to have gotten out, but I suspect it's a lie.

The turmoil around the coachman has attracted a crowd. The rumor of the lion envelops it and spreads. The Sanatorium Attendant appears.

ATTENDANT: I believe, Mr. Grude, you want to come along with me. It's my hunch that liquor is the cause of the lion more than the lion himself. (*Puts his hand on Grude's shoulder.*)

GRUDE: What the lion can do, I can too. Wheeee! (*Escapes.*)

ATTENDANT (*laughing*): One might think he let him loose himself, this cute Mr. Grude. A good guy, everything considered, but hard to figure out — not like the other nuts.

VOICE: You let a nut out, no wonder the nut let the lion out.

ATTENDANT (*pointing at Mankmoos*): There's your man, he gave the hue and cry. Get him! Hold him! All afternoon he's been harping on the lion.

MANKMOOS: I — I've got to go home. There isn't anybody with my dead wife, except she herself and the children. Grete, where are you?

GRETE (*from the crowd*): Here, Father!

A MILITIAMAN (*taking hold of Mankmoos*): Stop! Confess, you pisspot!

MANKMOOS: Ask the crazy Mr. Grude. He knows everything. I — I was there myself when he said the lion looked exactly like a big yellow dog. (*In trying to pull himself away, he drops the letters. They get stepped on.*) Oh me — oh my, now you've torn *that* off! Look for it, please, look, or you're going to be in trouble with the Grand Duke. My medal, my beautiful decoration!

MILITIAMAN (*releasing him*): I publicly maintain I saw no decoration. (*Scuffing the ground with his boots:*) Could that be it? The devil! It is. (*Picks up the medal.*) My name is Mamerov. I'm awfully sorry. Please forgive me.

MANKMOOS: Scratches all over! (*Polishing it.*) You bedpan — get it? That's what you are! Look, a deep cut right across the Grand Duke's face. Have you at least a safety pin?

AN EXCITED MILITIAMAN (*pushing himself through the crowd*): If the man's been decorated with an order, he's an extraordinary man. First we're going to catch the nut. This man is going to lead the militia. And his wife can still be buried later. (*Loud:*) Members of the militia: present arms!

Scene 4

A section of the fairgrounds. To the right, barely visible, a small merry-go-round; to the left, a shooting gallery with life-sized wooden Indians framing the entrance. There are several booths squeezed into the corners offering souvenirs and novelties. It is nightfall. Evidently the area has been hurriedly deserted. In the distance there is music from a barrel-organ, which approaches gradually.

GRUDE (*still in top hat and tails, carrying a large package under his arm — the lion's skin. He stands in the center of the area, looks about, unrolls the hide, and raises it high in both hands.*): Poor Caesar! But that's the way it goes — when fear no longer educates, an image must inspire fear. The man who cannot hear the still small voice has to have his ears reamed with the thunder and trumpeting of horns. A timely explosion for these humdrum times! (*Glances about.*) Look, Caesar, how they've made their getaway, every one of them. And your master, Caesar, drained a few bottles, so he's coping with it — at least he's set for the day.

He exchanges his top hat for a felt hat that is lying on the ground, and

117

his coat for a linen jacket he finds on the counter of the shooting gallery. He rolls up the hide and stows it under the counter inside the gallery. Two men cautiously turn the corner and approach the center of the square; they stop and listen attentively. As soon as they hear the noises that Grude is making within the booth, they race back. Grude, upon hearing their retreating steps, ducks and stays quiet for a time. At that moment a thief enters, laboriously dragging a bundle, which he sets down for a moment.

THIEF: I'm the honestest guy in the world. Nobody saw nothin' and as long as I'm the only one who knows what happens, who can say afterwards what *did* happen! I don't care long as my reputation don't suffer.

He rummages around in the booths and collects miscellaneous objects. Then he makes a second bundle that he ties with a piece of string to the first. Grude shakes one of the wooden Indians at the entrance to the shooting gallery and knocks it over. The thief wants to make off, but he cannot carry both bundles; finally he leaves them behind. Grude emerges from the booth.

A GENTLEMAN (*about to cross the square*): Have you seen anything?

GRUDE (*pointing in the direction of the thief*): He went that way.

MAN (*tips his hat in acknowledgment and turns around quickly*): Thanks a lot. (*Runs off.*)

Grude rolls the bundles over to the toppled wooden Indian and covers them hastily so that it looks as though a corpse were lying there. As one hears steps, he moves into the shadow of the shooting gallery. Sabina appears with boy scout Susemihl.

SUSEMIHL: Do you want to go even farther, Miss Eberstein? O God!

SABINA: Are you afraid, Mr. Susemihl? You've stopped playing your guitar.

SUSEMIHL: I know, but only because I'm pushing you, not because I'm scared — no, I'm not scared at all. But doesn't this place strike you a little weird — I mean for *your* sake?

SABINA: Look what's lying there!

SUSEMIHL: Where? Where?

SABINA: On your left. Isn't that a corpse?

SUSEMIHL: Corpse? Good God, yes — the only thing to do is run to the police for help. (*Drops the guitar and disappears.*)

SABINA (*alone in her wheelchair in the middle of the square, looks behind her nervously, and finally mumbles*): Dear — dear devil, come and help me — help me — but let's not have children.

GRUDE (*approaching her from behind*): What he can do I can do too, Sabina.

SABINA (*turning around quickly*): What are you doing here?

GRUDE: Trying to help, Sabina, that's all. (*He pulls the covering from the figure.*) You see, there are no corpses. We're alive and will love each other. If you help me I help you, Sabina.

SABINA: How do you know my name?

GRUDE: I can tell by looking at you that your name is Sabina.

SABINA: It just happens not to be my name at all — and it's none of your business anyway.

GRUDE: In that case, you'll simply be my own darling Sabina. Now do you want to see the lion?

SABINA: Is there really one?

GRUDE: Where devils are, lions can be too. I believe that, and if you help me believe, it's as good as if he were real.

Sabina shakes her head.

GRUDE: Old Nick has the lion already in his guts and so are the others full of him — and where was he? Far away, and only thought of as near.

SABINA: What do I care about him, anyway?

The barrel-organ can be heard approaching.

GRUDE: If you have the lion's love within you, the good lion's, whose majesty the desert lion merely apes, and compared to whom a living lion is no more than an ape, the good, the true, the only lion, why then, then —

SABINA: What then?

GRUDE: Then he opens wide his jaws inside you and eats you up, skin and all, and makes you a part of his majesty. Without lions, darling Sabina, there's no love, no life, no delight. Won't you help me hunt that lion, and if not that good lion, then the aping lion, known also as the conscience of savages?

Mrs. Grude and Sedemund appear.

MRS. GRUDE (*looking around and ready to continue, catches sight of her husband*): You — they claim you let the animal escape, they're all after you.

119

Sedemund steps over to Sabina in order to give the other two a chance for undisturbed conversation. Sabina examines him surreptitiously. His movements declare his willingness to make himself agreeable. One gathers by his clumsy gallantries that he is restrained by a kind of ascetic reserve.

GRUDE (*to Mrs. Grude*): They ought to be hunting the lion, and not the rabbit, don't you think?

MRS. GRUDE: Sounds awfully like you, Grude.

GRUDE: They're right, as far as they can ever be right. Where are the two of you going?

MRS. GRUDE: Doesn't matter — we're going now.

GRUDE: Have you any idea where my pursuers are?

MRS. GRUDE: They've divided into groups: some are not far behind us, others have gone to the graveyard; that's where they say the lion is hiding.

GRUDE (*with a glance at Sabina*): Was there anything else?

MRS. GRUDE (*shaking her head*): I have nothing against her, but how she greases her hair and perfumes herself! Lavender and witch hazel — disgusting hodgepodge.

GRUDE: You're right; she's a pitiful thing, and you know something: she really doesn't want to be a mother. Sedemund will take care of all of you as long as the fun lasts.

MRS. GRUDE: Take care of us — why?

GRUDE: Don't worry! He'll do it gladly; he'll protect you as one must guard a divine mystery, and you are that.

He returns to Sabina. Sedemund and Mrs. Grude go off.

SABINA: Was that your wife?

GRUDE: Wife? What do I care for women, dear Sabina! I don't ask for them, so you mustn't ask me.

SABINA: She's going to do me in.

GRUDE: Nonsense — think of the lion. If you love the lion, you love me. He's got me in his jaws and is gnawing away — who can be sure: am I still myself or already he? That's the length and breadth of it — of me, dear Sabina. Real life is a matter of gluttony, a miracle of metamorphosis and digestion and who knows what else!

A patrol of three militiamen marches in and comes to a halt. The

Organ-Grinder turns the corner, sets his organ down, cuts off a piece of chewing tobacco, and shoves it in his mouth.

ORGAN-GRINDER: Ah yes — guess the gentlemen are after the lion.

FIRST MILITIAMAN: Have you perhaps seen a man in a top hat and black coat? Well?

ORGAN-GRINDER: To be sure, many a time.

FIRST MILITIAMAN: But tonight?

ORGAN-GRINDER: If I'd been given the word they're looking for that type, I'd have kept an eye out. You bet. Maybe I bump into him — want me to deliver a message?

FIRST MILITIAMAN: Message, nothing! He's got to be picked up, he set a lion free — he isn't all there upstairs — you follow?

GRUDE: If it's a guy with a Vandyke, I saw him take off God knows where — to the graveyard, now that I think of it. Top hat is right, black also, but I couldn't swear to the Vandyke.

FIRST MILITIAMAN: What are you doing here, anyway?

GRUDE: Can't you see? I'm wheeling this young lady. When everybody started running, she was left sitting.

SECOND MILITIAMAN: What's all that stuff on the ground?

GRUDE: None other but the second statue, or the first, depending on your point of view. But you may want to take a closer look inside that merry-go-round — something keeps stirring in the dark. I've noticed it several times.

FIRST MILITIAMAN: Yeah, I get the same peculiar feeling that the whole works, poles and nags, keeps moving up and down. (*To Grude:*) Any ideas?

GRUDE (*pointing to Sabina*): The lady stole a couple of quick glances over her shoulder, and that was enough to scare me.

SABINA (*covering her ears*): I am beginning to hear him roar.

FIRST MILITIAMAN: Well, yes, what's to be done? Well? Is it "forward march!"?

SECOND MILITIAMAN (*thoughtfully*): We've only got a couple of cartridges, haven't we? If you got any to spare, let's have them.

THIRD MILITIAMAN: My gun is loaded; haven't got a shot beyond that.

FIRST MILITIAMAN: Same here.

1 2 1

SABINA: If you shoot, I'm going to have a fit. Oh, how clearly I can hear it, the snorting and the scraping.

SECOND MILITIAMAN: I'll be frank with you, men: I haven't got all this military courage it takes to shoot a lion. I'd just as soon take off this green uniform. You can do as you like, *I'm* not going to play the fool.

FIRST MILITIAMAN: You should be ashamed! How dare you say a thing like that so matter-of-factly! Well? Sir, I am resolved to report your conduct; take note of that, sir. Not a one of us brothers of the militia is going to purchase a thing from you after this; make a note of that!

SECOND MILITIAMAN: I quit. Play your piece without me. I'm not playing along and for that matter nobody can expect me to blow the trumpet if I'm winded. If the lady wants to go, well and good; I'll see her safely home; otherwise I'm going by myself.

Sabina shakes her head. Second Militiaman off.

GRUDE: That's what I say too: if one is afraid one should at least try to hide it.

FIRST MILITIAMAN: A regular militiaman is never supposed to be afraid. Well?

GRUDE: Well said, and now what are you planning to do?

FIRST MILITIAMAN: An attack on the enemy with my two guns is out of the question. We have one and only one objective, that is, to locate the lion's whereabouts.

ORGAN-GRINDER: How about letting me and my apparatus plaster a tune in there? I turn the handle like this, see? And the clunkhead won't 'preciate it — this I guarantee you.

GRUDE: I think he's got a point.

SABINA: I do too.

FIRST MILITIAMAN: I do too. You march ahead then and give it a volley of your thunder. Ready?

ORGAN-GRINDER (*spits*): Well, isn't one of you gentleman soldiers going to convoy me?

BOTH MILITIAMEN: Of course, that's for sure. (*They look at each other.*)

ORGAN-GRINDER: All right then; forward with a stiff upper lip!

He turns around and marches with music upon the merry-go-round. Each militiaman urges the other to precede him, until finally neither moves. The Organ-Grinder stops in front of the merry-go-round.

ORGAN-GRINDER: You can move up, safe and sound. Nothing to see in here, except what's always been here.

FIRST MILITIAMAN: I knew that all the time. I never expected anything else to show up, no sir.

THIRD MILITIAMAN: Same here.

SABINA: Same here.

GRUDE: And I bet the man didn't expect anything himself! How else was he going to find so much courage!

FIRST MILITIAMAN: If you knew there was no lion, what did you sick us on him for? Well?

GRUDE: If you're so sure there's no lion, why don't you go up closer? All the things you're going to report about your pal — because he stayed here so steadfast until he had played his game — didn't he show more courage than you? He believed in the lion.

FIRST MILITIAMAN: I too. I also thought *then* something was stirring in there.

THIRD MILITIAMAN: Me too, I was convinced of it then too.

SABINA: Me too.

ORGAN-GRINDER (*approaching*): And me, I still believe it. I didn't want to electrify the gents and the young lady, and that's why I said I'd seen nothing — but hear, hear something, that I did, oh yes; because in the dark you're more apt to hear than see, y'see. A colossal set of fangs working away in there, take my word, a couple of crunching jaws it's all one and the same if they make mincemeat of bones or flesh. The lady, she heard right. (*To First Militiaman:*) Go on, go on up; he can't do you no terrible damage. He's chomping away and won't be ready for another serving right away.

The militiamen look at one another. The Organ-Grinder winks at Grude.

GRUDE: Well, if you say so, I'll have to believe you, like it or not.

SABINA: Me too.

THIRD MILITIAMAN: Me too.

FIRST MILITIAMAN (*takes heart and goes halfway to the merry-go-round, but turns back quickly*): Yes, the case is solved and settled; I have located the presence of the lion. He crouches in the dark, I even saw his fiery eyes sparkle. One can smell him.

1 2 3

GRUDE: Just like witch hazel and lavender; I can smell it too.

ORGAN-GRINDER: Me too.

SABINA: Me too.

The sour-faced owner of the merry-go-round approaches in a leisurely fashion, carrying a bucket of water. When he catches sight of the toppled wooden Indian, he sets the bucket down and rights the figure.

OWNER: Go home, everybody — it's all right. The chase is headed back that way. To the graveyard. And the police showed up, thank God, and plenty of them. (*He is about to go to the merry-go-round.*)

FIRST MILITIAMAN: Sir, I draw your attention to the fact that you are exposing your life to imminent danger if you take another step. I have reconnoitered; I am dead certain the lion lies in ambush in there. You hear?

OWNER: What, in *my* place? (*Reaching for the bucket:*) Then it's high time we fixed that. (*Goes inside the merry-go-round and begins to rummage. From behind the horses:*) If you're so cocksure of being sure I'd like to see that cock you wore out with your cockiness.

GRUDE (*picks up the guitar and plucks away at some discords*):
> Inside was a dirty pig, gorged himself up full,
> Gobbled up garbage and eels' heads too,
> Gobbled up a bellyful.
> His lion's eyes sparkled — who got a view?
> Whose courage caught sight of his prickly mane too,
> Waving in the dark? Yes, who? Yes, who?

Sabina laughs. The Organ-Grinder gives an occasional turn to the handle of his organ.

> Open your ears and listen, friends,
> To this jingle-jangle song,
> But hold your noses, hold them tight
> When the militia's heart goes — bong! —
> Into his pants.
> All of you know the militiaman's no frog
> But of knightly virtues a catalogue.
> Garbage and eelheads stink like hell
> But the smell of the militiaman stinks twice as well.

(*To the First Militiaman:*) Say, man, can't you smell anything? It stinks, fellow, not like a lion, but more like a human. Are you going to report your own conduct too, or shall I praise it in another original composition?

Sabina laughs. Organ-Grinder grinds away.

FIRST MILITIAMAN: Nothing like this has ever happened to me in my entire life. Well?

THIRD MILITIAMAN: You think to me?

FIRST MILITIAMAN: What do you think, brother, should we arrest him?

THIRD MILITIAMAN: Well, you know, brother, this slippery customer has the mouth of a lion, and if it ever comes to taking an oath he's going to chew us to ribbons. Let's forget it. What he has fiddle-faddled in his foolishness my dumbness has driven home to me privately. I'm going to be all ears to what I'm going to say to myself — whether I shouldn't give up my green coat too. (*Goes off.*)

FIRST MILITIAMAN (*yelling after him*): Your conduct will also be reported, you hear? (*To Grude:*) No point in dealing with a fishmonger like you. About face! (*Goes off.*)

GRUDE (*to Organ-Grinder*): You born lion-hunter you! Look, don't squeal on the girl, will you? She goes gaily along on a lion hunt and feels safe and sound protected by your blunderbuss. Give us your support cheerfully!

He pushes Sabina forward. While the Organ-Grinder makes music, they move off together.

Scene 5

The graveyard. An area in front of the Sedemund mausoleum which resembles a luxurious villa for the dead of that family. At the left a thick hedge fences off the section alloted to suicides. Young Sedemund and Mrs. Grude.

YOUNG SEDEMUND: But I do think in the end everything in the universe harmonizes into a delicious feast for the ears — only the rest is silence.

125

MRS. GRUDE: The rest?

YOUNG SEDEMUND: Yes, the rest belongs to it too, the pause — the pause between breaths, between creation, the caverns of nothingness, which punctuate all the splendor of the something. My uncle is such a rest, a silence in the universe, and this despite his cheerful chatter — yes, a pause. And — my father, who knows: perhaps he has something clamoring somewhere or clattering or clinking away announcing the coming of something better.

Mankmoos stumbles in, panting, glancing repeatedly behind him. Mrs. Grude withdraws a few steps, waiting. Mankmoos clutches Sedemund.

YOUNG SEDEMUND: What's the matter, man?

MANKMOOS (*looks at him uncomprehendingly*): Man? You talking to me?

YOUNG SEDEMUND: If you're otherwise no man, you *are* the husband of your dead wife. Why are you holding me so tight?

MANKMOOS: She is pursuing me here, there, all over.

YOUNG SEDEMUND: Pursuing? Who?

MANKMOOS: She — the one you say is dead. I hear steps here, steps there, and when I look behind me —

YOUNG SEDEMUND: Your wife?

MANKMOOS: She's haunting me, round and round. Who else but her? There's nothing, and still it's something — why, I'd just as soon have the lion running loose. (*Discovers Mrs. Grude and registers shock:*) What — does — she — want?

YOUNG SEDEMUND: That's Mrs. Grude — open your eyes, fellow.

MANKMOOS: But what does she want of me? My wife hung all the children round my neck; I am stuck with them; I can sit and see to it that they get a start. And who'll give me anything for myself?

MRS. GRUDE: One of those rests you mentioned has shown up, Mr. Sedemund. Must the poor children suffer merely because their father is such a rest of a man?

YOUNG SEDEMUND: But it does astonish me that his thoughts fit so snugly to the form and shape of his wife. A rest is aware of nothing. Look, there she is. (*To Mankmoos's horror, he speaks to the empty air:*) Surely, Mrs. Mankmoos, everything will be done properly, nor will the children pine away. Mrs. Grude gives her word too. Mrs. Mankmoos,

126

you can leave your husband in peace now. (*To Mankmoos:*) Tell her, you're going to look after your children, go on, but speak loud.

MANKMOOS (*shaking*): Yes — Helen — yes — yes, — I want to — leave it to me. Grete is going to get a good new black dress right away.

YOUNG SEDEMUND: She's making a sign, now she turns away, reassured — she's gone. You're rid of the ghost, Mankmoos, but make sure she finds peace. Please come along with me later and I'll figure out what I can do for you.

Mankmoos wobbles off beyond the hedge to the suicides' section.

YOUNG SEDEMUND: A rotten place, where the suicides lie in unhallowed ground. Suicide — a word that shall rise up against us, as the ghost of Mankmoos's wife rose against the rest of a man.

They both go toward the back and disappear. Grude comes with Sabina and the Organ-Grinder.

GRUDE: Now then. Sabina here will serve the lion as a sacrificial lamb. (*To Organ-Grinder:*) You stay and watch over the lamb — I — (*he removes his coat and cap*) — I enter the service of lionkeeper Candido in shirt-sleeves and run after the runaway.

ORGAN-GRINDER: And I — I intend to dazzle the girls, even when I'm old, with today's monkey business.

Grude in shirtsleeves disappears behind the vault.
Greedycock and Glorylane come armed with guns.

GREEDYCOCK: I've got to kill someone, anyone, if not Coachman Karl, that bum, then that bastard of a lion.

GLORYLANE: You are too hotheaded, brother Greedycock. We ought to be quieter.

ORGAN-GRINDER: Yeah, the gentlemen might play it a little quieter because whether we are bums or bastards makes God knows no difference to the lion. He has a sweet tooth for bums as he has for bastards. We're all equal to him, as we are before the good Lord.

GREEDYCOCK: Hello! The girl in her wheelchair — what's the matter?

Sabina dries her tears and looks up gratefully.

ORGAN-GRINDER: The poor thing — the lion chased off her guide — well, it came to me right away why God has extended my happy life to this very moment. Something that you gents of the militia will understand, for nothing better can happen to militiamen and poor organ-grinders than to look after such a sick, sweet child. Am I right, gentlemen?

GREEDYCOCK: You expect to snag the lion with your grinding? Let me pass, man — where is he?

ORGAN-GRINDER: Don't be sore if I lump an organ-grinder and two such elite members of the guard in one mouthful. The lion? Well, he isn't so far off at all if we can take the word of Mr. Chief Assistant Lion-keeper, who's stalking him back there in the bushes, a monstrously brave person, to be sure, but then of course he's trafficked with monsters before.

GREEDYCOCK: I'm not asking about the lion-catcher — I'm asking about the lion!

ORGAN-GRINDER: I beg you, don't shoot bang! bang! if you see something white, because that's the shirtsleeves of Mr. Chief Assistant. The lion, he didn't put on any shirt. That's so, isn't it, Miss? In the bushes he is; right, lady?

SABINA: Yes. But I don't agree he is so awfully brave. He kept wiping away perspiration. And even you keep making the sign of the cross whenever I seem to look away — are you maybe Catholic? (*To Greedy-cock:*) Oh, I implore you, sir, good sir, don't leave me alone with him. Listen to this: (*Greedycock bends down close to her. She speaks softly:*) I heard him skitter past, and I saw the huge tracks he made in the sand, and they were an abomination to behold.

ORGAN-GRINDER: Most terrible thing about the lion is his speed: remember, Miss, how he whooshed across the road: swish, and into the bushes.

SABINA: Oh yes, yes.

ORGAN-GRINDER: And how your guide figured to catch up with him — took off like the wind — pale as lightning.

SABINA: Please stay here in front of me, and as soon as he shows up, let go with the music, loud, so I won't hear the shooting.
Organ-Grinder stands in front of Sabina.

GREEDYCOCK: Move away from there! I'm in charge here. With your god-damn carryings-on you're only going to draw the beast.

ORGAN-GRINDER: All the better, said the cockroach, scratching his left bottom cheek. I'll stand near you. (*Stands near Greedycock.*)

GREEDYCOCK: The hell you will! Get away! On the double!

ORGAN-GRINDER: You trying to tell me I should improve the landscape with my sweet absence?

GREEDYCOCK: Precisely — fresh air instead of you.

ORGAN-GRINDER: All righty. If I go behind the wall, I am less liable to be in your way. Let's blow a little salvo of a flourish for my good-by.

Grinds away and marches toward the suicides' hedge. Before he disappears, an anxious Mankmoos, flushed out of the bush and panting for air, shows up.

ORGAN-GRINDER: Don't wait, man, or the lion will bite you in the rear.

GREEDYCOCK (*screaming at him*): Damned rabbitfoot — I'm going to shoot you in the guts — out with it: what have you seen?

MANKMOOS (*his hands turning in all directions, doesn't know whether to go forward or backward*): Hey, Caesar, nice Caesar, nice, nice.

GLORYLANE: Don't shoot him, brother Greedycock, don't shoot if you have any love for me.

GREEDYCOCK: I've got to get rid of this bullet — again: I'll count to three — where is he? (*Raises his gun.*)

GRUDE (*from the back*): Don't shoot, people, it's my job to capture him alive — he's squatting behind the hedge. Drive him here, yell, but spare his life.

GREEDYCOCK: I'll give you spare, wise guy! (*Shoots blindly into the hedge.*) That was dumb — brother Glorylane, your gun! Take mine. (*He exchanges guns and jumps behind the hedge.*)

ORGAN-GRINDER (*to Mankmoos*): Roar, man, show the beast how an expert roars or your skin will be a lion sandwich — there, there, there, oops, he's slipping through the trees, fizzing along like a fiery fury.

GRUDE: Yell, everybody, loud as you can. (*Confusion, shouting.*)

GLORYLANE: Brother Greedycock, brother Greedycock, help, help!

Greedycock breaks through the hedge.

ORGAN-GRINDER: Room, please, for the royal master shot. He's bleeding, Mr. Sharpshooter — one more into that damned hide. To the lion-killer!

Grude hides himself again.

GREEDYCOCK: It was an accident, people, there was something looked like a moving shadow — now . . .

129

GLORYLANE: Not so reckless, brother Greedycock; remember these animals go mad if they're wounded.

ORGAN-GRINDER: Crippled on his left hindpaw, Mr. Grimycock, lamed him on the left, means he can't jump right no more. Mr. Chief Assistant slid just like that onto his track, like a rabid greyhound.

Greedycock ranges about, scenting. The shooting and noise have drawn people. From the back appear Sedemund and Mrs. Grude; Sergeant Lambkin breaks through the ring of onlookers.

SERGEANT LAMBKIN (*to Organ-Grinder*): Come here, you! Have you any part in this mess?

ORGAN-GRINDER: Hardly worth mentioning, Mr. Colonel-officer. A barrage of noise come out of this music box, maybe, but no explosive-type shots. (*Points to Glorylane:*) With due respect, take a look at Mr. Shotgun-Proprietor.

SERGEANT LAMBKIN (*takes Glorylane's gun and sniffs the barrel opening*): This gun has just been fired. Why has this gun just been fired?

GREEDYCOCK (*stepping up*): I whammed one into the lion's hide, Sergeant. The gun belongs to me.

SERGEANT LAMBKIN: Oh, Mr. Greedycock — aren't you Mr. Greedycock? Very well, so far so good. About the lion — I take it it's true.

GREEDYCOCK: Absolutely, Sergeant, you may depend on me. (*To Glorylane:*) Brother Glorylane, the two of us are all the witness Mr. Lambkin needs, right?

SERGEANT LAMBKIN: Oh, Mr. Glorylane — of course, Mr. Glorylane, I'd have known you right away had you simply mentioned your respected name. Indeed yes. We are going to take down a proper deposition. Everything in its turn. First I have to prevent all these people from spreading into the danger zone. (*Loud:*) All of you stay where you are and obey Mr. Greedycock's instructions — that clear? No one leaves this area until the arrival of the police.

ORGAN-GRINDER: I feel safe in Mr. Grimycock's bosom like it was Abraham's.

SERGEANT LAMBKIN: All requisite official authority has been vested in Mr. Greedycock. Whoever comes here later is also subject to this order. (*To Greedycock:*) I'll send here every single person I encounter; each has to report to you.

GREEDYCOCK (*to Sedemund and Mrs. Grude*): Nobody leaves! Step up, everybody; close it up!

Sedemund and Mrs. Grude come closer. Old Sedemund and Uncle Waldemar arrive with wreaths.

UNCLE WALDEMAR: Mistah Gweedycock, you can hahdly imagine what pleasure I take in yoah good fohtune. Congwatulations, and moh congwatulations! You ah, without a doubt, the hewo of the day. (*They shake hands.*)

GREEDYCOCK: My profound thanks, Mr. Sedemund. If you and your brother are going to the tomb, you'd be smart not to expose yourselves to danger more than necessary. Best hurry back.

UNCLE WALDEMAR: Piety, Mistah Gweedycock, twiumphs with disdain ovah the twials of danger. (*Pointing to the Old Sedemund:*) A tendah soht of pilgwimage to the gwave of his happiness.

They go off to the family vault. Uncle Waldemar unlocks it, then pockets the key. Young Sedemund approaches.

YOUNG SEDEMUND: Does it go that quickly, Father — one, two, three, in; one, two, three, out?

OLD SEDEMUND: Yes, my boy, haste has been urged upon us, but we won't hurry.

UNCLE WALDEMAR: To hallow the memowy of the deah depahted, Gewahd, with a sowwowing sigh.

YOUNG SEDEMUND: If a sigh can do that, are *you* going to heave a sigh?

UNCLE WALDEMAR: Gewahd, couldn't you show a little less spite toward me, at the gwave of your mothah at least?

YOUNG SEDEMUND: Yes. There is your sarcophagus, O God, Mother, they've come to hallow your memory with wreaths!

UNCLE WALDEMAR: One thing I must ask you to wealize, Gewahd, is that the pwesent large cwowds do not fohm a suitable backgwound for these fits with which you like to baby yoahself. Not so loud, Gewahd.

YOUNG SEDEMUND (*steps into the entrance as though taking the role of gatekeeper. Quietly*): You keep out, Uncle Waldemar; you too, Father. Haven't even wiped your feet, and you want to enter my mother's silent, immaculate chamber, the single spot on earth that has remained hers.

Bit by bit he has begun to raise his voice. The people have begun to

131

pay attention and have approached unnoticed. The Organ-Grinder plays a few notes. Old Sedemund shifts the wreath from his right to his left hand and passes his hand over his face.

YOUNG SEDEMUND: Oh God, Father, for a second I imagined you were going to strike your face with your fist!

He steps aside, leaving the entrance free.

UNCLE WALDEMAR: Bwothah, say a wohd to Mistah Gweedycock. He's a fair-minded citizen, he'll give you pwotection against this stony-hahted outwage waised by yoah son against you.

Old Sedemund looks around, casting his eyes over the assembled crowd, then turns away. He seems to be about to enter the tomb, but hesitates and then stops.

UNCLE WALDEMAR: Deah Mistah Gweedycock, you must find, don't you, as I do, such an altahcation befoah our tomb, and in the pwesence of so many eyes and eahs, a little catastwophic?

GREEDYCOCK: Step back, people! Up against the hedge! Don't crowd around an affair that doesn't concern you.

They move off slightly, lining up alongside the suicides' hedge.

YOUNG SEDEMUND: According to canon law pertaining to burial, Father, wouldn't Mother have to be interred beyond that hedge? Is this what you call my genuine Sedemund formula that can't be done away with and that keeps glowing like tinder?

UNCLE WALDEMAR: Do I heah awight, bwothah — and so fah I've not only heard wight, but known enough to dwaw my own conclusions — if I heah awight, Gewahd is on the point of contesting the wight of the deah depahted's body to wemain in our splendid family vault. Bwothah, the sight of poor you makes me twemble. Although yoah haht wefuses to entertain the possibility of yoah not going neah, allow me to entah in yoah place. And let me offah the weath as a gwieving accusation against that mothah's son.

GREEDYCOCK: Be glad, good people, this isn't *your* family tomb. Such a family can give one the creeps, that cannot bury such atrocities in good time. You can hear quite well back here, can't you, what's taking place so nice and publicly up there and what should have remained private?

Old Sedemund rejects Uncle Waldemar's offer and slowly goes himself

*to the gate of the vault. He turns suddenly, without entering, and
shouts:*

Why do you people stand there? Go and gape somewhere else!

GREEDYCOCK: Mr. Sedemund, do proceed without fear. Round up a
smidgen of good conscience; then you'll be able to do it.

UNCLE WALDEMAR: Oh, Mistah Gweedycock, you should also build
yoahself a family vault in which you can eventually intah yoah son.
Good Swingcohd has aweddy lost *his* taste for child-buying, as he
just now confided to me so nice and publicly. That's wight, Swingcohd — child — twade; twading yoah — vewy — own — child away for
money, Mistah Gweedycock!

The Organ-Grinder cranks away.

GREEDYCOCK: Child-trade? Oh Mr. Sedemund, if I were you, and had a
mind to disguise my own misdeeds with that of another, I would never,
no — never, drag in such a monstrousness which no one would expect
the devil even capable of conceiving. Child-trade, eh? But do tell us
how it stands with your own affairs.

Sergeant Lambkin appears in the background.

UNCLE WALDEMAR: Good of you to gwant me a wohd, Mistah Gweedycock. Pehchance you wecall our solemn bweakfast in the Ahchduke,
where we wegaled each othah with all sohts of cuwious and intimate
confidences. But you weally took the cake with yoah twucking business. When yoah twucks move onto the town's weighing-plate — well,
but do twy to wemembah, if you please — then between the second and
third load you pwoduce yoah famous bottle, and afterwahds what do
those stout hahts know? — whether the second load had aweddy been
weighed or had only just then been moved onto the scale — and foh
the sake of making doubly sure — the second load is weighed twice
ovah, and cwedited to you. And all this entirely owing to yoah bottle,
and, I sweah, nevah to yoah detwiment. Ah, Mistah Gweedycock, we
were all so ecstatic ovah such alert business sense! So how does it fare
with you, so happily, I mean on such a nice and public occasion, eh?

Organ-Grinder cranks away.

GREEDYCOCK: What does this have to do with public business, Mr. Sedemund? (*Turns around.*) Sergeant Lambkin!

133

UNCLE WALDEMAR: G'd evening, Mistah Lambkin. Have you also heard about Mistah Gweedycock's child-twade?

SERGEANT LAMBKIN: Gentlemen, gentlemen — I would think, though perhaps they're not wholly private matters, they don't belong here tonight. First things first! What's going on at the tomb?

YOUNG SEDEMUND: Mr. Lambkin, from compassion, from a sense of universal human brotherhood, and from other considerations, my father has irrevocably set his heart upon establishing a philanthropic foundation. Beyond this hedge so many a wretched mortal lies buried in unhallowed ground. I shall not try your patience with details; in short, my father shall place a modest tombstone on each of those neglected graves. This very instant he'll survey the grounds; right, Father? Weren't you about to count the graves? Or do you first want to — lay down your wreath?

Organ-Grinder cranks away.

OLD SEDEMUND (*glances about. Everyone is holding his breath. He turns suddenly upon Uncle Waldemar*): Where's the key? Lock it up.

UNCLE WALDEMAR (*whispering*): Bwothah, if you don't place the weath where it belongs, our pwestige in the place will be buwied wight heah and now. Think of that. Go inside and come back. Face the music!

OLD SEDEMUND (*violently*): The key! I tell you, if I could I wouldn't do it — whether I can't do it or why I run makes no difference — take the wreath.

He hands him the wreath, receives the key, turns it, locks the gate, and pockets the key. As the bystanders make way, he steps toward the suicides' hedge. A murmur rises. Uncle Waldemar follows him and tries to stop him.

UNCLE WALDEMAR: Bwothah, ah you in full possession of yoah senses? Do you weally mean to twavel this path of penitence?

OLD SEDEMUND (*stops and shrugs*): I can't think of a reason not to. But if you know better, I'll withdraw. Might as well put up the stones since my son has fixed it so nice and publicly in my name — without my protest.

UNCLE WALDEMAR: If only you had pwotested!

OLD SEDEMUND (*to himself*): Protested! Why, who thought of stones when the question was of stones? Extraordinary how much goes on in Waldemar's head all at once.

SERGEANT LAMBKIN: Gentlemen, this matter which looks more like a private personal matter may now be considered closed. I can't allow you any more time. (*Loud:*) All those present will proceed into the chapel for the time being. It is lighted: I saw the sculptors working there. Everybody forward march!

He marches ahead. All follow except the Organ-Grinder and Sabina. Mrs. Grude hesitates.

ORGAN-GRINDER (*turns crank and shakes his head*): Been expectin' more fun from all these high jinks — well, how did it please you, Miss?

SABINA: I haven't seen enough of the world, you know, so I can't even tell: was it sad or funny?

Mrs. Grude quickly comes over and starts to push the wheelchair, with some difficulty, in the direction of the chapel. Grude jumps out of the bushes and embraces her from behind. She is frightened and prepares to defend herself. But when she realizes who it is, she lets him kiss her heartily and lengthily. One can hear approaching steps, whereupon he jumps back into the darkness.

A MAN: Sergeant Lambkin sent me. He was mad because nobody pushed the wheelchair. He ordered me to take it — who was that man in shirtsleeves?

MRS. GRUDE: That? That was only my crazy husband.

MAN: Away, quick, before the lion gets us.

All go off.

Scene 6

The interior of a crumbling Early Gothic chapel which has been cleaned out and now serves as a storehouse for all kinds of antiquated and useless town properties like old crosses for graves and cracked wooden statues, as well as for more recent discards like remnants of festive decorations. The actual church fittings have been removed. In the background are two exceedingly narrow, pointed windows, and at the right a giant wooden crucifix rests against the wall. It is an ancient and severe piece of carving now in the process of restoration. Sculptor Bromann stands before it upon a small stepladder, lighted by a few candles which throw a faint illumination upon the rest of the interior. He is engaged in fitting his own carving, an arm of Christ, into place. He steps down and checks the over-all impression. The crowd is dispersed throughout the chapel. Most people have found seats on miscellaneous pieces of rubbish. Old Sedemund is sitting at the left atop an old wooden cross. Uncle Waldemar stands next to him, while Young Sedemund has begun to speak to the sculptor. Mrs. Grude walks up and down. Sabina is nearly in the center of the chapel. The Organ-Grinder can hardly be noticed. Because of its angle the wooden Christ figure appears about to soar upward.

BROMANN (*to Young Sedemund*): Tomorrow we'll be visited by the county building inspector, and then he'll look over my Christ. That is, the Christ figure itself, he says, belongs to the very best period, and many say he himself is a great connoisseur and admirer of that period, which he considers the very best. His specification was that my arm has to be also as of the very best period, but it turned out the way I learned it at the academy. Makes a substantial difference, if you'll kindly give it a moment's thought.

YOUNG SEDEMUND: This Christ was fashioned in anguish and toil; the arm is the arm of a parasite who never in his life said no to a free meal. Excuse me.

Mrs. Grude has heard this conversation and steps accidentally beneath the arms of the cross.

BROMANN (*rapturous*): Ah, look, look — that lady standing there — that's the place for Mary, the mother, whose son, larger than life, above her but turned from her, disregarding her pitiful motherhood, looks out over the world. You see, my respected friend, our sons — all mothers and finally all fathers must realize this — our sons are the judges and avengers of our failings. All who would be mothers must tell themselves that — am I right?

YOUNG SEDEMUND: Perhaps you have something there.

BROMANN (*pulling at his cigar*): She pleads for a glance, but he — stares above and beyond her insultingly. Women do not think of their children as by spiritual right — they poison them in their wombs with common humanity. They have no faith in spirit existing as conscience beyond and within them.

Because Sedemund notices that Mrs. Grude is taking this personally, he puts his hand on Bromann's shoulder to silence him. To gloss over the break in their conversation, they take a few steps back, as though to gain a broader perspective on the Christ figure. They stop near Old Sedemund.

OLD SEDEMUND: Turn around and do reveal to me more of those fatherly failings in the face of higher childhood. But be straightforward. I'll appreciate that.

They turn toward Old Sedemund. Slowly Mrs. Grude goes, her head bowed as though passing beneath a low archway, to stand in front of the Christ figure. She looks up. Young Sedemund quickly walks over to her, glad to leave his father.

MRS. GRUDE: Do you know what he says? He says: everyone born shall at one time or another be nailed to the cross. Therefore you must give your son such a start that he can look up in his most trying hour and soar above the world. I hear more.

YOUNG SEDEMUND: Of course, Mrs. Grude. There are enough evildoers in the world.

Engaged in conversation, he walks her toward the back.

OLD SEDEMUND: Well, Mr. Bromann, Christ here, Christ there — if he were living today, they'd lock him up in the clink as a hobo and rabble-rouser — and rightly so.

BROMANN: But perhaps he'd first find the occasion to say to you: "Thou shalt see, Mr. Sedemund," as to the blind.

OLD SEDEMUND: Come on, he struck a match and showed him the right way, that's all there was to it. In darkness we all need crutches, the blind as well as the seeing — there we are all stone blind.

BROMANN: You say Christ here, Christ there. Thousands upon thousands have been crucified. That's what's been done to man. Have you no compassion?

OLD SEDEMUND: Has he compassion for me? He's no worse off than I am. (*Spreading his arms.*) We don't have to look like that, every time we feel rotten lousy.

BROMANN: You?

UNCLE WALDEMAR: His vewy own son, Mistah Bwomann, has, so to say,

137

nailed him to the cwoss of public notowiety. Cwuelly and most un-filially.

BROMANN (*shaking his head*): How is that, Mr. Sedemund? What could his son bring against him to mark him like that?

OLD SEDEMUND: So you feel there must be something to it?

Bromann stares at him speechless.

OLD SEDEMUND: You see, you've already taken his side. And why not! We are all sinners, as you must know, all of us. Let it go, but have the kindness to move a little aside so I can get a friendly-like perspective of your freshly varnished Christ.

Bromann steps aside.

UNCLE WALDEMAR: Oh my bwothah, that was twuly stupid, that was wong, a stwategic miscalculation.

OLD SEDEMUND: Strategic? Damn it, Waldemar, what strategy are you talking about?

UNCLE WALDEMAR (*imploring*): Weally, you're sitting there like a wetched sinnah — that's no good, bwothah. Wather, you should be twying to pull the wool ovah these people's eyes. You should exploah if love and zest foh gossip help yoah case.

OLD SEDEMUND: The stinking carcass, you mean, should seduce the maggots with rosewater? A really bright carcass, that, Waldemar.

UNCLE WALDEMAR: Listen to me. You can gain the uppah hand if you make use of this golden opportunity that has bwought us all together. I have dwopped many a good wohd on behalf of the house of Sede-mund. The people ah in doubt and don't quite know how to take what happened at the tomb. Pull yoahself together, mingle with them un-obtwusively, and get it into their heads that the answer to the puzzle is pwofoundly unexceptionable.

OLD SEDEMUND: That slicker, that boy, he tied a bag of cement to my leg and you keep saying: alley-oop, jump, jump!

UNCLE WALDEMAR: What a fusspot you ah, old boy. Yoah ovahdeveloped sensitivity makes you squeamish. Just think what faiwy tales ah going to dwown us tomowwow morning.

OLD SEDEMUND: An orgy for horror painters! Anyway. (*Loud:*) Have to move my legs a bit — am going to walk around this place some.

He passes through the crowd. People move aside and look after him covertly. Others nudge each other and point to him.

OLD SEDEMUND (*to a young woman who is carrying a spade and a watering can*): Been planting potatoes? Rather late in the season for that, young lady.

WOMAN: I've been looking after my grave.

OLD SEDEMUND: And the lion came between, eh? I daresay you didn't finish?

WOMAN: Yes, I did.

OLD SEDEMUND (*about to ask a hearty question, he grows confused, coughs, looks about him, turns to an old man*): Were you about to say something to me?

MAN: About you I could have said something, all right.

OLD SEDEMUND: Well — haven't had rain in a long time. Farmers very droopy about that. Always are. Know what the flower man said when I bought the wreath? Because I bought one this afternoon for my wife, and why not!

MAN: To place on her coffin, and why not, eh?

OLD SEDEMUND: Well, it's like this, you see. From time to time, when memories crowd back, one has to do something. You read old letters or tell yourself a story or two of past days or take a bunch of flowers . . .

MAN: If you spent all that money on such a grand tomb and are all set with the flowers, how come you turned away right before the gate?

OLD SEDEMUND: Oh, ask me again tomorrow! (*To another:*) Why are you grinning, what's there to sneer at? A jolly place, this!

A WISEACRE: Why not amuse yourself according to your inclination? I have my own ideas when I think of death: your grave's going to make a rather pleasant whorehouse if the dead like each other — according to their inclination. What, does that offend you, old man? Does it?

OLD SEDEMUND: All of you are acting so damn affable, as though I were lugging a ton of sins on my back and needed a whole pack of father confessors. Now what are the facts? (*To a fourth:*) Would your eminence care to lend me your ear? (*He whispers something. The man reacts with alarm, having obviously heard something monstrous.*) Well, what's so surprising and shocking about that — hasn't happened more

139

than a dozen times. (*To another:*) You — my worthy — listen to a confession — no, please give me a hearing, I'm not going to bite your ear off. (*Whispers.*) It's hard to do but refreshes a weary soul. (*To still another:*) You wait, I'll confess to you such a piece of delectable derring-do, and spicy at that: how I got my beautiful sister pregnant while I was sick — the lay sister in the hospital, that is — what did you think I meant? Whoever's got a hankering — I can keep it up cheerfully — indefinitely.

OLD SEDEMUND (*putting his hands in his trouser pockets and looking around*): Look, you people, *now* do you see what you know? Your own peccadilloes, and in the best of faith! Why, each knows the other fellow's, knows them every time, the neighbor knows the neighbor's. And now tit for tat: we'll see I'm right. (*Laughing, to the bony Miss Ehrenreich:*) We know a ghost story about you — listen, everybody. (*Points at her.*) When her mother lay in her coffin, they put a delicately embroidered soft pillow under her head. She — this one — take a good look at her — she found it a pity about the pillow — she rifled her mother's coffin and shoved her bristly old sewing basket under the head instead. Nice, eh?

MISS EHRENREICH: Can you possibly have heard of the eighth commandment: "Thou shalt not bear false witness against thy neighbor"?

OLD SEDEMUND: Heard it? Of course I have. But think: being what you are, you can afford to be good and just. That's why it's so much easier for you than for one of us.

MISS EHRENREICH: How easier? Why for me?

OLD SEDEMUND: How — why? Because only nine commandments apply to you. Every schoolboy can demonstrate to you on his fingers that nine commandments are easier to keep than ten.

MISS EHRENREICH: But I should think all ten commandments apply to everyone, regardless.

OLD SEDEMUND: Well, in a manner of speaking. But what of the sixth? You're not in a state — never were, if my eyes don't deceive me — to imperil a marriage. Not with your figure! You could stand on your head and never even cause a crack in one. What is my conclusion? The sixth commandment does not apply to you. Wherever *you* are, *it* is not. *Miss Ehrenreich retreats enraged into the background.*

140

OLD SEDEMUND: None of you here is better than I am. None of you knows all about everyone. Only *one* lives, that is true. (*With his eyes he seeks out the Christ figure and he points to it.*) There's the lion, there he hangs, and that's bad, that's worse than if he were roaring or biting. Yes, indeed, that is my youngest son who is not well pleased with me. I ordered him made of wood so at the next Flood he can float on the surface — for thirty pieces of silver — what a bargain! (*Preaching:*) O my beloved, what thoroughly good creatures you are so long as no one knows what big swindlers you really are. *He* knows, and that's why he is so lean — one doesn't grow fat from so much secretiveness — and yet he is still so heavy with the weight of your sins that his hands are sorely pulled and torn.

UNCLE WALDEMAR (*has approached and drawn him forward*): Ah bwoth-ah, bwothah, you make it wohse and wohse!

Young Sedemund approaches.

UNCLE WALDEMAR: How yoah haht would melt if I were to name in public, as you ah doing, things which will be misintehpweted as shohtcom-ings.

OLD SEDEMUND: You — you're a phony. What do you know of sins?

UNCLE WALDEMAR: Ah bwothah, I do, I do — there ah oaths, certain oaths — don't push me — who knows if I could stand the test?

OLD SEDEMUND: Do you think, Waldemar, that that one's ears back there are merely wooden? Take care: he can't stand such Sedemund doings, though he endures everything else. He'll be sick and puke on us and bespatter himself — what disgrace for us. (*Notices his son.*) How do you think Grude would diagnose my case?

YOUNG SEDEMUND: He would say the lion is biting you. The good lion is changing you inside himself into fodder; that's what I heard rumored from the mouth of the little wheelchair saint, in truly Grude-like fash-ion. Isn't that a little word of truth?

OLD SEDEMUND: You think so? Unfortunately I am not in a position to give out the little word of truth — so obviously expected of me — like my billfold. (*Pulls out his billfold and hands it to his son.*) These en-dowment dollars remain in my pocket, burning my legs. That's all that has come from this hocus-pocus.

YOUNG SEDEMUND: Do the dollars burn because your son has struck your pocket in public? Because the lions' jaws of scandal are baring their fangs?

OLD SEDEMUND: Aren't you weighing the wallet as though it were my shrunken pouch of a heart? Mr. Sedemund's heart no less! I do wish to submit, however, that this my present splendid figure is not Mr. Sedemund's only one! There is another, as mighty as a point. This nameless point is at one with Mr. Sedemund, so much at one, indeed, that it is his essential self. Therefore it follows that Mr. Sedemund is not at all Mr. Sedemund, but this very point, which no fist can enclose; that Mr. Sedemund is merely the porter of his own self, which, like a point without ears, without breath, without pain, pure like nothingness, sinless like the sun, is sitting quite comfortably within. Mr. Porter Sedemund has no inkling where the point is to be delivered — the so-called Mr. Sedemund, whose clever son will no doubt dig up his own besmeared answer in a compost pile of foolishness. Now I'll quickly pay my respects to the wheelchair saint. (*Goes to Sabina.*)

YOUNG SEDEMUND: I heard you speak of oaths, Uncle Waldemar . . .

UNCLE WALDEMAR: Be genewous, Gewahd, don't mention that, not heah!

YOUNG SEDEMUND: Why not? Can't I clip the wool off my worthy uncle's words? How about a deal? Take this purse of money, add yours to it and with it distill a drop of comfort into Master Mankmoos's grief — but be nice about it. (*Gives him the money.*) Then we'll trample those oaths to death.

UNCLE WALDEMAR: A pleasure, Gewahd, gladly. (*Goes to Mankmoos.*) *Young Sedemund joins the center group consisting of Sabina, Mrs. Grude, and Old Sedemund.*

OLD SEDEMUND (*to Sabina*): A little exercise might be welcome, eh? My insignificant self could find no better employment than in the service of sanctity. (*Sabina shakes her head.*) You mean to say you're no saint. But of course: saints are in heaven, while you are sitting, as I am, in hell. Yes, yes, in the very center; nothing to be done about that: hell-roasts both of us. Now permit me, to prevent you from catching cold in this chilly hell! (*He pushes the wheelchair through the center of the crowd, faces front, and stops.*) And both of us know all about Lord Satan; I don't believe in him either, but actually I know better.

SABINA: So do I.

OLD SEDEMUND: You see, my dear, I'm a bad father but a capital hell-brother — therefore trust me. Haven't you just been confirmed?

Sabina nods.

OLD SEDEMUND: Then you know how it goes in the Lord's Prayer — "our daily bread . . ."

SABINA: The fourth petition.

OLD SEDEMUND: Quite right, the fourth. And then the interpretation with that grand list, beginning with eating, drinking, clothes, shoes — what virtue comes next?

SABINA: "Peace — health —"

OLD SEDEMUND: Health — a healthy, long life in a wheelchair, eh? (*Sabina bows her head.*) Go on.

SABINA: "Modesty — honor . . ."

OLD SEDEMUND: Honor and modesty? By God, there you have nothing to fear, don't have to go to the trouble of praying for those. They belong to you as a leash to a dog. Go on . . .

SABINA: "A devout husband, devout children."

OLD SEDEMUND: I advise you, my dear, when you're praying, use the fourth petition to catch your breath. It isn't for you, and it'll shorten the Lord's Prayer.

Sabina slumps.

OLD SEDEMUND: Yes, it does look sad; but then there's something about "good weather"?

Sabina nods.

OLD SEDEMUND: Good weather, to be wheeled out — I assume you have some use for that. Yours is a pitiful little piece of daily bread — I'm afraid it's not going to satisfy your hunger. Oh, oh.

Sabina cries.

OLD SEDEMUND: A pretty moldy piece of daily bread, but what more can you expect on hell's diet! (*He pushes her again in a circle.*)

Mrs. Grude steps up and takes Sabina's hand. As the chair makes a turn, Mankmoos stands in its path.

OLD SEDEMUND (*to Sabina*): Isn't this one of our brood?

Sabina looks at him, shudders.

OLD SEDEMUND: No? Then he belongs to the others. Out of the way, most honored sir, hell rejects you. (*He pushes on.*)

143

Mankmoos moves aside, but trots after them.

OLD SEDEMUND (*turning around*) : But he seems to take to our company. Does it without singing or praying, follows us loyally. (*To Mankmoos:*) Something important you want to say?

MANKMOOS (*showing the billfold*) : I wanted to express my gratitude for your contribution to the funeral of my wife. If it upset Mr. Sedemund when I asked questions early this morning in Mr. Sedemund's sickroom, whether Mr. Sedemund might not perhaps be willing . . .

OLD SEDEMUND: Brother, you're as good a hell-roast as any. Forget such ideas, but keep a tight hold on the money, wherever you got it. Join us on the road to hell, but behind, as rear guard. (*He pushes on, Mankmoos trudging behind.*)

OLD SEDEMUND (*whispering*) : Don't tell anyone, my dear, but you're not the only one crying here in the caverns of hell. It doesn't run sparkling down my cheeks — that's the only difference between us — and perhaps my way of crying is more violent than yours. You can be open about your sorrow, whereas I, even if I wanted to — my jowls merely start to twitch.

SABINA: Tell me why, but don't speak so horribly about your crying; you frighten me. Go on, tell.

OLD SEDEMUND: Should I? Very well, but we'll make another round. (*He pushes her, stopping in front of the Organ-Grinder.*) How well off this one is! He is able to blow his sorrow out his noisy air pipe. Loud or low — the grinding comes easy. (*To the Organ-Grinder:*) Regale us with a lullaby of love, good man. (*The Organ-Grinder is about to do so.*) No, not yet, but I bid you enter my employ as the musical accompanist to our journey to hell. Stay at hand behind us. (*Pointing to Mankmoos.*) He's the paymaster. Report to me if he shortchanges you on payday.

He pushes on. The Organ-Grinder falls in behind. Some curious people follow and a procession is formed. It circles slowly, half as a carnival parade, half as funeral procession.

OLD SEDEMUND (*to Sabina*) : Look, how many feel at home in hell. They all want to — give way to their grief. But you and I, we two, are the ones who suffer most. It's our turn to speak, isn't it?

SABINA: Is it time?

144

OLD SEDEMUND: Yes. (*He pushes her chair in a circle and instinctively seizes her hands.*) My dear, what is to become of us when people like that Mr. Sedemund run around loose in hell, eh? That'll have to be looked into. By the way, did you know I had a wife?
Sabina nods.

OLD SEDEMUND: But she is dead and in her own heaven. There is no Mrs. Sedemund and one day there won't be any Mr. Sedemund, may God be gracious to him, eh?

SABINA: Believe me, he will be. It is certain.

OLD SEDEMUND: Are you really so certain? When that Mr. Sedemund is no longer Mr. Sedemund, he'll have nothing to do with grace or disgrace — but all the same, Mr. Sedemund put on a little show for his wife — sickness, deathbed — (*Sabina looks puzzled and doubtful.*) Oh, that's easy, very easy; Mr. Sedemund did a thorough job: he is clever and well educated. He acted desperate.

SABINA: Really? Why did you do it?

OLD SEDEMUND: Shhh! *He* did! Because he evidently had to die: it's not easy to die suspecting one's wife of — of what then? An evil comedy — that's it! A stale but stirred-up tale out of the past, raised by the yeast of suspicion — whose suspicion? A willed suspicion that lashes out rather than being leashed, sung to the tune of "As I do to you, so you do to me" — you follow?

SABINA: No, I don't.

OLD SEDEMUND: Look, Sabina, I wanted to accuse her of what I did to her, make it alike in kind. Mr. Sedemund demanded a confession for the impressive reason that the dying always produce: I cannot die peacefully unless you say yes. And so she said yes, out of mercy and — well, kindness, merely to shorten my suffering because, you see, Sabina, she thought: he's dying and he needs to forgive for the sake of his own peace and comfort because he ascribes to others what came easily to him. That is how she reasoned — just as I had planned. (*He waits while she looks at him questioningly.*) Why? Heaven, I had inflicted so much on her, I was so hellishly in her debt, that I was aching to have something to forgive *her*. I wanted to even things out — holy God, don't you understand that?

SABINA: Wasn't that evil?

OLD SEDEMUND: Evil? Not at all. I was exactly as Mr. Sedemund had always been, nor did I become, by what he did, either better or worse. And so she said: Yes, I did it, because she believed my mind was fixed on it. By admitting to evil she did me an act of grace. Yet that did not make her evil, for she was good and remained —
Sabina shakes her head.

OLD SEDEMUND: Ah yes — do you begin to see part of the reality? She was upright, blameless, and competent.

SABINA: But not good.

OLD SEDEMUND: Ah, child, how do *you* know? Well, whatever she was, she branded herself with a blemish, grew leprous as though infected by my rotten taint, and my son says she died of it — (*He makes a face.*) You can see how sharply the claws scratch and how deep the pits are that they dig in places where indestructible villainies have far from rotted to dust. (*To Uncle Waldemar and Young Sedemund who have stepped near:*) What do you want? You — who has anything to do with you? This child here, who cannot utter the fourth petition, paymaster Mankmoos there, brother Organ-Grinder Nonpareil and all the other roasts and comrades of hell are under my care. It shall be my job to lead them — and myself with them — safely out of hell. (*To Organ-Grinder:*) You first, and blow your trumpets so the walls of hell may crumble. Nothing remains of the lion's claws but stumps, his fangs are chewed to impotence: he will hobble home at our scorn, and our drums shall break his roar! And with this I commend you all to Satan!
He pushes the Organ-Grinder ahead who plays at his loudest. The procession of spectators who find themselves protected by those in the van are gradually encouraged to follow. The leading group disappears quickly through the side door.

Scene 7

At the intersection of two paths in the churchyard. Dense bushes on both sides. The procession of the hellish crew, led by the Organ-Grinder, enters from the back and swings to the front. Grude, dressed as in the beginning in top hat and tails, and dragging the lionskin, meets the procession. He brings it to a halt.

GRUDE (*spreading out the skin and lying down on it*): Down, Caesar, nice Caesar! What are you all after? That's the way of the world: it's in your pants and coats that your true self is suspended; your hide is merely your color, but your color causes all the stir. This lion-fur produced the lion-fantasy. Caesar's clothes and fame were as good as his very roar — he who has ears can see it. Dead is not dead, for how could death be shocking if he were dead, eh?

OLD SEDEMUND: Who was it said so impudently that the lion is devouring us? Now it is clear what fat sheep we are, if lions lose weight like that one from it. In a way, to devour and to be devoured seem to be one and the same. (*To Grude:*) But if things are so nearly their opposites, we hell-brothers can take comfort: good is bad and bad is good — a mighty tender tune. Give us room and stop primping yourself with another bird's feathers! (*To the Organ-Grinder:*) Blow your bugle and make this trophy-cuddling hero shut up. Let hell roar! Up and away, up and ahoy, over hides and hoi polloi!
Organ-Grinder starts to play.

SERGEANT LAMBKIN (*hurrying in with Greedycock*): Who is responsible for this barefaced buffoonery? (*To Organ-Grinder:*) You are guilty of desecrating a graveyard, do you know that? Who gave you permission to play your organ here?

OLD SEDEMUND: I did, Sergeant. He and I are conjointly leading the roasts of hell on an exodus and a procession. He serves me as musical court jester. A virtuoso for the ages. You look surprised, Sergeant, but glance around you: yes, we have all of us truly returned!

SERGEANT LAMBKIN: Respected Mr. Sedemund, I am compelled to give you a serious warning. Don't you remember? I had put you under strict orders to stay in the chapel, and here you mention roasts of hell. How can you account for such a response?

OLD SEDEMUND: Easy, Sergeant. Like this: you have encountered a legion that has broken out of hell, that laughs at the lion. Don't be afraid: we're in our right minds, clearheaded, and none of our bodies riddled

by bullets. All hides are sound, not a flaw, except that of the lion himself, if you will just take a look . . . (*Points to Grude.*)

SERGEANT LAMBKIN (*to Grude*): You? We are looking for you everywhere, and you are *here*? Aren't you the man in a black coat from the
insane asylum? You are the one supposed to have released the lion.
What's that lying there?

GRUDE: A lion, Sergeant! He himself, alas, stayed home, but he most considerately bequeathed to me his hide, upon which I went for a ride
posthaste, however crazy it may seem. Here is Caesar, this lionskin.
(*Gets up and shows the hide.*) That's his muzzle, that his tail, there's
his belly, and here his legs, but his body is lifeless: we all have his soul
within us, you understand. There are other ways of saying it so even
fatheads get it.

Sergeant Lambkin sniffs at the skin, while Greedycock presses closer.

GREEDYCOCK: Where does he get the gall to appropriate this pelt? Altogether — a sinister character, if we consider what it takes to operate
secretly and without help in the dark.

SERGEANT LAMBKIN (*to Grude*): How did you acquire this skin? Let me
see your paws.

GRUDE (*showing his hands*): No blood there, Sergeant, and even the cuffs
all the way up to the shirt, every crease visible or hidden — all clean,
not a spot. (*Pulling out a piece of paper, good-humored:*) I purchased
the skin fresh from the lion, in a manner of speaking, still warm —
look: the grossly ungrammatical but nonetheless legal receipt of ani-
mal-circus proprietor Candido Franchi — so, take a look yourself, I
am going to strike a match. (*Does so.*) Here, take it: dead in the morning, skinned at noon, in the evening mine . . . Well, now, wasn't it
more like a rabbit, rather than the king of the desert, before which our
world tottered?

SERGEANT LAMBKIN (*reads the paper, returns it mechanically, then half
to himself*): By now the Congressman must have received our report,
and a deposition signed by Greedycock — (*To Greedycock:*) No, I
wouldn't have wished it on you, but you needn't have raised all this
to-do over such horse manure.

GREEDYCOCK (*stammering*): If you regard my infinitesimal part in this
matter of such importance, Sergeant . . .

SERGEANT LAMBKIN: Greedycock, in a minute the fire brigade will arrive; the entire police force is advancing upon us, only because you've seen the animal — so you claimed. You fired a shot and you lied. It was me you bamboozled, because I practically arrested everybody here on the basis of your word. (*Shrugs.*)

GRUDE (*to Sergeant Lambkin*): And is that all, Sergeant? Your ears were exposed to the accusation concerning the bribery of the Commissioner of Public Scales; your nose was stuffed with the stink of Greedycock's child-trade; your eyes could not but notice Mr. Waldemar Sedemund's readiness to produce further evidence — all those arrested have become alert to these things. But you, you were privileged to enjoy it all with grand-ducal ears and eyes and an official nose.

SERGEANT LAMBKIN: I don't seem to recall your having been present.

OLD SEDEMUND: But I was.

VOICES: Me too! Me too!

SERGEANT LAMBKIN: Oho? Who is this "me too, me too"? Up front!

ORGAN-GRINDER: Me too, Mr. Inspector-Sergeant. Myself I was here as I stand before you in that self-same person. If you're looking for witnesses, I'm ready and willing.

SERGEANT LAMBKIN: This matter can proceed without you, rest assured. I want to know why there were shouts of "me too," "me too." If anyone questions my handling of the case according to prescribed channels, step forward. You, Mr. Sedemund, why you too "me too"?

OLD SEDEMUND: A mere whisper of a "me," Sergeant. As the trumpet blows on Judgment Day, it may be the time for a louder "me," provided I don't have to save my breath for my own concerns. Ergo, I haven't been present — I draw in my tail.

SERGEANT LAMBKIN: Anyone else? Step forward! (*Complete silence.*)

SERGEANT LAMBKIN (*striking his breast*): You must all realize that Mr. Sedemund's brother spoke expressly of pranks and anecdotes related at breakfast in the Archduke.

UNCLE WALDEMAR (*from the back*): Quite wight, Colonel, that's cow-wect!

YOUNG SEDEMUND (*stepping forward*): But the construction you put on it, Sergeant, is completely wrong. There was talk of jokes, true, but not in the way of joking. It was a malicious charge, and of a kind to

149

make one puke, but there is not the slightest reason to change a vulture into a swan, as you so considerately seem intent on doing.

ORGAN-GRINDER: Did they sprinkle us with slop when they baptized us?

SERGEANT LAMBKIN: I see you're the young Mr. Sedemund. You are not going to get into trouble for nothing. Do, do continue.

YOUNG SEDEMUND: I have finished with you, Sergeant.

SERGEANT LAMBKIN: But I haven't with you, sir. You'll hear from me. (*To Greedycock:*) Have you put together *your* case? How am I to present the case to the Congressman? (*To the bystanders:*) Since there is no more danger, you can all go home.

The people walk past Greedycock. He glances at those in front as though he expected them to turn and look at him. They nudge one another with their elbows and now crane their necks. Finally one impudent teenager stops dead like a road sign and points his finger at Greedycock. Greedycock draws himself up and turns aside. He stands, his lips compressed, until the last one has disappeared. Old Sedemund, Sabina, Organ-Grinder, and Mankmoos slowly go off on one side. Young Sedemund goes with Grude to the other side. Finally Glorylane plucks Sergeant Lambkin by his sleeve, winks, and draws him familiarly aside.

GREEDYCOCK (*alone, looking around*): I wish I had the guts to cut off my nose so nobody would recognize me when I walk in the street tomorrow.

He stamps on the ground. There is a hollow sound which re-echoes beneath the earth. One hears the dead in their graves whisper to one another.

A SUBDUED VOICE: Hey, who is that lout?

Finally the subterranean whispering turns to quiet laughter. One hears talk and individual words like "Greedycock" and "Glorylane" — "the worthy Greedycock." Then a dark shape appears, coming to a stop before Greedycock.

THE SHAPE: They're telling tales of Greedycock and Glorylane down below. They laugh at you. How then can I rest in my grave without grief?

GREEDYCOCK: Mother, help me, at least to get rid of this fancy document!

He reaches into his breast pocket and pulls out the paper signed by Swingcord. He tears it to pieces and places them in the outstretched hand of the shape. But the pieces fall to the ground.

THE SHAPE: Much, much too heavy: I can't carry it. It wouldn't help if I took it with me beneath the earth. They have been pointing their fingers a long time at your doings and dealings, but you don't see it. They are mumbling at your misdeeds, but you don't hear it. Yet *I* have to listen. Now they're laughing and they will be laughing a long time. Let me ask if you intend to burden me with still more sorrows?

GREEDYCOCK: They know everything down there? What else do you know about me?

The Shape shakes her head.

GREEDYCOCK: Have the others told you nothing? Is there no whispering in the ground about — about — (*He strikes his mouth.*)

The Shape slowly withdraws. Greedycock follows.

GREEDYCOCK: Do you or don't you know — are you after all blind and deaf — the story about — out with it! I've got to know what the caverns and air and earth know about it.

The Shape has apparently come to a stop near a dark tombstone. He comes closer, but there is only the tombstone.

GREEDYCOCK: Who knows where she went! A spook is nothing, a spook doesn't have to take an oath, and whatever a spook says . . .

A new hubbub arises beneath the earth, this time in harsh, accusing tones. Greedycock is frightened and covers his ears. Then he listens again, and stamps his feet, whereupon the murmuring ceases. He looks around relieved, is about to go, stops, takes a step, stops again, bends down to the earth. Shaken and trembling, he listens.

GREEDYCOCK: She's crying, O God, she's crying, can't you hear? Damn you for her crying. (*Listens.*) Do I really deserve having the old woman in her grave crying her eyes out for me? God, she's still crying! Do what you want to me, but not that! How I would want her to dream good and blessed things about me! I wish I were a child again, so she could quietly smile down on me. (*Listens.*) Quiet again; perhaps she went to sleep. I would want her to dream a thousand years and forget altogether who I am and that I am. If only she wouldn't notice me! Away with you, Greedycock and Glorylane! (*Slinks sideways into the dark.*)

The two Sedemunds meet.

YOUNG SEDEMUND: I am looking for Sabina.

OLD SEDEMUND: And find your father — well, Gerhard, what does the son say of the prodigal father? Aren't you actually ashamed of yourself? I would think you had avenged your mother adequately. Does the picture of me pilloried afford you sufficient amusement? The candle-light back there in that hellish quarter was shabby, but it sufficed, didn't it? Here in the dark we could fight it out properly, but, my boy, if I were to tell you the whole truth, not in pretty words, no, but in words that fit the case, then we would both — blush before each other, even in the dark. She was a good mother, Gerhard, but a miserable wife.

YOUNG SEDEMUND: You disgust me, Father!

OLD SEDEMUND: All right, after all, what could you know about that! Learn to understand that the proximity, the relentless intertwining of life, is a dangerous thing; that an abyss thrusts people apart, only because they failed to keep distance between them. Learn to know those things that push themselves soundlessly into being and irresistibly gain ground. What have we committed, man, that we always spy on each other through the keyhole of our relationship? Have we nothing else?

YOUNG SEDEMUND: From this day on it shall be one Sedemund and the other Sedemund — nothing of father, nothing of son.

OLD SEDEMUND: Suits me. My fatherhood turned rotten and rancid in you. I did your mother an injustice: with the help of Professor Latchbolt I seized the staff of her self-righteousness from her hands and threw it to the dogs. Ah, you don't know how wonderful the world is, and neither did she. Call me sinful: God himself loved sinfully, since he created the world in horror and in beauty. And there was neighing like thunder as from a rutting stallion.

YOUNG SEDEMUND: And yet a moment ago I saw you deeply shaken — no, you had condemned yourself — how was it? — as a brother of hell?

OLD SEDEMUND: Perhaps so; I have to admit that.

YOUNG SEDEMUND: And do you now talk so contemptuously of your own confession?

OLD SEDEMUND: Who knows where our realities lie! I often accuse myself in the people's voice. Yes, it did shake me to stand at the tomb and to hear the myth that wanted to be born mumble quietly.

YOUNG SEDEMUND: No passer-by wonders about the spirit of a house if there's no ghost at the window, but if there is a ghost — the murderer's payoff — craning its head through an attic louver, everyone knows instantly. A possibility?

OLD SEDEMUND (*mocking*): You can put it this way: what I didn't say is as good as though I had said it, or whatever I do is as good as though I hadn't done it, or what I failed to do is as evil as though it had occurred. And now you know exactly whose the spirit of this house is. But have you any idea what things *you* will accommodate yourself to one day? Indeed, haven't you dealt badly with me — very, very badly?

YOUNG SEDEMUND: In being so certain that I won't ever accommodate myself? Let that be my worry.

OLD SEDEMUND: Is it not conceivable that one day we shall be rewarded for having been wicked — as compensation? That goodness must suffer for its enormous good fortune?

Mrs. Grude enters with Sabina.

SABINA (*to Old Sedemund*): After taking me out of hell you promised to lift me to heaven. I am holding you to your word, and that's why I asked her (*inclining her head toward Mrs. Grude*) to wheel me here.

OLD SEDEMUND: Ah child, I did indeed promise you that. So I shall give you a foretaste of heaven — more I cannot do, despite my best intentions. You shall have a child, and by me — — a son, a learned son. (*Reaches quickly for Gerhard's hand.*) Look, he shall be your son, I make him over to you, my single offspring. You saw how singularly he dealt with me because of his love for his mother — — and you, as his new mother, will — —

YOUNG SEDEMUND: Father, what an absurd fantasy!

OLD SEDEMUND: No "father"! That's over. Take her in your arms and make the poor thing rich. (*Whispering to him:*) She turned to the devil and meant it, she told me herself. That is how cruelly loneliness crushed her. Don't deprive me of the pleasure of doing something for her. Look at her closely: doesn't she sit in her chair like a young broken-winged sparrow? (*Young Sedemund looks at Sabina.*) Indeed, what is there but to conjure for her some fool's paradise one way or another; nothing less will truly restore her. She is exiled to her little island — — one must swim across without bag or baggage. Go ahead! Don't be a slug.

153

YOUNG SEDEMUND: Can a human being be so alone and still remain human?

He takes a deep breath, quickly steps over to Sabina, and kisses her hand. She is frightened. He bends over her, embraces her, and kisses her.

SABINA: And what may your name be?

YOUNG SEDEMUND: I am called Gerhard.

SABINA: Gerhard is good, but then good isn't good enough. I'm going to rename you for as long as I am your mother. Be named Henry. Gentle Henry, and be like a gentle, refreshing rain.

OLD SEDEMUND: And just think, soon your Gentle Henry will get married and then you'll be a grandmother, and you'll have more grandchildren than your arms can hold.

SABINA: Has the time come so soon to marry? He will have to ask my permission. But first I must tell him something special. (*To Old Sedemund:*) If you don't mind, it's only for him.

Old Sedemund steps back.

SABINA: Come here, Henry; give me your hand, and promise — here — will you promise?

Young Sedemund gives her his hand.

SABINA: Good! Now listen: it is a most urgent, yes, a sacred deed that you do this old man back there — a good man, really a very good man — better than good — that you do that old man some good, something better than good, something wonderful. There it is, Henry; otherwise you'll never have my permission to marry.

YOUNG SEDEMUND: Do you really think he is good?

SABINA (*turning away*): Leave me, I don't want to see you, go away. Ugh, you kissed me. (*She wipes her mouth.*) I want none of your grandchildren. (*Stamping her feet:*) Away, off, you make me sick. (*To the Old Sedemund:*) Come back, please stay with me. You are good, and he is bad, because he doesn't know what is good — ugh — he has no idea. If you cannot lift me up to heaven, I want you to take me back to hell.

OLD SEDEMUND: From one place to another. There are many stops between heaven and hell.

He moves her off. Mrs. Grude follows. The Organ-Grinder and Mankmoos march back and forth in front of Young Sedemund.

ORGAN-GRINDER: This crazy old man has a dose of the devil in his guts. You, mister, why don't you go squat astride a weathercock and let the four howling winds cuddle you a bit? That pretty little one, she's got a hellishly sharp nose: crippled legs can happen, but life gobbles away in her guts like a holy hallelujah complete with stuffin' and trimmin's. Come along, Mr. Paymaster — grease your joy rides with eye and nose droppings.

Goes off with Mankmoos.

Mrs. Grude returns, excited.

MRS. GRUDE: They're unbearable, those two. He pushed the organ-grinder and tailor aside; she made me such peculiar faces that I caught on right away. If it weren't too disgusting, I'd say they were trying to be by themselves — looking for a hideaway. Where is Grude?

YOUNG SEDEMUND: Up there somewhere — running after his beloved wife before going home.

MRS. GRUDE: Home? Heavens, what does he mean?

YOUNG SEDEMUND: His own, *his* home, *his* heaven. He is hale and hearty, like a mountain stream, and thoroughly restored. You merely need to present yourself.

MRS. GRUDE: I won't let him wait. (*She hurries off.*)

Glorylane and Sergeant Lambkin enter.

GLORYLANE (*whispering to Young Sedemund, in the belief, because of the darkness, that he is Greedycock*): Brother Greedycock, brother Greedycock, relax: everything's fixed. Mr. Lambkin proved friendly to me beyond all expectation and praise.

YOUNG SEDEMUND: That's excellent, Mr. Glorylane. Let it be a little darker and Mr. Greedycock's comfort will serve me too. Really, Mr. Lambkin, they don't praise you loud enough! Weren't you supposed to hear from me, or I from you — remember? Or doesn't it make any difference?

SERGEANT LAMBKIN: Dear Mr. Sedemund —

YOUNG SEDEMUND: Oh no, that's not my name: merely Mr. Sedemund.

SERGEANT LAMBKIN: Very well: Mr. Sedemund, if you prefer. Since you offer me the choice *you* shall hear from *me*. Is it your purpose to humiliate me? It seems you uncover dereliction of duty, you catch me in official negligence — — I can see you assent, despite the dark. Assume

155

then I ignore Greedycock's doings and dealings so long as they don't become generally known. Mr. Glorylane and I know the ins and outs — such enterprises click and mesh with us like well-greased gears. We stand amidst mute graves: ears cannot hear and mouths do not ask to be heard. (*To Glorylane, who is picking up scraps of paper:*) What rarities are you discovering?

GLORYLANE: I have a feeling I ought to collect these scraps. Ah, yes. (*Searching eagerly.*) They are such remarkable rarities they deserve to be put in a safe. Although you are entirely correct in maintaining we stand among mute graves. (*Putting the scraps in his pocket:*) Ears cannot hear, mouths cannot — —

GREEDYCOCK (*rushing out of the bushes*): Shut up, you loudmouths! What do you mean — mute graves, deaf ears?

GLORYLANE: Brother Greedycock, brother Greedycock, what a scare you gave me.

GREEDYCOCK: Brother Glorylane, brother Glorylane, what is my mother's property doing in your pocket?

GLORYLANE: Strange, what a son you are to be speaking of your mother who has been dead so long.

GREEDYCOCK: A brother's pockets are open to his brother. Please! (*He tears open Glorylane's coat and pulls out the scraps of paper which he throws back upon the ground.*) Listen, brother. (*Tears out the lining.*) You recall my recent troubles, you recall how you stood by me in brotherly solicitude to let me slip past like an eel. (*Tears his coat into pieces and pulls off his waistcoat.*) But was it not really my son who had troubles at the hands of his father? Such a clean job we put together in brotherly harmony! And just as I was about to rinse that cleanness off my hands, you come along with "Brother Greedycock, brother Greedycock." Do you understand, brother Glorylane, my dead mother shall finally rest in sleep, you wretch! (*Pulls his suspenders loose.*) Hold on to your pants or you'll have to skip home in your shirttails. There — now run and yell in the streets: my brother Greedycock did this to me!

GLORYLANE: Sergeant, he's really gone crazy.

GREEDYCOCK: Earth and sky are murmuring of it; there's rumbling in the ground and it goes "Brother Greedycock?" Shut up, I say, or she'll begin to weep again.

YOUNG SEDEMUND (*to Sergeant Lambkin*): There's nothing funny about this. Mr. Lambkin, he's throwing a big monkey wrench into those well-oiled gears of yours.

SERGEANT LAMBKIN: One word, Mr. Glorylane!

GREEDYCOCK: He has no longer any say in matters Greedycock! And he who hasn't got any say isn't going to produce any more words, right? What word, Mr. Lambkin? (*To Glorylane:*) Go to the devil, you — what word?! (*Grabs Sergeant Lambkin's shoulder.*)

SERGEANT LAMBKIN: Don't you manhandle me like Glorylane! Let me go, good friend, no nonsense; let me go, I say!

GREEDYCOCK: O Heavenly Father, help me, prevent me from killing this living Sergeant Lambkin lion-dead. (*Embraces him in a convulsive rage.*) Help thou me, keep me from doing it! (*To Sedemund and Glorylane:*) For heaven's sake, help him; move, get someone! *Glorylane rushes off.*

SERGEANT LAMBKIN (*half-choking*): The catch on my revolver is off — out of the way, Mr. Sedemund — I'm going to shoot!

GREEDYCOCK: Shoot? God be praised, now I can let him go. (*Releasing him, quietly:*) Don't shoot, pal, no noise, please! I only came to make you pipe down, and now — (*Listens.*) Everything is quiet, they are asleep in their graves, let's part. I don't care to know what the word is, I don't care for anything that'll waken the dead. *Jumps into the dark and disappears.*

SERGEANT LAMBKIN (*laughing*): Isn't this funny after all, Mr. Sedemund? I didn't even have a revolver on me — just a little military strategem. (*Confidentially:*) You see, we don't want to trouble our most eminent citizens needlessly merely because they've cut corners here and there. A good reputation means a whole lot more to us than the letter of the law. Mr. Greedycock is an example of a proven, good citizen: we must take good care not to throw a wrench into things as they are. A sound appearance shields a sound enterprise, and a sound enterprise is our shield and shelter.

YOUNG SEDEMUND: You mean of course that to seem good is to be good? By the way, I told you earlier that I had finished with you. Remember?

SERGEANT LAMBKIN (*comfortably*): Why so angry, Mr. Sedemund? Greedycock is by no means the worst. It would be a pity to lock him up when there are so many running around who ought to be in jail. And what of punishing those sinners who fail to commit their sin for lack of opportunity? Should they be left happily riding up and down the countryside merely because they found none? Get off scot-free and brag of it? By rights the very ones above suspicion ought to be punished — they first and foremost.

He decides to go, but collides with Uncle Waldemar, who runs into him in excitement and terror.

SERGEANT LAMBKIN: Hallo — who's that? Look where you're going, man! Oh, good evening, Mr. Sedemund.

UNCLE WALDEMAR: Where is he, if you please?

SERGEANT LAMBKIN: Where is who? Your nephew is there.

UNCLE WALDEMAR: Oh, Mistah Lambkin, if you only knew — yes, evewything is in the best of ohdah, Mistah Lambkin. Go, please.

SERGEANT LAMBKIN: Do you mean me?

UNCLE WALDEMAR (*getting hold of himself*): Excuse me, Colonel, it concerns — — ah — confidential family mattahs.

SERGEANT LAMBKIN: Certainly, Mr. Sedemund, of course. G'd evening, Mr. Sedemund. (*Goes off.*)

UNCLE WALDEMAR (*clinging to Young Sedemund*): Oh Gewahd, Gewahd! Come and help me, Gewahd, to take yoah fathah away. Imagine, he talks on and on at wandom with that Sabina, and tells her she's a sweet little soul and such twaddle. O God, O God, and in passing, to make her listen bettah, he says: my bwothah pehjures himself. Yoah bwothah? she asks and acts in love. Yes, he himself, the vewy Waldemah, he says, as though that were nothing, and then he goes on talking about himself. Oh, Gewahd, Gewahd, come quick!

YOUNG SEDEMUND: Leave me alone, Uncle; I don't think your oaths are my oaths.

UNCLE WALDEMAR: But I'm yoah uncle, Gewahd, — Gewahd, I'm going to hang myself if you don't help me.

YOUNG SEDEMUND: And for the time being I have decided to put myself, as a favor to my father, in the care of Dr. Grabbold. Sabina put that idea in my head. And so, Uncle, you'll have a job making the rounds,

158

embroidering upon the tale of horror at the graveside and whatever else happened. Perhaps something like this: Would you believe, you'll say, what whimsies, what impossible follies, not to say lunacies, wallowed — you'll say — in my poor nephew's head? And what was left for my poor brother than to react to the fantasies of his own son as to a very serious matter, even if this meant profound humiliation, not to say degradation — you'll go on — no, you'll put it even stronger — the profanation of his own person in front of the rabble. Yes, he went so far that I myself, the uncle — you will say, Uncle — could not be spared, that is, we became the victims of his raging madness while trying to save him from his very ravings. That's what you'll say, and it will be as true as one of your oaths. Both of you are in fact most eminent citizens, and one musn't throw a wrench into things as they are. Come along, Uncle, but not to frighten Father from Sabina. If you mean to put your energies to Father's best use, you'll reconsider your own sensational hanging.

UNCLE WALDEMAR: Oh Gewahd, deah boy, how good of you — you — you genuine Sedemund.

YOUNG SEDEMUND: Genuine Sedemund? Yes, that's what they are — incorrigible. The Sedemunds stink to high heaven like a mass of excrement. A lion's jaws open and a lion's gullet howls wrath upon us, and you call me a genuine Sedemund! And yet at this moment any name in the world is more praiseworthy than ours. The play of color on a speck of soapsuds, the pretty glitter of a soap bubble are, for the time, more substantial than our standing. Where does that leave our genuineness, my father's and mine, since we remain genuine Sedemunds? *Young Sedemund and Uncle Waldemar go off. Grude and Mrs. Grude emerge from the background, arm in arm. Suddenly he takes hold of her and dances a little way.*

MRS. GRUDE: Now don't! Step softly — you can dance later. First let's get away from these graves.

GRUDE: Pooh! Straight across the graves! And right through the horror! And away with the horror into the ditch under our feet! The old have had their day — are stamped into the ground. Now it's our turn, and after us our children's. Everything will be radically different. Hurray for the new day and the genuine Grudes! *Off.*

THE BLUE BOLL

A DRAMA IN SEVEN SCENES

Cast of Characters

LANDOWNER BOLL

HIS WIFE

GRETE GREENDALE

HER HUSBAND

OTTO POMPMASTER

WOODFRESSER, A SHOEMAKER

VIRGIN, A WATCHMAKER

MAYOR

ELIAS

HIS WIFE DORIS

A GENTLEMAN

MRS. UNK

GUESTS

SUCKLEWORM, A COACHMAN

TOWNSPEOPLE

THREE CORPSES

WEHDIG

PIPELOW

Scene 1

The town square with shops on one side; in back the base of the church tower is visible, fronted by a wide arching portal.
Boll and his wife are crossing the square.

BOLL (*stopping*): There is still this light fog — actually not at all unpleasant, eh, Martha?

MRS. BOLL: Except that it's chilly. When we left Krönkhagen it did seem to me the least little bit too brisk.

BOLL: That's so, Martha. Anyway, look at this hazy perspective, it appeals to me — more can hide behind it than one thinks; it can all turn out differently than planned. When one comes right down to it, what ultimately is the lasting good of an easygoing life, fully insured against broken bones — what do you think, Martha?

MRS. BOLL: I don't know and nobody else knows what good purpose is served if things turn out differently than one thinks. But that's why I don't provoke it, and that's why I don't lose sight of my self-respect — no, on that score I understand the good Lord far too well to believe he had something different in mind for me than I can grasp — oh no, never!

BOLL: Well, here's the store: Beerneck & Co. Should I take another chance on being snubbed by the salesgirl? She has the taste, you make the decision — what am I doing here?

MRS. BOLL: You know perfectly well, Kurt, that we have to pick something suitable for Aunt Emma's birthday.

BOLL: Quite right, Martha. So it falls out, a fall that may cost one's neck, and with my tendency to high blood pressure and dizziness — you do see that, Martha, I know you do, no? May I at least get the door for you? (*He opens the door.*)

MRS. BOLL: Let me see, Kurt . . . oh, of course, we have a dinner engagement with the Pompmasters, and Bertha and Otto are always so delightfully punctual — obligates us to the same — oh, don't act like that, Kurt! (*She disappears inside.*)

BOLL (*hesitating, to himself*): It's in the air, the air takes it, the air returns it. (*Follows her.*)

Woodfresser and Greendale run into each other.

GREENDALE: Golly, if it isn't Uncle Woodfresser!

WOODFRESSER: Look — and if it isn't Greendale — just imagine, Greendale!

GREENDALE: Well — what about it now?

WOODFRESSER: What *can* be done, Greendale? Best leave it all alone. If your Grete ran off, Grete will return. Leave it alone! Yes, she did come to me crying, crying, crying . . .

GREENDALE: Then everything is all right. Let's go to your place, Uncle, so I can take her home. Have to get back to Parum. Imagine the racket the kids have made.

WOODFRESSER: *You* try to find her. As I was leaving she just sat down and stopped crying and said: "Uncle, please go. I want to leave too, Uncle," she said. Why is she upset this time? Is she having ideas again? Ideas, Greendale, are matters you know nothing about, nothing at all. Is all this commotion about flesh *again*?

GREENDALE: Exactly — nothing but flesh blocking her. Away with flesh, she keeps telling the kids. Bacon and ham and sausages, she says, they want to make bacon and sausages of you. Are you entrails, or what? And then she covers her ears, asking Can't you hear what they say? — meaning the kids — and when I ask her what it is, she tells me to shut up and let them wail, let them cry, let them have their way. That, in short, is how things stand at home, you see.

WOODFRESSER: Indeed I do see.

GREENDALE: And then she says Beasts that need fattening, they're the ones who should gorge; it's a glorious life for pigs, but are children pigs? Away with flesh, she keeps saying; the minister's right, for he

THE BLUE BOLL

says it too. She had just come from church. — So she wanted to leave you, Uncle Woodfresser? Then why didn't you lock her in?

WOODFRESSER (*nervously*): Here comes the mayor, straight toward us. Go, Greendale: I have to tell him something. Mr. Mayor!

Greendale waits. Mayor comes hurrying round the corner, returns the greeting, and continues.

WOODFRESSER (*unperturbed, blocking his path*): Something is not right!

MAYOR: Calm yourself, Mr. . . . Mr. . . . aren't you master-shoemaker Woodfresser? I have to be at the council meeting, Mr. Woodfresser.

WOODFRESSER: . . . definitely not right, Mr. Mayor.

MAYOR: Come, we're going in the same direction. You obviously want the police, I'm going to the town hall. Did you notice him too — just now? Wasn't that landowner Boll with his wife, entering that store together? It's important that I have a word or two with him.

WOODFRESSER: Boll is doing some shopping, he has the money, and he's going to take his time. Here they call him the Blue Boll.

MAYOR: I know, but . . .

WOODFRESSER: But if anyone loves his life the way he does, well, he has to give it the best of care as long as he's got it. Good deeds pay interest, and if he continues to do as well by himself as he has up to now, there's going to be a slam-bang of an interest, Mr. Mayor, that is to say, a bang-up shooting interest!

MAYOR: I haven't time to wait till he's finished, after all — good-by, Mr. Woodfresser.

WOODFRESSER (*severely*): If Mr. Mayor has not enough time to wait for landowner Boll, then an ordinary citizen of this town has even less claim upon the left *or* the right ear of the mayor's time.

MAYOR: I see. You want to make a report, Mr. Woodfresser. Please do — what is it?

Greendale is about to say something.

WOODFRESSER: Quiet, Greendale. How can your wife's running away interest the mayor? (*To Mayor:*) He's actually my brother-in-law and a swineherd in Parum, nothing more. — Mr. Mayor, three or four days ago a man comes into my workshop — I live in Grünwinkel.

MAYOR (*resigned*): Indeed. Continue.

WOODFRESSER: . . . he comes upstairs — I have my workroom above a pigsty — comes up, how should I say, skipping or bouncing or dancing. No matter. He places an order for footwear for his right foot, a club-foot, Mr. Mayor, a genuine clubfoot — if not a horse-foot — gives the order, leaves the foot and leg behind, puts on his hat and skips or bounces or dances down the stairs, my workshop being above a pigsty in Grünwinkel. Down and gone!

MAYOR: I hereby direct you to deposit said leg forthwith in the police chief's office.

WOODFRESSER: The leg? No, Mr. Mayor; that's what it's all about, that's why I'm running through town and find something is not right, because that leg has disappeared from my workshop like a living dancer's, bouncy and shamelessly happy, attached to a genuine Satan's hind-quarter. So now this leg is galloping somewhere, and that, Mr. Mayor — no, Mr. Mayor, a search, a hunt must be organized, or else things are not as they should be.

Boll comes out of the shop and offers a greeting.

BOLL: Have you a moment, Mr. Mayor? Oh — I see you're busy.

MAYOR: In a second — right away, Mr. Boll. (*To Woodfresser:*) I shall certainly have this report investigated, Mr. Woodfresser. Depend on it, rest assured.

GREENDALE: Let's go, Uncle, the mayor has had enough of our family affairs. (*Both off.*)

MAYOR: Well, Mr. Boll, how is Mrs. Boll — and yourself?

BOLL: Oh, so far, you see . . . thank you, Mr. Mayor, but . . .

MAYOR: But?

BOLL: What incredible goings-on, Mr. Mayor! I solemnly and openly de-clare that I am chewed hollow, my insides scraped sore, only because matters stand thus and not otherwise. Mr. Mayor, it is shocking.

MAYOR: I am truly sorry, Mr. Boll, that matters stand thus and not other-wise, especially since I or another member of the municipal adminis-tration seems to be responsible.

BOLL: Certainly, Mr. Mayor. Someone must be blamed — therefore, you! What hair-raising nonsense!

MAYOR: I am profoundly indebted to you for your candor. But what is the precise cause, if I may ask?

BOLL (*his face swelling and turning blue*): A confounded, inexcusable, foolishly entangled cause is the precise cause. Is "foolishly entangled" excusable, eh? Is it possible to defend a foolish, a botched cause? A fine defense that would be!

MAYOR: I trust that no defender can be found for such an indisputably grave cause — at least not in our town.

BOLL: Bad, very bad.

MAYOR: Without doubt. But what specific part of this regrettable cause is owing to my guilt?

BOLL: What part? Today, you see, I deal only in wholes. A part here, a part there — let's not bother with parts! Eh? What of the heart of the matter, Mr. Mayor? Better alive than dead, that's what the cause is about. How disgustingly out of place a creature is in this existence, put here as though into a calf's life — his permission asked perhaps? His consent given? Calf's life — how? Don't we do well, oh, very well, and better and still better and always still better, and suddenly what do I see? Why, it won't get better and always still better, but worse and still worse and worse yet. What a shoddy indecency and — look, Reverend, how the trap with its greased joints and spiked jaws snaps at our flesh and bones — snap, snap! And we must hold still. One begins by living well, too well, and then . . . that's how it is.

MAYOR: I understand completely, Mr. Boll. With your prophetic eye you take one look and scan the far horizons.

BOLL: Why is landowner Boll held accountable for being a landowner? He has not been asked, not — been — asked, whether he wanted to be land-owner Boll. An impudence, sure enough, making landowner Boll into landowner Boll — for what does he have of it, Reverend? He has himself as master, nothing more, and how can a servant serving himself be satisfied with such a master?

MAYOR: Yes, yes.

BOLL (laughing): He'd better watch out, Doctor! Isn't it true you said that Boll drinks, Boll gambles, Boll sits untiringly upon, and reigns grandly from, the majesty of his behind, that Boll makes friends with none other than his enemy — twisted life?

MAYOR: Just as Boll rode his strength to a limp and now must make do with his weakness . . .

BOLL: Quite so. Boll has shot all the stags and now pops his gun at a denuded forest . . . As a matter of fact, Boll has collared Boll — ahead of him is only the leanness of his great expectations, ahead of him is everything except what is good and welcome and kind — only devil's brew. Let him deal with it as best he can. (*He offers cigars:*) Brand Coffin-nail.

MAYOR (*refusing*): You too, Mr. Boll, should restrain from heavy smoking.

BOLL: How "should"? Isn't it "Boll must"?

MAYOR: Mr. Boll, although it is you who have borne the chief burden of our conversation, it is I who am out of breath. My concern for you . . .

BOLL: Boll is the one who is killing Boll — can you prevent that?

MAYOR: Perhaps he should prevent it himself? Dear landowner Boll, an overflow of frank cordiality enables me to tell you that, in truth, Boll apparently is killing Boll. But why, good sir, is one of the two a harmful Boll? Couldn't he be one who slyly devises for Boll in years to come the realization of every pleasant potentiality, like a good and honest lawyer protecting his client with seasoned care? Couldn't Boll be precisely the best help to Boll?

BOLL: There's my wife. Let's leave Boll to his own devices, let him manage, as I believe I have already said, for himself.

MAYOR: The councilors are waiting. The meeting is set for eleven on the dot. Mr. Boll, I wish you a good day. (*Goes off.*)

Mrs. Boll comes out of the shop.

MRS. BOLL: Hardly half an hour until we . . . Kurt, are you listening?

Boll looks at his watch, nods.

MRS. BOLL: And right at the beginning the endless rush. It seems to me it couldn't have been any longer, or was it?

BOLL: I'm going to stop a little at Grotappel's, for an hour or two. Will you join me?

MRS. BOLL: I don't know what to make of you, Kurt!

BOLL: Oh well, I have to drink myself into courage. This affair with cousin Pompmaster will be long — therefore, drink into courage! You know, it's lucky that I'm at least brave enough for that. Someone who has lived it up for so many years should be allowed to call it a day and get drunk on extreme apathy.

MRS. BOLL (*alarmed*) : But how can I do my shopping with peace of mind if I have to keep wondering . . . what did you actually mean last night when you said — it came like an explosion: each one is nearest to himself, especially on an estate where neighbors are hours away — or something like that? Then you said: myself, I wouldn't want to be such a one. Now tell me if that wouldn't upset a person! You begin by obviously speaking about yourself, then you say you wouldn't want to be in *his* skin. What does it all mean?

BOLL: No, I wouldn't want to at all, under no circumstances.

MRS. BOLL: I am growing quite dizzy — what kind of an answer is that again! I would honestly like to know why you keep thinking up new means of torturing me.

BOLL: Could hardly happen better than it does.

MRS. BOLL: Happen? What happens?

BOLL: Look, Martha, how the tower rises and rises and then again doesn't rise. The fog lends it such a hazy outline that it seems the tower had his little joke with the spire, pushing it out of sight. I feel well, like that tower, because I am quite certain *it* feels well.

MRS. BOLL: Kurt, I'm so easily frightened. Didn't you mention that silly dizziness? Is your blood pressure building up a little?

BOLL: Why should it! Why should I waste my time with a thing like that!

MRS. BOLL: Oh God — again what an answer! It could give a person strange ideas.

Watchmaker Virgin passes by. He unlocks the church door, enters, and leaves the door ajar. Both glance in his direction casually.

BOLL: The strangest idea is probably this, that in some cases it is impossible to be sure whether the idea is strange or common. For instance!

MRS. BOLL: Stop it, Kurt. I have still so much shopping left to do. All right, Kurt . . . what did I do with my list? Couldn't you help me look? Ah yes, here it is; well, thank God! All right, no later than four o'clock for dinner at the Golden Ball. (*She gives the word dinner a hysterical note.*) The Pompmasters are certain to be there by three. Remember that. Now I really have to . . . (*Goes off.*)

BOLL: Remember? Yes, but in a strange way. (*Looks up at the sky.*) It's in the air, the air takes it, the air returns it. (*Laughs.*) Not for a long time have I felt this well. Dizziness? Seems to me someone mentioned dizziness — did anyone?

Grete Greendale appears, dressed in her Sunday best, with a colorful kerchief over her head. As she passes Boll she looks boldly into his face. Boll reaches into his breast pocket, takes out a cigar case, removes a long, fat cigar, and lights it while his eyes follow Grete.

BOLL (*looking behind him*): That way leads to the doctor . . . therefore, about face!

He turns around and prepares to follow Grete who has hurried back and quickly passes him. Greendale, following her, lays his hand on her shoulder.

GREENDALE: Been taking quite a little time, Grete, out on your walk.

Grete attempts to continue, whereupon he puts his other hand on her and makes her turn around.

GREENDALE: To Parum, Grete. Perhaps you've forgotten we're going to Parum. And the way to Parum is there, Grete — straight ahead.

Boll pushes him aside. Greendale turns around. They stare at one another. Grete slips into the store.

GREENDALE: Sir — or whoever you are!

BOLL (*brandishing his cigar*): Hands off, you know, hands off the lady — that's all.

GREENDALE: She happens to be my very own wife!

BOLL: All the more, all the more, hands off, just *because* she is your own wife.

Greendale looks around, leaves Boll, and runs around the nearest corner.

Grete emerges, looking at him questioningly.

BOLL (*pointing with his cigar*): Yes, they're looking for you.

GRETE: Is there any place to hide?

BOLL (*indicating the church door*): The tower is open — just push against the door.

Grete slips through the portal.

GREENDALE (*returning*): Where is she, where could she have gone?

Boll points in the opposite direction. Greendale runs off.

BOLL (*throwing away the cigar*): One can't be responsible for everything. If the cigar wants to be burned all the way, it has to find another smoker. Not to the doctor — on the basis of principle; not to Grotappel's, on the basis of prudence — but to the tower, and to the tower once more! (*Goes off into the tower.*)

Scene 2

A narrow room half-way up the tower. The rear view is into the shadows of the church roof. To the left is the narrow spiral staircase from below; in the right wall are stairs leading higher. There is a window with a Gothic arch. A slow ticking of the clockwork is heard throughout the room and walls. Grete sits cowering at the bottom of the stairs leading to the roof. Boll, breathing heavily, appears from below.

GRETE: Are you somebody?

BOLL: No one — never was anyone — nobody!

GRETE: If you are somebody, have you anything to do with this place?

BOLL (*pointing to the window*): He's down below snooping into every corner. But to look up — no, that doesn't occur to your husband. Have you any children?

Grete cowers even more into herself. Silence.

GRETE (*mumbling*): Everything smothers in flesh — you too: in flesh.

BOLL: Let us ignore flesh, forget flesh! Look, Madam, even I am something apart from my flesh, something elevated, towerlike, substantially something else.

GRETE: Do you have any business here? Do you belong here?

BOLL: I stay where I feel well — I feel well here, so here I stay.

GRETE: Ought I to go back down?

BOLL: As long as you feel well, you stay too.

GRETE: Anyhow, where would I go?

BOLL: If you have children, why not go to them? Flesh to flesh — tower to tower. I'm going to stay.

Grete gets up.

BOLL: Your husband is still down there. He will beat you.

GRETE: That he has never done and never will. I'm not afraid of him. But he's going to take me back to the children.

171

BOLL: If that hurts, who is hurt by it?

GRETE: The poor souls . . .

BOLL: Yes — say it!

GRETE: The poor souls whimper and cry, begging me to let them go — they keep begging and pleading, they want to be let out, they wail that I have brought them misery — misery!

BOLL: They whimper, the poor souls?

GRETE: They keep calling, they cry, and just when all is asleep, then in the darkness I hear them the loudest.

BOLL: Have they any reason to be crying?

GRETE (*in a monotone*): The poor souls cry while the growing flesh chokes their voices, but still they torment me to deliver them from flesh.

BOLL: How many are there?

GRETE: Three souls have I borne into cursed flesh.

BOLL: I am another such poor soul.

GRETE: I suppose. But why do you say that about the tower?

BOLL: The moment I lie I feel better. It's like this: I punish my flesh with lies — I slice myself with lies into a thousand shreds and then throw these shreds before dogs. And then, just as the dogs fall on them — a jolt, a jog, and all is back in one piece. It's in the air, the air takes it, the air returns it. Am I the same, or am I no longer, or, for that matter, did I ever exist? My blood is red, but in my face it's blue. By the way, who *are* you?

GRETE: In my village they call me the witch — I don't know why. Something like this keeps running through my mind: if there's to be dying, it cannot be worse than living.

BOLL: And I have always lived well, but I shall have to die badly, according to a damned strict system. I wish I began to find gradually a little pleasure in dying. But being what I am I cannot help being afraid — I await my death without enthusiasm.

GRETE: He who exists no longer in flesh is in bliss. And I must deliver my children from flesh.

Breathing heavily, Boll looks at her. He turns to the window and glances outside. Then he approaches hesitantly and uncertainly, reaches into his breast pocket, and pulls out the cigar case. But he pushes it back instantly. With his arms extended, he appears to fall toward Grete. She presses her hands against his chest and holds him back.

BOLL: Don't choke me — now it's better. Something crushed me to the floor, whatever it was. I had to hold on to you for support. (*He withdraws and leans against the wall.*)

GRETE: Shouldn't I get help?

Boll waves a no and shuts his eyes.

GRETE: You ought to be in bed.

BOLL (*suddenly opening his eyes wide*): I am standing! What else are these legs good for! I don't want to lie down, but hold me tight for a moment. (*Grete supports him.*) It helps, your touching me; I thought it would. That's why I stretched out my hands for you when blackness fell before my eyes. (*In control again:*) Can't let go of this dear flesh. (*Thoughtfully:*) What *did* happen? Bumped my nose into a lamp-post at the corner, struck it and lost my sense of direction for a second — got muddled, eh? Well, it turned out all right, and now I'm on a familiar street again.

Watchmaker Virgin descends from the upper stair.

VIRGIN: Good Lord, do my eyes deceive me — Mr. Boll?

Grete releases Boll but remains standing near him.

BOLL: Not as far as I know. (*To Grete:*) There's an excited gentleman for you!

VIRGIN: My name is Virgin — Virgin, the watchmaker.

BOLL: A remarkably beautiful name.

VIRGIN: As beautiful as, if not more beautiful than, yours, Mr. Boll.

BOLL: Boll? You'll have to ask elsewhere if a person by that name is known here.

VIRGIN: If you prefer — you should know. Do forgive my mistaking you for that man. It's not exactly flattering.

BOLL: And what sort of man is he, this Mr. Boll, if I may ask?

VIRGIN: I believe he considers himself an instance of the unsurpassable in every sense, that Mr. Boll.

BOLL: An enviable person, no doubt.

VIRGIN: This confounded machinery of a tower clock went on the blink. So I am up here doing with my time what Boll — Mr. Boll — does with his . . .

BOLL: The same Mr. Boll?

VIRGIN: The very same. For how can a man appear more honorable than by giving himself up to dissipation? Am I speaking too softly? I am a trifle asthenic, and going up and down these stairs — you follow me?

BOLL: Don't worry.

VIRGIN: Well, what I was going to say . . .

BOLL: More about Boll, I hope!

VIRGIN: Naturally, but you may have heard this elsewhere, this business with Baron Ravenclaw and Boll?

BOLL: Ravenclaw — Ravenclaw?

VIRGIN: Baron *and* Viscount Ravenclaw, the patron, you see, of our new evangelical assembly — I am also a member, therefore . . .

BOLL: I understand.

VIRGIN: Now the Baron had made a number of official speeches, unfortunately not without setting in motion all sorts of illwill.

BOLL: I would have thought so. They discussed him more than the entire baronial speechifying deserved.

VIRGIN (*startled*): Hm — yes, if you like. Boll first and foremost; Boll boasted that he had smoked out the evangelical nest and thereby — permit me — deeply hurt this good old noble gentleman. And what do you think happened next?

BOLL: Couldn't be more anxious.

VIRGIN (*gesticulating*): Listen. During last year's horseshow, after the first race, Boll comes marching from his side straight across the field toward the grandstand, which only Boll would have the nerve to do. Just like that! Bloated with self-esteem, resplendent with self-adulation, he makes his solo triumphal march. The sun is reflected in his gleaming face, and his legs — why his every step shakes the foundations of the world. Magnificent! As fate will have it, Baron Ravenclaw feels impelled to take the same direction and make his way straight up against him.

BOLL: Presumably he had some business on the other side?

VIRGIN: Certainly. They march toward each other, and the grandstand holds its breath. With his eyesight weak as it is, the Baron finds himself a few steps from Boll before he becomes aware of him. He turns

174

— turns his back on Boll and returns to his former place. That's how it was.

BOLL: So far I discover nothing upsetting, Mr. Virgin.

VIRGIN: But Boll — my dear sir! What was Boll left to do? In order to complete his journey, was he to follow the Baron, though publicly cut, at three paces, politely and obediently — obediently, mind you! — was he, his bearing and walk deferential, to accompany the Baron so? He did just that, but . . .

BOLL: But?

VIRGIN: But the manner, sir, the manner! The sun, which until then had sparkled on his face, chilled. The splendor of his airs disintegrated. His face, until then the most glowing flower of the occasion, discolored, dipped in shadow, ink, and shame. He put up with it, sir. What do you say to that?

BOLL: Say? I wish I could have watched it from the grandstand myself.

VIRGIN: You'd have beheld a once-in-a-blue-moon miracle.

BOLL: I am not so surprised as you are that Boll put up with it — perhaps he isn't so bloated with self-esteem as you assume. He put up with it! I take it the old gentleman gave his evangelical assembly some right excellent tips?

VIRGIN: Tips, my dear sir? He dwelt on man's becoming, not being. That was his subject. You call that tips? Our being, he said, is nothing but a fountainhead, and our life a stream of becoming, and there's no goal except renewed becoming. That's what he said: eternal becoming! The now is but a threadbare tomorrow, and tomorrow is canceled by the day following. Something of this sort has — I suppose, has never remotely reached your ears?

BOLL: Me? I thought we were talking about Boll.

VIRGIN: Law, constraint, ineluctability — well, I really must go, Mr. Boll.

BOLL: My greetings to Mr. Boll, if you happen to run into him, and tell him to look me up. Then I can explain to him this matter of tomorrow and the day after. Don't slip on your way down.

VIRGIN (*hesitating*): How long, if I may ask, do you intend to view the tower? I am only asking.

BOLL: You may leave me the key. It will be returned to you promptly.

VIRGIN (*giving him the key*): Very well, Mr. Boll. (*To Grete:*) What are *you* doing here, by the way?

Grete stares embarrassed into one corner.

BOLL: That will do, Mr. Virgin.

VIRGIN: Of course, Mr. Boll, if you will answer for her . . .

BOLL: Certainly. I shall answer for her and assume every responsibility.

VIRGIN: It's all right with me. (*He climbs down.*)

BOLL: He has learned his catechism very nicely — how did it go? Eternal becoming? Very pretty. It reminds me how with a simple instrument, a mouthorgan for instance, one can make quite tolerable music. — Yes, here we stand, not even a place to sit. Let's take a look. (*He peers through the window.*) God, this Sternberg, what a pile of rubbish, what a speck! There to the right is the way to Grotappel's; just below, so near one could spit on it, the roof of the Golden Ball — ah, and there: Monsieur Virgin! Look, child, something blackish pushing itself across the square, can't tell from here about that asthenic chest, but the bent back is recognizable . . .

Grete suddenly puts her arms around his neck.

BOLL: Hey, what's that, what are you doing?

GRETE: You are Mr. Boll, aren't you?

BOLL: Did you doubt it?

GRETE: I want to beg Mr. Boll for a favor.

BOLL: Beg? First-rate, child, beg!

GRETE: Mr. Boll can do it, he can, he must.

BOLL: Yes, what I can do, I do. What is it?

GRETE (*still holding him tight, whispering*): What I need is . . . people call it poison.

BOLL: Poison? Not for the children?

Grete nods and in a choked voice mumbles something incomprehensible.

BOLL (*trying to free himself*): That — that your children may die, I should . . .

GRETE: You must! (*She pushes herself close against him.*)

BOLL: Have you thought it through?

GRETE: You must!

BOLL: Oho — Boll must?

176

GRETE: Yes, you must do it, so it will go without whimpering, without suffering — and — (*she pushes herself still closer*) — it must be finished before I leave the house.

BOLL: I understand, a little white powder or something to take with a spoon.

GRETE: Quickly — it must work quickly.

BOLL (*trying to disengage himself*): I will consider it, child. Be satisfied with my promise to think about it.

GRETE (*holding him tight*): You *must* promise, and you *must* do it. No need to think.

BOLL: How can I promise if I don't even know whom to turn to — and, how shall I put it, under what pretense ask for it?

GRETE: Mr. Boll has promised and agreed to do it.

BOLL: Now tell me just this: having done it, what will you do after you're out the door and the deed behind you?

GRETE (*releases him and looks at him surprised and incredulous*): I — I — I? (*Stammering:*) When it's all done?

BOLL: Well, you know, you must be aware that you'll be prosecuted.

GRETE: When it's all done! (*She throws her arms around his neck, sobbing:*) I will do nothing but offer thanks and more thanks.

BOLL: To that we haven't come yet.

GRETE: No, it's as good as done: accomplished! You can get hold of it by tonight.

BOLL: Listen, child — incidentally, what is your first name?

GRETE: I am Grete.

BOLL: All right, Grete, my dear witch, have you thought what's going to happen to me afterwards? After all, I'll have taken part in it.

GRETE (*releases him and walks slowly to the stairs*): You permitted the Baron to humiliate you. Go on, walk about in dishonor. You're worthless! Boll must, you keep saying, but you only say it.

BOLL (*restraining her*): And what if I do bring you what you ask?

GRETE: So the deed may be done?

BOLL: Easily, quickly, and surely — a deed accomplished.

GRETE (*looks at him half-smilingly and places her hand in his*): Bring it tonight.

BOLL: If I do, will you like me for it?

177

GRETE: Yes, if you do it, if you do it by tonight — yes, then.

BOLL: Tonight . . .

GRETE (*shaking*): Where?

BOLL: After nightfall in Church Street.

GRETE: After nightfall, without fail after nightfall in Church Street.

BOLL: We'll find each other.

GRETE: You'll have it.

BOLL: I hope to have it by then.

GRETE: By then he shall have it!

Scene 3

Street. Woodfresser with several townspeople.

WOODFRESSER: . . . believe it or not: down the stairs — one, two, three — skips, bounces, dances down, and a genuine Satan's hindquarter stuck to it — believe it or not!

A TOWNSMAN: Did you actually see this, I mean with a clear head?

WOODFRESSER: Am I running up and down streets for physical exercise, or do I have to make my living by my occupation, eh? Am I known as trustworthy or am I not? Am I not on my feet all blessed morning long in strictly professional work?

Greendale turns the corner.

WOODFRESSER: Is it possible — Greendale? Still in Sternberg? Did you happen to come across my leg running about?

GREENDALE: Have you seen Grete?

WOODFRESSER: Oh yes — Grete. What should she want here? She returned to Parum long ago.

GREENDALE: And your leg, Uncle, has long ago gone back to your workshop and is now squatting on its hindquarter. Do you think it will allow itself to be chased all morning by the dogs of Sternberg?

They move to the side and stand about.

Mrs. Boll arrives, followed by Suckleworm, the coachman, who is loaded down with packages.

MRS. BOLL: He didn't go to see the doctor either. Grotappel knows nothing. Do run over to Ohls, please, Suckleworm, yes? And say that the Pompmasters have arrived long ago and would like to eat as soon as possible, yes? Go to the left by Penitents' Lane, you understand, yes? *Suckleworm leaves. Boll arrives from the opposite direction.*

BOLL: There you are, Martha! Are you waiting for anyone?

MRS. BOLL: Kurt, I've asked for you everywhere! You weren't anywhere. Where am I supposed to look for you if you aren't anywhere?

BOLL: If I am not anywhere, Martha, I don't exist. I lost my way, that's all.

Mayor comes.

MAYOR: Ah, Mr. Boll, how fortunate to meet again! Good day, dear Madam! Could you spare us a moment's patience? We men of affairs, you know . . . and so forth!

MRS. BOLL: As long as you won't keep him from dinner, Mr. Mayor, him and me and several more — well and good. I lend him to you, but please do remember we must eat.

MAYOR: Oh, it's something quite trivial, something that just came to me. Now then, Mr. Boll, I ought not to have forgotten it this morning: the agreement regarding the bull should be settled as soon as possible. (*In the meantime Greendale approaches slowly, eying Boll.*) If you were to give the representative of the pastures committee or Town Councilor Walnut a written . . . better yet, if you saw each other personally.

GREENDALE (*to Boll*): Aren't you the gentleman, sir . . .

BOLL: Quite so, Mr. Mayor. I would only ask you — may I accompany you to the corner? (*They go, followed by Greendale.*) I might even today find an opportunity to visit Councilor Walnut in his office. (*To Greendale:*) All right, wait your turn — we're talking business. Now then, Mr. Mayor!

MAYOR: That would be excellent, would please me enormously . . . (*To Greendale:*) My good man, less impatience!

GREENDALE: Pooh . . . I have altogether something else in mind. Impatience can wait.

179

MAYOR: In any case, let me assure you you will never succeed with that tone of voice. (*To Boll:*) I'll return with you in order to take my leave of your wife, Mr. Boll.

Greendale also turns back and walks at the Mayor's side.

MAYOR (*stopping*): Well, I must say — I find this impudent!

GREENDALE (*also stopping*): I don't mind being told off. So, I am supposed to wait — I'll do that right away, I sincerely and religiously promise to do that.

MAYOR (*to Boll*): Do you know anything at all about this, Mr. Boll? (*To Greendale:*) What do you actually want of us?

GREENDALE: Good; you've concluded your business, and I can begin mine. (*To Boll:*) I think I'd like to ask that gentleman something. It makes sense to direct questions where there are likely to be answers.

BOLL: Questions? Answers? Who are you, for that matter?

GREENDALE: This is what I said to myself: only be polite to this gentleman, and you can twist him around your little finger. I merely want to say I don't want to hold him up, and if he doesn't mind my talking straight . . .

BOLL (*to Mayor*): This character has been loitering about the streets for quite some time — I'll settle this little matter later privately. Martha, the mayor wishes to bid you adieu.

Mrs. Boll steps closer, but Greendale places himself in between.

GREENDALE: This business with my wife comes first, as the gentleman knows only too well.

Boll pushes him aside. Greendale clutches the Mayor's arm.

MAYOR: A physical molestation — let go!

GREENDALE (*letting go*): It doesn't matter. Ooops, did I get you dirty? (*Slaps him on the shoulder.*) You see, my hand being so dirty, if I physically dirty anyone, I promptly clean him up physically too, which is only as it should be. That other gentleman there isn't that fussy.

MRS. BOLL: For heaven's sake, Kurt, let's go. (*To Mayor:*) I fear he may kill him on the spot.

GREENDALE: Relax, lady. If you're afraid he's going to kill me, I can soon talk you out of that; he won't do anything less than tell me where he's keeping my wife. That's all.

MRS. BOLL: You dare say such a thing in broad daylight at noon in public?

GREENDALE: He fixed it up with my wife in public too, except that it was morning. Furthermore, I happen to recollect most distinctly it was *my* wife and no one else's wife.

BOLL: . . . anyway, quite some time since! (*To Mrs. Boll:*) He was guilty of improper behavior, you know, and I took him to task.

GREENDALE: Yes, that much is true. That's how it began, but then sir, where did you and my wife go?

BOLL: Someone has put something over on you.

MRS. BOLL: Kurt!

BOLL: Not worth your attention — leave it, not worth it. But listen, what *is* worth telling is what came to me as I turned the corner earlier. When once the old biddies stand on the tower blowing their trumpets at us furiously . . .

MRS. BOLL: God, what you come up with! What old biddies?

BOLL: Well, I mean angels — those who on the last day will scare all the deaf corpses out of their graves. What an almighty howling and shrieking in the market place then, I thought. God in heaven! Then it won't be let's eat, let's eat — but rather: putrefaction won't get you out of it — come, corpses! Fortunate is he who can then say: why me — I am another? Take care, children, watch out how you manage, strive to become such that they cannot question you. (*To Mrs. Boll:*) Imagine, we won't be able to drive up in our carriage, and all your finery will serve you no longer. You may not even have a shift to cover you!

GREENDALE: But as far as the worthy lady is concerned, no one doubts she will be presentable all right in God's sight without a shift.

BOLL: Enough! Some time is yet left us. And in the end perhaps a shift *will* be necessary.

MRS. BOLL: I keep asking myself how you can let that fellow get away with all this! How dare he take such liberty in our presence! Just tell me this: how do you *ever* expect to make up for it?

BOLL: Let's not worry about making up — where would there ever be an end to that! No, listen to me, people: I am one of those who are another — why question me? And you talk of making up?

MRS. BOLL (*to Mayor*): Don't you find this downright strange?

MAYOR: Mr. Boll! Mr. Boll!

181

BOLL: Mr. Boll? Then it's still Boll and not another. What a misfortune, and not a moment's peace before one. You see, Martha, whatever I do, Boll remains Boll. The more I disown Boll the more exposed do I stand before you, naked and exposed. I am even coming to suspect the shift. No, Martha, it is impossible, there's no hiding far and wide, not even under a shift. Boll always — always Boll.

GREENDALE: Dear lady, you realize that he now admits he took liberties. All of us have to face up to that, depend on it. And therefore one can depend on Boll. There's dependability with your gracious presence *and* without. (*Laughs.*)

BOLL: I want you to know that both my wife and I can do without your compliments. There must be respect! So shut up!

GREENDALE: In a jiffy — a respect of that sort, you see, will also find time to scratch its own bottom. It is quite possible that your wife wears a clean shift, but my wife Grete certainly does . . .

MRS. BOLL: Help, Mr. Mayor — after all, he is my husband!

MAYOR: Only too willing, Madam, but I am reluctant to presume upon Mr. Boll's duty.

BOLL: Let me handle it. (*To Greendale:*) What's on your mind, man? Respect or no — I could almost find a certain respect for your effrontery. Where did you ever get that? Don't you find too, Martha, that something like respect grows on you?

MRS. BOLL: My only answer to that can be no answer. If I endure shame for your sake also, I do it silently, urging my pride to come to my assistance. Because I am proud enough for the two of us, don't you see, I can do it and feel shame privately.

BOLL: But Martha, what grousing motives becloud your skies. (*To Mayor:*) Am I already so much another that I fail to recognize my wife? Proud! Silent!

MAYOR: Nevertheless, and however that may be, your wife's motives for pride and for a silent demeanor . . .

BOLL: But that man is really quite honest, Mr. Mayor; in short, he's right. Obviously my wife can't help the fact that he's right. No, Martha, leave your lip alone, don't do that — you offered pride and silence, and there's nothing better. So you were right again. You always are.

MAYOR: With that, I trust, this unedifying interlude has come to an end. I hereby return to you, Madam, your devoted and most proper husband. (*To Boll:*) In any case, am I correct in assuming it concerns a purely private matter?

BOLL: It does, Mr. Mayor.

MAYOR: And so — dear Madam!

BOLL (*to Greendale*): Still here? I thought we were done. You were perfectly right, and I am willing to put that in writing. Now be off, with your rights in your pocket.

GREENDALE: You've been so generous with me I wouldn't want to depart ungrateful, sir. Therefore try to be nice and add the little that remains.

BOLL: If I put my mind to it — your wife's name is Grete, isn't it?

GREENDALE: An unalterable fact. Grete is her name and Grete she's always been called. And Grete's been on several such binges before. But she snapped out of it every time. The doctor said it means nothing, he said. After each she's quite subdued, but later we have a good time — then Grete is the liveliest woman in the world.

BOLL: You know you're not the only one? God, what do you expect! We've all got one type of bit or another in our jaws, we can champ at the bit — we get that free of charge. But the bit stays, regardless.

GREENDALE: Yes, Mr. Boll, it's pleasant to swap stories with you. Maybe that's all true about the bit. And if the whole street here wants to stand on its head, I will take the bit out of my mouth and put it between your teeth. Then you can champ at it — and you get that free of charge. That's the responsibility to Grete: when you bite into it you're stuck with it.

BOLL: Responsibility? That doesn't suit me at all right now — does it have to be?

GREENDALE: It does, sir. You would come to the same conclusion if you gave it a little more careful thought. All of these ladies and gentlemen are witnesses that I put the bit between your teeth. I have to congratulate you on the way you look with it.

MAYOR: Watch out, Mr. Boll. For God's sake and your wife's sake defer your consent. I . . . I know . . .

BOLL: I too, Mr. Mayor, I too know everything, but we are not of one mind. (*To Mrs. Boll:*) What I think you better do, Martha, is go ahead to the Golden Ball and order dinner. And put the wine list in Otto's hands and tell him to turn to the top of page 3. They list there half a dozen genuine French wines — let him pick the most unpronounceable. (*Looks at his watch.*) Yes, it's easy to waste a lot of time chatting with this man. I have to make only one more small purchase. (*Striking his stomach:*) Must be ready for all accidents, whether they occur after a meal or not. A few cents' worth of white powder or something for the spoon. (*To Mrs. Boll:*) I'll just skip into the pharmacist's. Mr. Mayor! (*Goes off.*)

Mayor and Mrs. Boll look at each other.

WOODFRESSER (*stepping up to Greendale*): Didn't take you long to make yourself at home in the finest society, Greendale. Now watch *me* have a word with the mayor. (*To Mayor:*) It's not your fault that none of your measures have had any effect so far, but who will from now on effect the measures?

MAYOR: Good Lord, Mr. Woodfresser, nothing works that fast.

WOODFRESSER: It's not a question of fast, but this, on the other hand, is very slow, couldn't be slower.

GREENDALE (*drawing him away*): Don't you see, Uncle, Mr. Mayor can't get to take measures only because you detain him? (*Both off.*)

MAYOR: Truly, Mrs. Boll, you are a lady to admire! What astonishing self-control in the face of your husband's deplorable attacks, indeed, lapses of memory — self-forgetfulness.

MRS. BOLL: You hit upon the right word: lapses of memory. You see he actually forgets who he is.

MAYOR: One might also say, lostness.

MRS. BOLL: As though he had lost himself. Often I just don't know any more — so entirely beyond showing all respect and consideration. Listen to this. Once he said to me: child, he said, you are a wonderful woman, let that stand like an ultimate sentence forever, let that be enough and be satisfied: a wonderful woman. But if you admit that, I said . . . No *but*, he shouted at me, no but's — a wonderful woman is much, very much — let no one dare question it. There!

MAYOR: Hm . . . well, Mrs. Boll . . .

MRS. BOLL: What was it you were going to say?

MAYOR: You remember we mentioned his having lost himself. Ought we not to move cautiously toward the question of considering whether the lost — so to say, the former — Mr. Boll was not the false one, whereas the present, the new, or new-found Boll is the real Boll? I mean it may at least be worth asking the question.

MRS. BOLL: Are you serious? That would be ghastly, don't you think?

MAYOR: The conversation I had with your husband this morning gave me to . . .

MRS. BOLL (*imploring*): No, Mr. Mayor, I cannot appreciate such a disclosure. What an idea! And what is to become of me if Boll, my good old Kurt, is no longer the old one.

MAYOR: All kinds of things come to pass unnoticed in the dark of a person's inner life.

MRS. BOLL: That — no, no, that is unnatural. If that were to happen it would be a case of the extreme, a cause for mourning. In that case I would rather have him dead and buried, because then I would always be sure who it was that lay there and who he had been, and then I would know how to picture him for ever and ever. But like this — oh, God!

MAYOR: Mrs. Boll, I deeply repent my having indicated to you such a distinctly remote possibility — no, no, without doubt your cherished husband has fundamentally the very same old trustworthy and familiar nature.

MRS. BOLL: You really do think so, Mr. Mayor, don't you? True, Kurt is, he is — — you have to admit that lately now and then — I don't mean, therefore, that he is entirely another, nor that he isn't, as you put it yourself, fundamentally the good old Kurt, his real self, that which he always was and always will be. (*Weeping:*) Oh God, I worry almost too much over him. And what you said just now was said in almost the same words by the old dairy hand Kidneyskin in Krönkhagen. The cook told me in confidence. — Now I must really hurry to dinner. We are most anxiously awaited, a very important appointment. Farewell, Mr. Mayor. I am simply rigid with hunger.

MAYOR: Madam!

Scene 4

A dark street. There are sounds of bowling behind shutters. From the house opposite comes plaintive singing. The outlines of the cathedral may be seen in the background across the roofs. Grete approaches from the rear, looks around, and dives into a dark niche in the wall. Boll appears in front, turns around, and stops. Grete disengages herself from the darkness of her hiding place and comes up behind him.

BOLL (*turning around quickly and passing his hand over her head*): Is it you?

Grete says nothing.

BOLL: At least your hand, Grete!

She holds out her hand.

BOLL: Yours is a good hand; it comes from you as though it had powers of healing. I feel better the moment I touch this warm trifle. Do you hear, witch? You can do me good.

GRETE: I don't feel a thing. Is it in your pocket? (*Her hand plunges into his coat pocket.*) Where is it?

BOLL: I couldn't get him alone, it's impossible.

GRETE: You brought nothing; why did you bother to come?

BOLL: Because you are helping me, Grete, helping me without knowing it yourself. If you wanted to . . .

GRETE: I want to, only if you help me.

BOLL: The words come more easily while I hold your hand — give it to me. I must explain.

She gives him her hand.

BOLL: Listen, dear, such a purchase is a joke. You say a few words, give him the money, there's nothing to it, it's done. But it takes cleverness to hit on the right words, and there wasn't a chance — I couldn't find a safe spot in which to speak quietly and confidentially to the pharmacist.

GRETE: But you said yourself, Boll must.

BOLL: And then they pursued me, my so-called relatives. Picture it: me with my frame in this little nest of a town, like an ox in an open field trying to creep into a mouse hole. I devised the most ingenious tricks to keep my person out of people's sight. All afternoon I denied myself my most regal habits. Please take that into account, Grete.

GRETE: Evasions, evasions — while I must and you must?

BOLL: You know, dear, I don't think this is a case of must for Boll. Nor, I believe, must you.

GRETE: Let me go.

BOLL: Not yet — I feel as I did in the tower; where I feel well, there I like to remain. And I feel well when I am with you.

GRETE: Disgusting how you feel well in the flesh! My husband and I know what hides in flesh, and there's far too much of that in you. Let me go.

BOLL (*releasing her*): Where to in such hurry? Walk slowly, Grete, and let us talk of better things.

GRETE: Did you think I ran away from my village in order to find flesh here? I'm determined to find what I want; away with flesh! (*Glances about.*) As it is, there are too many people about.

BOLL: People? What people?

GRETE (*pointing*): I saw them standing in front of the windows just then — there or not, it's people.

BOLL: Deep shadows only, Grete, more solid than the most solid people could make.

GRETE: Yet I did see them. I don't want to stay where there are so many people.

BOLL: Please, I *did* want to help you.

GRETE: I am going to go and I am going to keep going until I have found what I'm looking for. Some there will be who will do better than you did. It's only that I like your voice: it spoke of fulfillment.

BOLL: Does my voice not come from my flesh?

GRETE: Your voice comes from the world that's good, and you, after all, come from that same good world. But your flesh I abominate.

She walks up the street and disappears in the darkness. Boll, unnoticed, goes with her. A door opens on the left, throwing a strong beam of light that creates an illuminated area across the street. Elias half leans out the door, listening to the singing opposite.

ELIAS: Sounds like a coffee grinder today — that old woman Unk is at it. Her neck is a rusty rattrap crushing a sad hallelujah to pieces.

187

VOICE FROM WITHIN: Today I thought they'd manage without this nightly racket because they were auctioning off the Baron's pisspot.

ELIAS: It's time, I think. Let's get everything ready. Maybe we'll get a handout from the heavenly bank-loan outfit.

In the meantime Elias and his guests have been carrying a table and chairs into the street and placing them in line with the light so that the party is glaringly illuminated. Elias brings glasses.

FIRST GUEST: Or the bad penny come home!

SECOND GUEST: Can you tell me who the man was with the jawbone of an ass?

THIRD GUEST: A pointless question. We don't have to keep what produces deformities.

FIRST GUEST: Quiet! They're coming.

Across the street the door opens. Members of the evangelical assembly disperse into the darkness.

ELIAS: Number One has exercised restraint and for once praised someone besides himself. Number Two has trumpeted himself into a hernia and in the excitement bespattered his waistcoat. Number Three — ah, number Three! Has a forehead like no one else. You dip him with his nose into his own dung and he says, anointed am I, anointed! Number Four — you are only number Four, but you're helping number Five. Two nothings add up to little, and that at least is something. Number Six — rise, friends, to honor number Six! Long live Aunt Unk!

They rise.

ELIAS: Now Aunt Unk, come back a step! These people know something about flute melodies. This is the cozy Devil's Kitchen. Squat awhile! Have a seat, let the chair kiss your devout rump.

MRS. UNK (*as she passes*): You can in no way insult me, sir. Perhaps you know what it says: enter into thy closet and shut thy door?

ELIAS: That's been attended to for today. I use that special closet just once a day. (*Laughter.*)

Mrs. Unk departs hurriedly. Woodfresser appears with Gentleman.

WOODFRESSER: I hope you don't mind, sir, my not losing sight of you — but I couldn't afford to.

GENTLEMAN: It's easy to tell you want to get acquainted. Shall we sit down here with these people?

WOODFRESSER: If you really don't mind, with pleasure.

They sit down.

WOODFRESSER: I've been running around all day; my legs are sore. You don't walk very fast either, sir.

GENTLEMAN: This leg is somewhat stiff, can't quite keep up with the other.

WOODFRESSER: I see that, I saw that right away. Have you — are you — what kind of footwear have you got? I happen to be an expert. (*He looks under the table.*)

GENTLEMAN: Oh, this is well-made equipment I'm wearing. You hardly notice that one leg is shorter.

WOODFRESSER: Yes, that's it, sir, that's what I thought right away. Where did you get that leg?

GENTLEMAN (*laughs*): Why do you ask? Happened all quite in the course of things — a birth defect.

WOODFRESSER: Don't try to put something over on me! Three days ago this leg was entrusted to me personally for repair, and it somehow disappeared. When I accepted it, I took complete responsibility. I have summoned municipal authorities to recover the leg.

GENTLEMAN (*laughing*): Let's leave it at that. Please accept a glass of beer from me.

Elias brings glasses.

WOODFRESSER: Leave it — no, sir. I am personally responsible for that leg. Are you forcing me to call the police?

GENTLEMAN: I'll save you that trouble. If you suspect me of appearing on a stolen leg, I am prepared to escort you with it to the police station. Does that satisfy you? To your health!

WOODFRESSER: But I have to reserve the right to keep an eye on it. That leg has a devilish pace about it, attached to a Satan's hindquarter. Cheers!

GENTLEMAN: So far, so good. So that's what it's supposed to be — a Satan's hindquarter! (*He strikes his thigh.*) Apart from that — I mean all the rest that goes with it, like bones and joints, deserves highest respect. Moreover, please know that I am a philanthropist.

WOODFRESSER: I didn't mean to have implied anything less.

GENTLEMAN: This incidentally is helping an analogy onto its feet. Growing and becoming find themselves strange paths.

WOODFRESSER: What do you mean?

GENTLEMAN: There isn't a spot you could spit on where something doesn't hover waiting to be thrust into existence, waiting to leave its cocoon. Why, look what became of that leg today — am I not tolerable company considering I grew out of a Satan's hindquarter? Becoming — that's the watchword.

ELIAS: Perhaps the gentleman is looking for a house of prayer?

GENTLEMAN: Quite so. I have friends here, but I rather fear it is too late. Anyway I am in good company here — everywhere I am among friends, in a house of prayer as in a tavern. We and you, all of us, are on the same road of becoming. We are all running toward what is better, be it even on devil's legs.

ELIAS: All this lovely edification comes free with the beer.

GENTLEMAN: Certainly, free of charge. Beer must be paid for while we are rewarded with realization. Always forward, always something fresh, always more out in the open — that's how it is with us — and, as I said, all completely free of charge.

WOODFRESSER: My name is Woodfresser, sir.

GENTLEMAN: Is it?

WOODFRESSER: But doesn't this becoming have its limits, sir? If we keep growing on and on to such an immeasurable grandeur, we finally won't be able to recognize ourselves.

GENTLEMAN: Why is that deplorable? Do you want to be Woodfresser forever? Is it worth it? But it *is* worth the trouble to become so that you would have to be ashamed of having once been Woodfresser.

WOODFRESSER: Ashamed, sir?

GENTLEMAN: No, not you, and not like this. By the way, do you know a Mr. Virgin who lives hereabouts, and could you take me to his home? First, if you like, we can stop at the police station. I will tell you en route what I mean by this shame.

WOODFRESSER: But for heaven's sake walk slowly with that devil's leg of yours. Mr. Virgin lives close by to the right of the town square.
Woodfresser and Gentleman off.

FIRST GUEST: Elias, I am still thirsty.

ELIAS: No more today. Your thirst is in a state of becoming. It is growing more and more grand-like while your credit remains in a cocoon. The two don't balance.

FIRST GUEST: Then goodby until tomorrow.

SECOND GUEST (*to the third*): We're going the same way. (*The three go off.*)

Grete returns, Boll behind her. He takes her arm. Elias is cleaning up.

BOLL: You're asking a great deal, Grete. After all, you're a smart woman, and you know that I'm somebody and don't usually listen to requests. But you shall have everything, you hear?

GRETE: How slender you are, Blue Boll — you like to hear that, don't you?

BOLL: Haven't I promised you all and everything, Grete?

GRETE: How young, Blue Boll — that pleases you, doesn't it?

BOLL: You think you have to torture me, witch?

GRETE: Aren't you the one that doesn't know the word must, Blue Boll? Does that please even better?

BOLL: If you say so, it has to please me. All right, Grete, say it once more.

GRETE: Must is not for you, even if you are the Blue Boll.

BOLL: Go on!

GRETE: I like you, Blue Boll — does that please you?

BOLL: Yes, Grete, it feels good — more than I can say — go on.

GRETE: Boll must — he must submit, he must be ashamed, he must let himself be told a thing or two.

BOLL: I am listening, Grete; say it once more if you wish.

GRETE: It comes from pleasure, ugly pleasure, Blue Boll, do you hear?

BOLL: I do.

GRETE: You shall have nothing from me, I'll give you nothing — even if you should promise again that you'll help me. Oh yes, Boll must, now this way, now that.

ELIAS: Friends, friends, what a life! Nothing better you could do than go to bed. And if you haven't reached that point, well, wait for the right time — tap its freshness — don't hoard old relics! Becoming is the watchword.

He pushes a chair toward Grete and urges her to sit.

BOLL: What kind of a place is this? Doing business in the middle of the night and on a public street?

191

ELIAS: Oh, the police close an eye — we're on good terms — I look after all kinds of types. Relax and sit down.

BOLL (*seating himself across from Grete*): What can be had here at this hour?

ELIAS: A selection of wholesome dishes, tidbits for the most regal stomachs. Merely make your wishes known.

BOLL: Ever hear of maraschino?

ELIAS: My wife, sir, is asleep, the sleep of the just. It's her habit always to put the keys under her pillow — I cannot get at the liqueur cabinet, alas, alas! But any ordinary pharmacy would appreciate your patronage.

BOLL: I have an idea what you would bring us. Keep your poison to yourself!

ELIAS (*planting himself before him, legs apart*): As I have already said, becoming is the watchword. No way of telling where such grandeur will take us. You too, sir, are destined to greatness. What I wanted to say was, do you wish to be the Blue Boll for ever? Is it worth it? (*Seeing Boll rise, he motions him to stay.*) No, you could bear improving until your becoming flourished furiously. Upon that pasture of consolation may you bravely do your grazing.

BOLL: Who told you who I am? I have basically very little to do with the Blue Boll, practically nothing.

ELIAS: As good as nothing. Does the same go for your sweetheart?

BOLL: That's her own business. I certainly have nothing to do with her. And even if I were the Blue Boll, would you care to change places?

ELIAS: Or perhaps you with me? People hereabouts call me Elias the devil. (*Whispering:*) And I want to tell you something, between you and me, in confidence: there's something to that.

BOLL: If that's so, let's forget about changing places. It would have to be the devil! How do you arrive at this devil-thing? What are the symptoms? Don't you agree that I talk to you, this being the case, in an altogether pleasant vein?

ELIAS: I'm quite used to talking to men of honor. But one must not overestimate the advantages of that. Well then, Mr. Boll, about being a devil. As long as one does it properly, it's all right. Each one is nearest to himself, assuming that that near one is decent and honest. If this works to a degree, why, then there is already a nice devil created. Take it further: it's a question of not becoming afraid, especially of oneself. Can a devil be afraid of devils? You who don't want to change places with a devil don't want to because you are a bundle of anxieties and don't realize that there's a wholeness to the devil. What you want to do, you aren't able to — what you must do, you don't want to. Half-people are no devils. (*Putting out his hand:*) Take it, and give me your half. In return you'll receive from me a hellish charge. For my part, what am I to do with a wretched half like yours? (*He blows his nose with his hand and stretches his hand forth again.*) Like this — and it's gone.

BOLL: Stop this confounded hocus-pocus — disgusting!

ELIAS: And your sweetheart? It seems she also wants to have nothing to do with half-people.

BOLL: Bah! Why, after all, should I cast off the Blue Boll? Each one is nearest to himself.

ELIAS: Yes, yes, exactly — away with the Blue Boll. In the end this would be best for him. (*Laughs.*)

BOLL: Why the silly laugh?

ELIAS: I am delighted that I am not the Blue Boll but only Elias the devil, and yet a wholeness, thank God! What Elias does, he must do; and what Elias must do, he wants to do. Think what you like of me while you're thinking; let me tell you that I heard earlier what your little sweetheart whispered, and she was right. In the darkness it sounded like "Boll must, now this, now that."

BOLL: Was it that?

ELIAS (*to Grete*): Am I wrong?

GRETE: Yes, it was that, and it is true.

ELIAS (*to Grete*): In you, poor little coffin, something deadly is hidden — that's a job for Elias, he'll help set it on its feet. My dear young lady, I've helped many here, here you're well taken care of. A pleasant room, and you're so tired — get a good sleep, stay as quiet as you like. You say no? Are you aware of what you're refusing? Note this: first look, then decide. Take a look first, and then make your decision — that's the time to say no, if bed and room don't please. You go in and

193

close the door behind you, and tomorrow is another day. (*Although she resists, he takes hold of her and pushes her into the house.*) Gently, gently, not to wake my dear wife. Quietly, and straight ahead. (*To Boll, who has jumped up:*) Perhaps you'd like to have some of my poison, after all? But it's too late, we're closing up, and there's no accommodation for such noble people as the Blue Boll. (*He closes the door behind him. Boll is left standing in the dark.*)

BOLL: Away with Boll! Is he not even permitted to ask whether he wants to or whether he must? Don't I have the bit between my teeth? No choice — must wait until he jerks the reins and points the course of the journey.

Virgin, Gentleman, and Woodfresser appear, the last in a humble attitude behind the Gentleman.

WOODFRESSER: Here the street turns and the light from the square thins out. Is someone there?

BOLL: Only myself.

VIRGIN: We're looking for Elias's place near here. Could you help us?

BOLL (*knocking*): Elias! Hey, Elias — customers!

ELIAS (*from an upper window*): Nothing doing, Mr. Boll. Let the customers take to their heels!

VIRGIN: Do my ears deceive me? Mr. Boll standing here in the dark? (*To Gentleman:*) The very same Boll whom you may still remember. You see, Mr. Boll, this gentleman is a stranger here, looking for a place to spend the night. Why just here is rather mysterious, but he is simply taking advantage of the opportunity to probe a little into poor Elias's melancholy disposition. We members of the evangelical assembly are neighbors of Elias and — well, my God . . .

GENTLEMAN: Hello, Mr. Boll! I take it you agree there's not much chance of finding lodgings with Elias?

BOLL: Try to talk him into it — Elias is possibly a human being too.

Gentleman speaks to Elias.

WOODFRESSER (*to Boll*): Mr. Boll, oh, Mr. Boll — such things happen, such things! That gentleman here, the unknown gentleman — who do you think he is?

BOLL: Well, who?

WOODFRESSER: In a word, God himself. As a simple pilgrim. Us all embracing, us all involving in — in — in short, the Lord himself. I was the first to realize it and for that do give myself a little credit.

BOLL: Am I supposed to marvel at that? A thing like that lies heavy in the air, the air takes it, the air returns it. If it isn't anyone else, it must be God.

VIRGIN: If you knew, Mr. Boll, what fears I have endured on your account.

BOLL: Deeply honored, Mr. Virgin. I thank you most humbly for so much — well, so much involvement.

VIRGIN: Only think: I waited hour after hour for the key to the church tower — waited and thought to myself: oh God, there is Mr. Boll clambering around in the tower and in danger of slipping.

BOLL: Or plunging?

VIRGIN: Or plunge — yes, plunge.

BOLL: Plunge down . . .

VIRGIN: No one knows what happens, you acted so extraordinary this morning both in speech and behavior, Mr. Boll. What about the key?

BOLL: The key, of course! But you see, in the dark I can't find my own way in my pocket; wait until morning. (*To himself:*) One says away with Boll. The other thinks he plunges like thunder and hail from the tip of the tower. I am curious to know how Boll's becoming will turn out.

GENTLEMAN: We must accept it — Elias is clearly unwilling to afford me accommodation. (*To Virgin:*) Where to now?

BOLL: To the Golden Ball with the gentleman — the Golden Ball, where I'm going myself. You are my guest, sir, even as Mr. Anonymous. I appreciate the opportunity of inviting the gentleman and of being of assistance to him as a result of my efforts. May I consider myself fortunate enough to have your assent?

GENTLEMAN: Yes, Mr. Boll. So that your friendliness will not have been in vain, I agree gladly.

BOLL (*to himself*): Grete has the devil for a bedfellow while I go home with the Lord — one could come to have strange ideas.

195

Scene 5

The dining room of the Golden Ball Hotel. Otto Pompmaster, surrounded by bottles, is on a settee opposite Mrs. Boll.

MRS. BOLL: True, Otto, if you put it that way, you see . . .

OTTO: After all, and . . . in short, after all.

MRS. BOLL: But I want to know what we women are supposed to do when men carry on like that. Then you say they do it without guile, in full innocence.

OTTO: Without guile is right. It's true men always have less guile than women. But are we, as a matter of fact, talking of particular men?

MRS. BOLL: But Otto, how you flirt with absent-mindedness! How can you cope with it if you drink all that wine — how, Otto?

OTTO: I'm not going to stop as long as my speech is clear enough to order more. Now then, Martha, how do you picture us sitting together in Goldensea? Bertha likes to go to bed early, that's her way, and she was doing it even before we got married. What am I to do? And how can I get around it? Except by managing to sit up by myself and by looking after the red wine by myself? Today I am in addition responsible for Kurt's portion. What do you think, Martha?

MRS. BOLL: Yes, we must wait for him. Even if he sends word that we shouldn't wait for him, it could only be in the nature of a suggestion, couldn't it?

OTTO: Dead right, Martha. Entirely of your opinion. (*He strikes the table.*) Just let him try and think I'm going to crawl off to bed scared as though I needed his permission to take off! Here I sit and here I shall drink until the matter can be settled, and it shall be settled at the latest very soon. Furthermore, it is characteristic of me that the more I drink the sooner can I empty the bottles and the more enterprising becomes the trajectory of my thoughts.

MRS. BOLL: Listen to me, Otto. Do you believe that people can change themselves — I mean in such a way that they become substantially different? I must tell you I am more anxious about Kurt than I can say.

OTTO (*laughing*): If it tickles Kurt to do something like that, let him debit

196

his own account. If he can't leave off but annoys us with it, why then I'm going to have to show him a thing or two. We have no use for him other than he is — become different — what next!

MRS. BOLL: Yes but . . .

OTTO (*striking the table*): I'm opposed to all change. Nothing can become better, and that's why becoming had better stay put. Period. Finished. Martha, trust me to straighten him out all right. Bertha is opposed to any change, too, and that's why she's gone to bed at her invariable hour. One of her sublime traits, you realize. Pipelow! (*The waiter comes; Otto points to the empty bottle and Pipelow brings another.*)

MRS. BOLL: You know Kurt often allows himself to be suddenly intimidated. On such occasions he says well, it must be so for it not to be so, or something like that, therefore . . .

OTTO: Quite right, Martha; therefore he shouldn't stint himself a thing or two. But I can't understand why he seeks out my presence only to flaunt his absence.

MRS. BOLL (*quietly*): Maybe he is a certain someone we don't recognize. And perhaps that's why he can't help it if we wonder about him. He may possibly be wondering more about us than we about him.
Boll, Gentleman, and Woodfresser enter.

BOLL: Look at that! Who would have thought — at this hour! I hope you haven't denied yourselves anything. All well, Otto? Good evening, Martha.

OTTO: All well? Now why, you know, I ask myself, do we arrange to meet if, in the first place, you don't show up, and, in the second, my wife — did you expect Bertha to wait up in the second place?

BOLL: I telephoned a number of times. Didn't they tell you I kept being detained?

OTTO: Yes, yes — over and over. Was phoning enough?

MRS. BOLL: Couldn't you have had me called to the phone, Kurt?

BOLL: Why? I had enough consideration, Martha, not to disturb you at dinner. Eat, I said to myself, let her eat in peace. He who is eating has his mouth full and would only munch into the telephone. No, I thought, leave her in peace. However, Otto, listen, and Martha. What will you say now? I must introduce you. This gentleman is my guest; his name remains a mystery and a secret, but don't let that alarm you.

He is God himself, of course strictly incognito — under cover, as it were. And here as a witness and pledge to my words, also without name so far . . .

WOODFRESSER: Woodfresser is my name, master shoemaker. (*Humbly, to Gentleman:*) With *his* permission!

GENTLEMAN (*to Boll*): If you want it so, Mr. Boll, I shall not lift the cloak of anonymity in which you have clothed me — but only a little in passing and in confidence between the two of us: well, Mr. Boll, God, you said — just between you and me — there is something to that, but only as a faint and meek reflection out of the infinite do I accept the name of the Lord, a weak, hardly discernible adumbration of God. Is not that the way you meant it?

BOLL: No unnecessary modesty, sir. I know how to honor my guests. Very well, Otto, you remain on the settee, the Good Lord next to you, which gives you two a majestic symmetry. Martha, remain seated where you are. Have you sampled all the nobler brands? (*They seat themselves as indicated.*)

OTTO: I always pictured God differently. For my part, it didn't occur to me to question him about his profession, but you can imagine, Kurt, what's on my mind. I am a landowner, you are a landowner, that's enough for today and for a while to come — what do we need with the Good Lord for company! You know, Kurt, each one is nearest to himself, and my wife for that matter has gone to bed.

BOLL: What beautiful bright teeth Bertha still possesses, Otto; but they are now with her in bed. May God save her dentures for many a year. I would by no means have grudged our dear God the opportunity of admiring them, but as you say quite correctly, each one is nearest to himself. She got tired and — — but on that score I'm not going to tease you or her any more today.

OTTO: If you honestly mean that, I might call her for just one moment. Of course, her teeth — there is truly nothing you can say against her teeth.

BOLL: Pour us some, Otto. (*Otto pours.*) Now don't mistake me, but when I see you handle that bottle, what a revolting family resemblance there is! I'm afraid we look bitterly alike. It has often occurred to me that this phenomenon of resemblance must fairly strike one — strike one down, that is — but listen, don't be angry, please! Now those teeth of

your wife — how long do you think will she keep them, and, anyway,
will she eternally remain Bertha Pompmaster? Is it worth it?

WOODFRESSER (*rising, humbly to Gentleman*): With *his* permission! (*To
Boll:*) Exactly, Mr. Boll, just so. It is not worth it; but to go further,
it is on the contrary worth achieving that point at which there is shame
at having ever been such a lady. Hence you're quite right, Mr. Boll.
(*He sits down.*)

BOLL: I hadn't exactly addressed myself to you, Mr. Woodfresser — that
is your name, isn't it, and you are, I believe, a shoemaker? Very well.
Strictly speaking, you don't know anything of the lady in question.

WOODFRESSER (*rising, humbly to Gentleman*): With *his* permission! All
of us sitting here together will one day be ashamed of ourselves, the
lady — thank God! — included. (*Sits down, more quietly:*) It doesn't
matter whether I know the lady or not as long as I know in what respect she has to be ashamed, namely, in face of the glory to be. All
ladies are in the same state.

OTTO: Neither here nor there, Kurt, all this fancy talk — agreed? (*To
Woodfresser:*) If you keep jumping up and down like that, you'll knock
over the bottles. Kurt, when you come to Goldensea, you must not fail
to take a look at Antonia — a Danish breed, you know — a first-rate
milk producer — and — well, what else was I going to say!

GENTLEMAN (*accepting a glass*): You have an extraordinarily steady
hand, sir; I remarked it right away. If you'll permit me: to your health
and of course to the health, above all, of the ladies present and not
present. (*They clink glasses.*)

OTTO: Oh yes, sure, a most sure and steady hand, and why not! But don't
you have an idea what I was going to say? (*To Mrs. Boll:*) Good Lord,
Martha, we talked of it all night. What was it?

MRS. BOLL: No, Otto, absolutely not, do me this one favor and drop it for
the night.

OTTO: Ah, that's it — a favor, a case — no, not a favor, it had something to
do with a case, and it was the case of a woman. (*To Boll:*) Kurt, do
you know what woman that was — a woman, I believe, for whom
you've assumed — possibly the same woman, Kurt — assumed responsibility? (*Triumphantly to Mrs. Boll:*) You see, and you thought I'd
forget such a crucial issue!

199

Mrs. Boll covers her eyes.

WOODFRESSER (*rising, humbly to Gentleman*): With *his* permission! This woman, this same woman, is Grete whose uncle I am. (*To Boll:*) Mr. Boll's responsibility is as sound as a municipal undertaking's — as sound as Mr. Boll is sound. They call my niece Grete the witch of Parum, but that has nothing to do with the responsibility. Mr. Boll got the bit of responsibility stuck between his teeth, and my nephew Greendale, the husband of this same woman, returned cheerfully to his three children in Parum, the same who're also Grete's three children. (*He sits down.*)

OTTO: Much too few children in that story to tell *me* about it. But, Kurt, who is she, and this Uncle Shoemaker? Do you mean it, a witch, an honest-to-goodness witch? (*He rises.*)

BOLL: Yes, yes, and what of it! Not enough? I would think it's enough and more than enough. Sit down, Otto.

OTTO: A bona fide witch?

BOLL: And to crown it, I found her accommodation with a bona fide devil. (*To Gentleman:*) I hope you will not conclude there was intention to entertain you with such company. (*To Otto:*) Sit down, Otto!

GENTLEMAN: As it happens, I am friends with both devils and witches. We've all set out upon the same road.

OTTO: Kurt, I'm *not* going to sit down. That much I had to promise Martha and seal with a handshake. I must not sit down as long as I consider myself a decent fellow. And what you said about a bitter family resemblance is neither here nor there since I can accuse you of it on the same grounds. I'm ashamed, thank God — it's a frightening observation — I'm ashamed of the family resemblance. Martha, poor Martha! (*He gives her his hand; she sobs.*)

MRS. BOLL: Do sit down, Otto. It's far too late for us to get even a minimum of sleep. Shall I have them bring us coffee?

OTTO: Please, Martha. Coffee does a man good and that's why you should properly do so. But sit down — no, that I'm not in a position to do. (*Mrs. Boll leaves in tears.*) Now you see, Kurt, how you've succeeded, what you've done! I'm ashamed that I even had to promise Martha a thing like that. Why can't we just discuss all this quietly among ourselves?

BOLL: But you promised her, I can't help thinking, that this should not be done quietly but rather under racking family pressure . . .

WOODFRESSER (*rising, humbly to Gentleman*): With his permission! May I, giving myself a little credit, draw your attention to the fact that our town has since this morning enjoyed a glorious becoming? Now, that coffee must be prepared at this late hour witnesses to a becoming put into easy motion by an eternally effortless vigor. In humbleness but not without a little pride I remind one and all of the presence of — (*bowing before Gentleman*) — as its prime mover. (*Sits down.*)
Mrs. Boll returns.

OTTO: Well, Martha, thank God, Martha. We're in dire need of Pipelow because, I assume, Pipelow is getting us coffee; or has he gone to bed, too?

MRS. BOLL: I couldn't simply pass by without a tiny peek into Bertha's room, Otto. Bertha forbids coffee categorically, and you're supposed to come to bed instantly. (*To Boll:*) Suckleworm is putting the horses to the carriage — we've never yet driven so late.

OTTO: So — no coffee? You had to tell Bertha about coffee, did you? I consider this an inexcusable act of thoughtfulness. (*To Gentleman:*) If you meant to get up, I'm ready to let you pass — did I understand you to have said something to that effect?

GENTLEMAN: Rather than trouble you on that account, sir, I should like to ask you something.

OTTO: I don't lend money on principle — please rephrase your question accordingly.

GENTLEMAN: It has nothing to do with money. I might, at that, be in the fortunate circumstance of rendering you, in case of need, modest financial assistance.

OTTO: Case of need? Do you really mean to say I — we — need money? In such circles I do not move. But you, on the other hand, seem to know that type of people. There are never cases of need in our circles.

GENTLEMAN: Unfortunately there are many decent needy people among my friends. Nevertheless we are all of us in, if not the same, then a related, case of need.

OTTO: This is getting more and more fascinating. Related? A whatnot relation with you? Or am I drunk?

GENTLEMAN: Neither in your present lamentable state nor in a sober one can you escape the fact that your recent words about the bitter family resemblance specifically indicate the need for a different quality in your family, that is to say, a better quality. Or put more simply, you feel that your state demands a drastic change.

OTTO: You know something, Kurt? Why don't we send these people away, huh? I mean this heavenly father has drunk enough wine he isn't paying for.

BOLL: Nonsense. Like you he's staying at the Golden Ball and as my guest. (*He slaps Otto on the shoulder.*) But my dear old Otto, what words you pick out of the heart and core of your wooden self — damn it: case of need — us! I should like to know what we are looking for in such a case, what we have need of. Let someone show us. A need for a change? CHANGE?

OTTO: Dear old boy — say!

BOLL (*to Gentleman*): I hope it hasn't escaped you that my cousin is innocent of the ugly words concerning family resemblance?

GENTLEMAN: He caught the word all right — but a good word, not an ugly one, Mr. Boll. There is a germ in it, readiness stirs, and becoming will sprout forth. (*To Otto:*) Oh, you too will soon face great changes; no, not you alone, Mr. Pompmaster, but all of us feel that we enjoy the same good will of fate. For don't we all stand together, mingled and scrambled in the pitiable condition of a universally human and bitter family resemblance?

OTTO: I'm not drunk enough to be so drunk I can't see through all his ludicrous godliness — he's a swindler, Kurt, a swindler, I tell you!

GENTLEMAN: Such a swindler, Mr. Pompmaster, and a witch and a devil are all taking the same road with you and with everyone else. Consider Mr. Boll's genial way of doing things: he assumes responsibility for the witch. In him too sprouts the urge of becoming, bursting its husk. Don't be offended, sir, but we're all of us together, in this deeper sense, witch-mates and devil-brothers, you included!

OTTO (*swinging his fists*): Kurt, I call on you, I beg you — eeeow! How my flag of outrage waves back and forth, how it shakes! I call on you, Kurt, renounce it — renounce the bond of any possible change! Stand tight, old boy, in the bond of marriage, in the face of marriage, behind marriage, and next to marriage. Catch hold of whose neck you want — witches', for all I care — but above all hold fast to the bond of irresponsibility. Hold fast to that! Renounce responsibility! (*Suckleworm appears in the doorway. Half-choking:*) Suckleworm! Luckily there comes Suckleworm ghost-walking. Old Suckleworm, do look into that left corner, there's a spittoon, eh? Bring it here. (*Otto places the spittoon before Gentleman and pours into it the dregs from the bottles.*) There, you fortune-teller, you trickster, you spelling mistake on a toilet wall, you digested dinner, you universally used convenience, you forgotten circumstance! I urge you, watch out for my steady hand and relish what my responsibility spits before you! (*To Boll:*) Do you swear to renounce responsibility?

At Boll's signal Suckleworm takes the spittoon away. Otto is about to speak, stops, and sits down.

SUCKLEWORM: The ladies and gentlemen may step into the carriage. (*Goes off.*)

MRS. BOLL: Praised be God that we can get away at last!

BOLL: Drive off? Home? No, Grete, no driving off.

MRS. BOLL: Did you say Grete?

BOLL: No, I'm not driving away — not now, not ever, Grete! But were I doing the driving it would be straight off to hell with me. Grete in the devil's claws, and I should drive off! Grete who doesn't know what she is doing, Grete whose guardian I am, Grete who wants to ignite the dwellings inhabited by the souls of her children, Grete whom I promised to assist in that task instead of standing by her to attain the opposite!

MRS. BOLL: Don't listen to him! For my part I will put my forgiveness by — he shall have it. But now he must, he must come along — must!

OTTO (*wearily*): I'd better drop my flag to half-mast. Is there any other way I can help you, poor Martha? Shall I plead with him once more? (*He puts on an air of being tough.*)

MRS. BOLL: Ah, what's the use, Otto? I almost don't understand the good Lord any longer. What could he have in mind for us since he obviously thinks differently than we do — no, oh no!

BOLL: Very well, dear Martha, so you will forgive me? But what is the use of your forgiveness if I don't forgive myself? There is my case of need!

The case of cases. Can't you picture this, Martha: the calm night outside, and I, Boll, torturing myself up the stairs of that tower? And what does the tower say? It says Boll must! And then the calm night releases a little morsel of air from up above, only one and a most private one at that. No one notices it, but a heavy black chunk of night collides with that little air and cleaves the pavement in two. Next morning they wash half a dozen yards of Boll's redness from the stones. Picture to yourself the possibly unnecessary complications; understand it thoroughly. Rather than drive with Suckleworm, with you close beside me, to hell, I would fly somersaulting through the air.

MRS. BOLL: You — you frighten me horribly. What am I to do?

BOLL: Don't you see? Listen closely, because this morning I was there when you, as a martyr, pained, proud, and silent — you do remember — and now you're to be honored before all people, because they shall know that yours is the great honor of the decision! The two of you — you and the tower — divide my fate between you. You two must talk and consider and decide. Arise triumphant, Martha, for you've been chosen!

MRS. BOLL: God, it scares me so terribly! Kurt, how can you expect me to understand it all just like that!

Boll raises his finger and shakes it as though he wanted to listen undisturbed. Everyone looks at him. Mrs. Boll searches for enlightenment on the faces of the others. The last one she looks at is Gentleman, who smiles at her.

GENTLEMAN (*quietly*): Boll must?

MRS. BOLL (*to Boll, with a brief sob*): You must, Kurt, you *must* go to her, I send you to her, go to Grete, Kurt, go now!

Scene 6

A guest room in the Devil's Kitchen Inn. There is a door in the rear wall, a bed and table on the right with just enough space for a window that faces the courtyard of the building. Left, an old easy chair. On the table is a kitchen lamp giving a faint light.

Grete, fully dressed, is sitting on the bed and appears to be listening to noises. Suddenly she covers her ears. A fist moves into sight behind the pane of the window. There is a knocking. Frightened, Grete looks around, goes to the window and opens it. Elias's head moves into the light.

ELIAS (*whispering*): Take it! Eat and drink. I'll be back soon. In the meantime you can . . . go on, take it, I chose nothing bad for you.

GRETE: I don't want that — you know what I want — I have no wish to eat, drink, or receive presents.

ELIAS: This isn't a present — eating and drinking are part of it, see? I'll like you better if you eat and drink. You're hollow-eyed and that makes you look so hungry. Be more cheerful, understand? — cheer is part of it. Is it a deal? (*She takes the package.*) There you are! Now you show more sense, we'll get along and be nice to each other. Look, I have to use this entrance from the courtyard because my wife sleeps in that passage and there are some loose floor boards. Got to take care of something: always something, that's business! (*Off.*)

Grete puts the package on the table. There is knocking next door. Grete listens, shakes her head. More knocking.

GRETE (*quietly*): I'm here.

WEHDIG'S VOICE (*behind the left wall*): Are you Grete?

GRETE: I'm here.

VOICE: Got such a hunger and here I keep hearing talk about eating and drinking. How am I supposed to sleep with this racket about food and drink!

GRETE: You can eat if you want to. Come and get it.

One hears a bedframe creak. There are sounds of shuffling and groping in the dark. Wehdig appears at the center door to the hallway; he is half-dressed and barefooted.

WEHDIG: Where?

Grete points to the table.

WEHDIG: Eat hearty, Cap'n Wehdig! (*He unwraps the package and shakes the bottle.*) This doesn't slosh like dishwater — glows a nice yellow — I'll save it! (*Chewing:*) Where is he? Gone? You two got anything planned? If not, I'll stay right here; how about it?

GRETE: Where do all those people come from?

WEHDIG: What people?

GRETE: You can hear them.

WEHDIG (*stops chewing, listens, shakes his head*): All I can hear is lice marching everywhere, but people — no. (*He continues to eat and stares at Grete.*)

GRETE: But he is among them, walking around, telling them things. Elias is talking to them.

WEHDIG: What does he say?

GRETE: He's scolding them and swearing.

WEHDIG: That all? As long as he swears he's got something to put his mind to — good thing he's swearing.

GRETE: He seems vicious.

WEHDIG: Vicious — oh, yes! Blow out the light or he's going to make trouble. (*He blows out the light himself.*)

GRETE: But there's still light coming through the cracks. (*She points to the left wall.*)

WEHDIG: Behind that wall is the hole he put me in. (*Laughs.*) He forgot and left me my shirt! Well, it won't make any difference to you — I'm the same with a shirt or without, huh?

GRETE: Still more people!

WEHDIG: With that many, a few more don't matter — forget them.

GRETE: But what could they be doing there? Is there enough room for so many?

WEHDIG: Do they bother about me? I don't bother about them.

GRETE (*going to the wall*): I can see through the cracks — ah, there's Elias again, running back and forth, hard at work carrying dishes.

WEHDIG: Better come here. You may sit on my lap, Grete.

GRETE: Oh, dear God!

WEHDIG: What more do you want, I'd like to know? I told you my room is behind that wall — nobody there, no people, no Elias — all foolishness. Come, Grete!

GRETE: Aren't they playing with golden cards? I think they're holding golden cards. They jingle when they throw them. Why, sure: golden cards!

WEHDIG: Say what you like. I'll be done in a minute. Then you'll see.

GRETE: Yes, they're playing with golden cards and Elias — look, look — he's grabbing them by their legs and tears off their boots. And now —

he's dragging in tubs, steaming tubs, pushes them under the tables, one tub for two people. He's making them stick their feet in the tubs. I really believe those tubs are glowing! There, there, there — he's coming with a bucket full of red coals! And that one there — why, I know him, it's Flourcake, Flourcake with that beak like a raven's, and he's got to get in it — oooh, aaah, what singeing — he's sweating pearly fat like bacon in a pan and the hot droplets jumping all over like fleas. Flourcake too has golden cards in his fist and plays them out — but makes such a face! I wouldn't want to play with such golden cards!

WEHDIG: Yes, bacon in the pan, that sizzles nicely — makes you prick up your ears. Does it smell like it too, Grete?

GRETE: Oh Lord, what faces they all make! They're trying to show they're having a good time, that's part of the game. Now they're shuffling their golden cards and keep right on playing. Oh yes, friends, have to look tickled pink even though the going is hard. Yet I have to admit you do what you can; you don't want to be called spoilsports.

WEHDIG: My feet are cold. I can take it longer than they can.

GRETE: There comes old Splint and another behind him — I know him too: Cheeseman from Klüz, and also Groundperch, yes, that's him — but he's long dead, and I myself saw Splint and Cheeseman buried! How did they get here?

WEHDIG: Why don't you ask them, Grete, they may remember how.

GRETE: We always called Cheeseman Brambleberry, he still has those red tassels dangling from his cheeks — oh oh oh, there's Elias about to raise a fuss — is it because one of them doesn't want to play along? There he comes, pushing Elias aside — and I believe I know him too. That must be Boll, but a youthful Boll, slender and red. He's lighting his cigar and blowing smoke at Elias's outbursts. I'd love to see what he's got there, looking for something in his pocket — it's a golden ball, now he bounces it on his hand. He's twisting his head around — I'm scared; he's looking for me.

WEHDIG (rises): Now comes the chummy part of the evening. Let's investigate what's bubbling in that bottle. You'll have to drink too, Grete.

GRETE (moaning): You — you too, all three of you? Ah, you poor little ones, what do you want in hell? Your feet are so dirty from all this running around, and you grabbed the worst raggedy clothes! How you stand there so lost! No one cares! What luck, Blue Boll, your head turns around, you discover them and wave to them with your long cigar. Now Elias is letting go of Boll, Elias understands, he laughs at them, and now he pulls up such tiny little chairs — sit and rest your tired feet, children! He's taking off their dirty boots, first Al, then Lena, then Pete — takes off their boots, reaches out an arm, now he's got hold of — of a bucket of hot coals? (*Screaming:*) Hey, Elias, what are you doing? They're my children, Elias, Elias, Elias — damn you, Elias!

WEHDIG: Shut up, woman! It's the middle of the night! You'll wake the whole house!

GRETE (*crying out louder*): Take pity, Elias, or I'll stick your own head . . . take pity on my children, the poor souls are looking for me. They're nothing to you! (*She pushes herself against the wall and strikes it.*)

WEHDIG: That's not how we were going to play it — I'm dealing myself out of this game! *And* wash my hands of it! (*He tries to make off with the bottle, but it slips from him. He makes an unsuccessful attempt to find it.*) May you poison whoever finds you! (*He slips out; the door remains open. — Elias comes with a light.*)

ELIAS: You trying to wear your tongue to a frazzle? Want to scream your head off? Choke, you witch!

GRETE: Who allowed you to deal so with my children, you devil, Elias! (*She squeezes past him to the door, but he takes hold of her and pushes her onto the bed. He places the light on the table.*)

ELIAS: Children? Your children? Are you bewitched?

Elias's wife Doris, a portly woman with a deep voice and an utterly imperturbable manner, appears at the door.

DORIS: This traffic in and out of her room! Let someone take her away, Elias, but first she must pay.

ELIAS: Go back to bed, woman; I'll handle this.

Doris turns slowly and goes.

GRETE: Didn't you know they're all three my children?

ELIAS: I know about the children. You told me before. (*Quietly:*) Be sensible, Grete, you hear? Speak quietly. But children? Where are your children?

GRETE: In there, playing with golden cards, their feet in bowls, there behind that wall. Bring them here right away, Elias!

ELIAS: Did you eat?

GRETE: He ate instead — he also went in to those people; Boll is there too, and he plays with the golden ball.

ELIAS: Naturally. That pack's belly is always open, ready to shovel in slush and mush.

GRETE: Bring them here, Elias, I beg you! Bring all three!

ELIAS: Right away, in a second; but Boll is there to feed them. Boll will find something for them.

GRETE: Let me go, Elias. Believe me, I'm not afraid of those characters, not of Cheeseman, nor of the other corpses — I want to feed them myself.

ELIAS: Relax — you're so out of breath.

GRETE: Tell me, where did you put your poison? No chance that Boll could mistakenly get hold of it and feed them your poison?

ELIAS: Boll will do whatever he pleases, now this, now that. Boll must, Grete.

Doris appears in the doorway.

DORIS: Elias?

ELIAS: She's drunk. First I must tie up her skirts. Go to bed. I'll be done in a minute. (*Doris goes off slowly.*)

GRETE: That woman isn't going to them? A terrible woman, that. She mustn't go to the children!

ELIAS: She hasn't eaten any children so far, and she isn't going to them. Has her own children.

GRETE: Her own? Some children they must be!

ELIAS: Regular children, healthy children, children like all children, Grete.

GRETE: Really good children?

ELIAS: None better!

GRETE: But where did you hide the poison, Elias? Children just take things, always looking for sweet stuff — what if they find the poison?

ELIAS: If they do, they're used to it from the beginning. It does them no harm, they thrive so one can see them grow.

GRETE: What kind of children they must be, what kind of people you are!

ELIAS: All part of the business: there's fun in hell. I trust you're coming around to see that everything here is as it should be. So let me tell you something — but I'll say it quietly not to lose sight of the main point . . . (*Doris at the door.*)

DORIS: Elias?

ELIAS: Go to bed, woman.

DORIS: Elias?

ELIAS: I told you: to bed!

DORIS: Have you done with her?

ELIAS: Go to bed; it'll be all right in a minute.

DORIS: I think it's all right now. Go and call the police. I'm going to keep watch with her. (*She enters.*)

GRETE: Boll — Blue Boll — help me!

DORIS: Her! Who'd have thought she was that kind! Forget the police. (*She catches sight of the bottle, picks it up and places it on the table. To Grete:*) You deserve a little thrashing to bring you to your senses. (*To Elias:*) Didn't she say something about children?

ELIAS: What of it! What are her children to us?

DORIS: It matters to them. We are losing sleep over her children. (*She sits in the easy chair.*)

GRETE: Tell her, Elias, she mustn't sit here, no!

ELIAS: Tell her yourself! She's the kind that's easy to get along with — that's her.

GRETE: I can hear her breathing, I feel her as close as if the whole room were filled with her, even though I know she's sitting back there. Elias, don't leave me.

ELIAS: It's all right to say anything, Grete; try, and see what happens. (*He busies himself moving chairs, picking up pieces of paper, fussing with the wick — every inch the innkeeper. But from time to time he makes a face.*)

DORIS: Everything in its own good time, you silly thing. You're a tough chicken, but I'll eat you up anyway. (*She shakes her finger.*) That's the devil, fool — get away from him and come sit in my lap.

GRETE (*clutching at Elias*): You hear that, Elias? On her lap, she said.

ELIAS: Do what you want, all comes to the same. (*To Doris:*) Can't you see she's afraid, woman? Time you left her in peace.

DORIS: Oh my dear Elias, how I know you inside out! Let her be afraid:

fear will help her; don't think it can do her any harm. It's a lesson one learns here.

GRETE: Ah, Elias, I know what she means. It is learned with coals under one's feet. Weren't you there when the children had their feet in the bucket? What were the coals supposed to teach them?

DORIS: Come, my Elias, no more about the children. Give me the bottle, just right for someone like her — your poison. Let's see, let's find out. (*Elias hands her the bottle. Doris drinks.*)

GRETE: In there? Is that it? It stood there on the table so bare and bright and you never said a word?

DORIS: By the taste I can tell how well you mean by her, Elias. Ah, you silly thing, so one has to put on a show like yours to warm oneself in his attention? There, let her drink. It'll drive away her fear, teach her about devils, teach her to get rid of something and stamp it out.

GRETE: Look, Elias, she's drinking. Do I have to drink after her?

ELIAS: Don't ask, and stop this playacting. You heard what she said. Here — take it! What, so eager? Look, she's drinking the poison like water!

GRETE (*drinking*): If it isn't exactly like that with the coals! Ah, you poor little ones, your mother will burn up with her coals inside her.

DORIS (*shaking her finger*): You silly thing, nobody is burned up by our coals. Our coals know what's what, know exactly. They burn where needed, they destroy nothing but what's spoilt.
Grete writhes.

ELIAS: None other than the scalding frost, Grete — it creeps into you, freezes your guts and scorches your fear. Open your mouth, Grete!

DORIS: She's drinking, Elias, stop torturing her.

GRETE (*drinking*): Yes, there's something to be learned from you people. It may be burning but it burns up the body's fear and gives pain without care. (*Looks at the door.*) I suppose they want their share, eh, Elias?
Three corpses enter.

GRETE: That would suit you, wouldn't it, you creeps — eh, Cheeseman and Splint and Flourcake? What a company you are! (*She laughs.*) What did you do with your flesh and bones? I wonder how you'll wish me good day. I won't touch anything that smells of what used to be, what's cast off, or what's growing back into itself.

The corpses look around.

GRETE (*laughing*): No mirror here, Flourcake. You, yes, you — you can still afford to be vain. Look at Splint, he's only got half what you have. Go on, laugh with the part of the throat that's left you!

FLOURCAKE: So, Grete, we've come to take your children along.

GRETE: That's why you came?

SPLINT: That's why and no other reason.

GRETE: All three of you?

CHEESEMAN: We'll take them and go right on.

GRETE: For you to keep? And turn them into such elegant shapes as you? But you must be starving, friends, to judge by the way your bare flesh dangles and by your damned, hollow-eyed, hungry looks. Hovering, waiting for my children, are you? Take a drink first, excellent poison, can't possibly do you any more harm; maybe it'll give you other ideas. (*Gives them to drink.*)

SPLINT: If the children are having their share, I don't mind. Room I have plenty. (*He drinks.*)

GRETE: A damned kind of life that must be, death — but you obviously know that.

FLOURCAKE: True, Grete. You fight your way through if you aren't too shy. We'll look after the children. (*Drinks.*)

CHEESEMAN: Oh yes, you catch on to the ins and outs soon enough and the young learn as fast as the old. First you get rid of your good flesh — then acquiring the putrid is a cinch. (*Drinks.*)

GRETE (*laughing*): Guzzle all you can, Cheeseman! You see you've licked off the last drop, not a crumb, not a drop left — — nothing, nothing, nothing is left, nothing for Al, nothing for Lena, and nothing for Pete! Take to your heels, friends, on your way — what more can you do under the circumstances than be honest corpses?

The three look at each other.

FLOURCAKE: If it hadn't all been agreed, Grete.

GRETE: Knock such an agreement out of your heads — I didn't call you.

SPLINT: Believe me, I do that gladly. Why? Because I'd rather not do *it*.

Grete, let your brats stay in their own flesh if you're not looking for anything better.

CHEESEMAN: Isn't it going to hurt us to proceed with this interrogation? People like us have their pride too. You can wait a long time for another such opportunity — I can't help you.

The corpses walk backwards out of the room.
Grete follows and shuts the door after them.

GRETE: Now let someone say I didn't manage that well! Do all the dead become so stupid when their minds begin to rot? How they looked! Why, they didn't even know how to get out the door. (*She stops before Doris and claps her hands.*) And all the poison has been drunk, and nothing left for Al nor Lena nor Pete — not a drop except what remains in your empty bottle.

Doris lifts her arms. Grete slides down and hides in Doris's lap.
Elias has got into bed and is soon snoring.

DORIS: Here, come closer, that way you'll be warmer. Let's forget which one of us is which, forget everything, forget about yourself, relax in that calm from which everything springs and where all is well. Give me what is false and evil in you, it won't affect me — Elias's Satan-woman keeps it safe. It'll grow over and become mine: I know how to carry it, I carry it without effort. Trust me to bear that of which you've been relieved. Come here, little blockhead, listen closely.

GRETE (*raising her head to Doris*): Boll is — Boll is dead. Is the Blue Boll dead?

DORIS: Listen carefully. (*She speaks quietly.*)

GRETE: Yes, that's true, I know it — the Blue Boll is sitting with his feet in Elias's coal bucket — ouch, ouch, Blue Boll! It draws up into your heart, the bubbles burst, the evil company is blowing with rounded cheeks — that's how, Blue Boll, that's how it has to be, she says. But what of the young Boll? The young and slender one, who gave the children the golden ball to play with — must he also to the coals?

DORIS: No, what *he* saves goes to the credit of the Blue Boll — listen. (*Whispers into her ear.*)

GRETE: Can't he? Can't he really let it be, can't forgive himself? Can no one? Not even he himself? Ah, you poor Boll, I do forgive you. Play with my children and be forgiven.

DORIS: It is the young one who is playing with the children.

GRETE: Yes, the young — he need not suffer for the sins of the Blue Boll. If you can do what you said you could, if you can bite and suck the evil out of me and bear that of which I am relieved, can't you do away with the old Boll too and bear him too without harm to yourself?

DORIS: Let the Blue Boll be his own judge. Enough. You fell into the hands of devils who live in the house of evil — there are many more evils that can get a lodging in that house. Elias is snoring, and I'm tired too. I've settled some things and bring them all together to a good rest.

ELIAS (*in his sleep*): Boll must, now this way, now that.

There is loud knocking at the outer door.

GRETE: Who would want to come here so late?

Doris has fallen asleep. Grete shakes her without effect.

ELIAS: Boll must . . .

GRETE: It's Boll. (*She jumps up.*) Boll, Blue Boll, wait, I'm coming. (*Off.*)

Scene 7

The interior of the church, of which only a pillar, a window, and pews are visible. A woodcarving of one of the apostles is attached to the pillar. Grete is sleeping on a bench while Boll walks up and down the aisle. The early-morning sun streams through the window and highlights the apostle. After a few seconds Grete wakes and sits up slowly; her eyes follow Boll who continues to pace. They glance at each other as he passes her.

GRETE: Isn't that the Blue Boll? Who else! But how did you get here?

BOLL: Aren't you here too, Grete? (*He gestures.*) What a building, what stony rockets rising high, and what joyful bounding there in the vaults of heaven! It's morning, Grete — did you sleep well?

GRETE: Didn't you give them the golden ball? And they kept running and running after it?

BOLL: Just so, right after the gleaming ball, and the ball rolling straight to

Parum, pointing the way in the dark. They've been back in Parum a long time, Grete, and are playing with the golden ball.

GRETE: But Boll was young and slender and red — and now it's the Blue Boll again?

BOLL: Why should that upset you? Yes, I was young and slender, as though . . . as though, Grete, I really *were* young and slender, and that's why you kissed me in the dark. Don't you remember what the night watchman said?

GRETE: We were running, and you said the children were ahead of us. That's why I ran. I was tired and getting faint but I wanted to run all the faster. Yes, it was dark!

BOLL: Very. But you didn't run for long. You dropped to the ground, didn't move a limb, didn't say a word, and I lifted you up — both the night watchman and I lifted you and carried you with some effort (*pointing to the wall*) there to the front of this building, in front of the Golden Ball. He got his tip and thanked me and suggested I should let my little bride get a good night's rest, she seemed to need it, and he laughed at that, just as any smart aleck would in a situation like that. He said bride, Grete, because that's the way his mind ran.

GRETE: And then I kissed you?

BOLL: In the dark — I was young and slender in the dark, Grete. Then it suddenly struck me what you meant when you kept saying over and over, poison, poison — I sniffed it, and I understood why you had begun with laughing and crying and coughing and ended with snoring. So I was young and slender, and glad to be so — in the dark.

GRETE: And then?

BOLL: And then I turned from the Golden Ball on the left, got the key out of my pocket, unlocked the door, and once we were in the tower, we got by ourselves into the belfry. It went against my grain: I would rather have taken you somewhere else, but I suppose it had to be. And you lay down and went to sleep, slept deeply and well, and I kept watch, up and down, in the dark. Can it be more quiet in heaven? Just think how quiet it was!

GRETE: Do you remember the uproar in hell and how they put the bare soles on the blaze? Elias knows all about it, Blue Boll. He gave me a lot of poison.

BOLL: Elias? True, he belongs to them too — what are you looking at? Why do you stare at that wooden mannikin?

GRETE (*glancing from the figure of the apostle to Boll and back, laughing*): How he looks! How you both look! The sun strikes his face, and his staring eyes are wide open. Is he looking for lice — why else is he fumbling around in his big beard?

BOLL: Ah, yes — him! Look, now the sun strikes my face too and there's a shadowy Boll growing large on the wall. That wooden saint and my shadow are face to face — it's easy to tell what flesh they come from. He too was flesh once, and I am still — take a good look, Grete.

GRETE: He's closing his mouth, his eyes wink.

BOLL: They glow, they glow! And mine?

GRETE: Yours? Ah, Blue Boll, they're not your finest ornament. Over them are such blinkers banging shut that one would be ashamed to peer through them. Apart from that, those eyes are genuine eyes; yet they've crept into hiding in thick walnut shells. He's got a mouth but he shuts it.

BOLL: Shut tight! It has nothing to say, wants to say nothing except a word now and then — no more than half a dozen watery words. And my mouth?

GRETE: Yours isn't bad, Boll — good for yawning and showing off teeth and getting all sorts of offal for those teeth. But your teeth are very good, ready to do their part. Now look at his sunken cheeks — no more room for teeth there! The walls of that chamber are thin, its beds empty. Perhaps his eyes glow because he has no teeth and searches for something besides flesh.

BOLL: No, he's hungry, Grete, and hungry — you have to admit — is not the way I look!

GRETE: His forehead is divided, if you look closely, into two beautiful, perfect shells.

BOLL: And mine?

GRETE: I do think you're a nice Blue Boll, but I wish I hadn't kissed you. Beneath your whiskers your cheek is smooth, and this is your forehead — because it's exactly where it should be. Just right.

BOLL: What were you going to say about Elias, Grete?

GRETE: It's like heaven here, really. I would rather be silent, and then I'm tired too. The poison still claws behind my eyes. I want to go home — home. How it hurts. (*She touches her forehead.*) I'll go as soon as I've rested a minute.

BOLL: You don't have to go, Grete. While you were asleep I walked across and woke up poor old Suckleworm. He's putting the horses to the carriage now. (*Looks at his watch.*) You leave very soon and drive to Parum, and Suckleworm will be back before the rest of the party have their shoes shined. But tell me what went on with Elias!

GRETE: You're going to hear what you want to hear. Tell me, and I'll repeat after you.

BOLL: Look, Grete, even if that shadow on the wall is not beautiful, the almighty sun drew it honorably and without mockery. Are you going to be angrier with me than the sun is? You know, this becoming is such a tough business. You will ride to Parum. You will get off there as though the owner of the carriage were the man in the moon and Boll a scarecrow elsewhere. This you may do, and it will be owing to Boll's difficult task — a task at which my becoming broke into plentiful sweat. But becoming and thriving shall be accorded their rights, and thus shall the Blue Boll leave his abnormal valley of misery and come to rest in the gleaming hall of the better norm. Long may he live in towering belfries!

GRETE: Continue.

BOLL: Ah indeed, Grete, you supplied the impetus, you gave Boll the occasion to taste the flavor of becoming. Now he will prevail all the more perfectly on such an ascent . . .

GRETE: Go on, Blue Boll.

BOLL: Because Boll no longer has a choice; he must prepare himself for the glory of becoming. That's why he has ordered the horses put to the carriage, and that's why Suckleworm will drive the beloved witch at a safe and sound trot — safe and sound, Grete, you are sure of that now — safe and sound home to her dear children. And Boll, waving his respectable right hand, allows her to ride away never to return, while he gives himself to the change from the beloved valley of misery and hurries upward to arrive safe and sound — where? In the festive hall of the ineluctable hereafter! That, Grete, is how it shall be. There's no other way.

GRETE: Say everything, Blue Boll.

BOLL: My God, Grete, dear Grete, how much sooner I would stay in the familiar valley of misery where I had so much fun but where I may no longer remain! Boll's will power isn't so bad, but how great his displeasure with the everlastingly rocky path of change! Not a word about Elias!

GRETE: I believe you completely and accept as true that you made me your first test case — and what hard work it was at that! But listen, what an impressive woman that Satan's wife of Elias's is! She plucked me from his claws. That's how it was, and let no one say otherwise. Does that please you? When the sun shines into your eyes, they glow better than that other one's. Of that I'm sure, if I look closely.

BOLL: Small wonder — can he do anything with his eyes except let them be seen? I, on the contrary, can see for myself, see you sitting there and hear you speak the truth, and, to judge by your eyes, you look like a hale and hearty woman. (*He glances at his watch.*) Time to be off. I'll take you there — come, let's go.

GRETE (*hesitating*): And what will happen to you, Blue Boll, if you can no longer have fun?

BOLL: Don't worry, Grete. Boll cannot refrain from bringing another Boll into the world, you wait and see. Boll's rebirth, Boll's towering change are ringing the doorbell. Each is closest to himself in his unfolding: *he* must discover how to bring it about.

The door to the tower creaks. They look around.

BOLL: This works out perfectly, Martha, we can have breakfast together — no, no, do come here, you don't disturb us in the least.

Mrs. Boll enters.

MRS. BOLL: But is it all right with her?

BOLL: Kiss the lady's hand, Grete. She's Boll's wife — now why so mincing? — do it, please!

MRS. BOLL (*waving her away*): I happened to glance out the window . . . and you were crossing the square and disappeared inside the church . . .

BOLL: Kiss her hand, Grete! (*She does so with the greatest reluctance, awkwardly and fearfully, with Mrs. Boll hardly able to put up with it.*) She's going to ride away never to return, Martha, never, the Grete that used to be. Suckleworm is waiting in front of the Golden Ball, I'm sure, as I trust you noticed. Never, never again!

MRS. BOLL: Wouldn't you rather not tell me about all this, Kurt? No, I really do fail to understand our dear Lord any more. (*She turns away and touches her forehead.*) Without the tiniest chance of sleep as the night wore on — don't such excitements regularly bring on my migraine headaches! (*Turning back:*) My God, Kurt — you don't seem to have the faintest idea what happened last night?

BOLL: I think I do — much happened, a great deal. Perhaps even more?

MRS. BOLL: Then you really don't know? I would never have thought it.

BOLL: What is it, Martha, if you please?

MRS. BOLL: Oh, how could you know . . . who would have told . . . (*To Grete:*) I must inform my husband, who unfortunately is totally unprepared, of a shattering family occurrence.

GRETE: Yes, Mrs. Boll?

MRS. BOLL: She doesn't understand, Kurt.

BOLL (*to Grete*): If you care to do one more thing for me, go up front and pray one Lord's Prayer for me. For me as for one who has no more time for it or who cannot summon the courage. Will you, Grete?
Grete turns away. Boll accompanies her several steps and points in the direction of the altar. Grete off.

BOLL: So you slept badly, and the migraine came back as usual, after such doings.

MRS. BOLL: Crisis after crisis, Kurt.

BOLL: If you will permit me the remark, Martha, they are occasions for taking medicines — but I interrupted you.

MRS. BOLL: Will you be able to cope with what I have to say? If your sight blurs the least little bit, or even . . .

BOLL: Never mind, it's my turn. Proceed.

MRS. BOLL: You'd better sit in that chair. Be resolved, make an effort to dismiss all feelings before I even begin. Oh God, time will heal it. One day you will say that what happened could have happened any time in the past or future — I should never have believed it!

BOLL: Very well, Martha. Now I'm prepared for anything — if you please!

MRS. BOLL: Perhaps you recall that last night you and Otto did not part in the friendliest of spirits?

BOLL: I and Otto? Why, this has happened before — it slipped my mind. Did he say anything else?

MRS. BOLL: Ah, Kurt, to spare you, how shall I tell you with sufficient gentleness? At first he kept on drinking by himself, saying that the liquor would dissolve the dear God from his inner linings, and then when he wanted to go to bed, Bertha had just gone off to sleep, so he disturbed her, on top of it all. Suddenly he dropped in front of the washstand, stretched out on the floor. Luckily the man they call God was right at hand, since he had the room next door and Bertha merely had to knock. Such people really come in handy in emergencies. We did everything that had to be done — now he lies quietly in bed, and that man sits next to him talking. But he's really remarkably changed, Kurt, and his hand keeps shaking. He's unable to speak. The doctor thinks he's likely to recover fairly well this time . . . I should never have believed it.

BOLL: You were quite to the point with your little joke: it could have happened any time in the past, present or future. Notice how much I am under control?

MRS. BOLL: I'm glad to see it, but I'm nevertheless terribly grieved over poor Otto.

BOLL: Could he be dead? Perhaps that fact is to be driven into my head in slow stages — as far as I am concerned, he might as well be dead. Living quarters in such a changed valley of misery can at best be only a pigsty.

MRS. BOLL: How dare you say a thing like that, Kurt! No, thank God, he lives.

BOLL: But very much changed? And his hand shakes? Just think, who would have thought that of Otto — no, I also should never have believed it. I bet that his change in this manner came easier to him than my hard trial with Grete came to me. This Otto . . . now he speaks as with the tongues of angels, and I can hear him roaring in my ears, I tell you, just as though one of the old biddies were holding her trumpet at his mouth and he were blowing into it with all his physical strength. (*Shouting:*) Can you hear me, Grete?

GRETE (*from the rear*): Yes, Mr. Boll?

BOLL: You must be done praying by now if it didn't take you too long to remember how it begins. I am no longer worried over courage. (*To Mrs. Boll:*) Strange how effortless my conversation with this witch has become. Can you explain it?

GRETE (*from far away*): Boll, I hear her again.

BOLL: I don't.

GRETE (*far*): I can hear again what the Satan's woman said. I prayed and cried, but she said he should be his own judge — but that you should have my forgiveness.

BOLL: Very well. Now I understand everything.

Grete returns.

Mrs. Boll is about to say something.

BOLL: Quite right, Martha. That's exactly how things are.

MRS. BOLL: But I didn't say anything.

BOLL: As though that mattered; you are always right, and I knew that to begin with. But I shouldn't have interrupted you — please don't be angry. (*He puts his arm around her and at almost the same moment takes Grete's arm. He walks up and down with both and comes to rest before the apostle.*) Children, look at the old sourpuss. A short while ago I was beginning to be frightened by his wooden grandiosity, but now I stand before him strangely apathetic. You, with your cavernous mouth of silence, I can show you my teeth and laugh at you, you sullen, toothless clod, whatever you say! Does he answer, Martha, can you hear anything, Grete? I have cherished what I had in my life, cherished it as it was given me and as it has become. Anyway — it had to be, it was a case of must, and Boll must — — look, he's shaking his head, can you see, Martha? No, in fact he knows better. Very well then: take another good look at him: a dryness throughout but no taint. He too has the form of his "must," he too has known must, he too must! What do you say, Martha?

MRS. BOLL: Do you want me to die of shame? I shall perish if you don't release me from this hell. I'm going to scream, Kurt!

BOLL: Don't Martha! You shall do more than merely not scream — you shall be good to her — and don't mention shame.

MRS. BOLL: I must scream, I shall scream.

BOLL: Consider, Martha, how much she has earned for us — consider that, consider that — and for that reason you must kiss her hand, that is the tribute you must pay her. She forgives, that is her part, you must honor her — your part. Kiss her hand, and then take her gently to the carriage. That is what I demand.

Mrs. Boll, weeping, utters a few unintelligible words.

BOLL: Still and all, you're right, right after all! A warm, heaven-descended power is at work. Status, did you say? A landowner's wife, you claim? Et cetera, et cetera? Let me tell you, you are Boll's wife and Boll's status has an upper and a lower limit. We are at the lower limit. The honey of humility can help you in your sour toil to a sweet becoming. Shake yourself, wake up! (*He shakes her.*)

Pushed by Boll toward Grete, Mrs. Boll takes Grete's hand and bends over it.

Gentleman's voice is heard from the rear.

BOLL (*without turning around*): How is Otto?

GENTLEMAN: Fine, never better, Mr. Boll. Without resistance your cousin yielded to the second of two quite faint signs by a gentle hand — it happened with the calmest of ease, just as a ready smile follows an obvious allusion — —

BOLL: There, there! Darkness falls before my eyes. (*He disengages himself and gently pushes the ladies outside.*) Do it, Martha, finish it, and take her to the carriage and help her — you do it on my behalf, and what you do for me you do for yourself.

Mrs. Boll and Grete go off.

BOLL (*to Gentleman*): The hand waved gently and Otto's own shaking right hand steadied? How the changes tumble thick and fast! With me, a quite sizable shoot has begun to sprout, but in Otto the becoming has indeed shot up into blades. I do thank you for all your care — — — I thank you but I need no more help. (*He points impatiently to the door.*)

GENTLEMAN: After you, Mr. Boll!

They look at each other. Boll hides his confusion with difficulty.

GENTLEMAN: And how does it go with you? Perhaps it is owing to the clarity of your masterful delineation last night of a plunge that it occurs to me to ask . . .

BOLL: Nonsense! Who would bother with such as that next morning!

GENTLEMAN: And yet — if you consider it carefully, what else is there for you to do? If you hesitate, certainly nothing will come of it — this I can predict. In two, three minutes it's done.

BOLL: Two — three — *what* two, *what* three?

GENTLEMAN: The more words, the more delay, and therefore the more torture. You hardly have enough strength, Mr. Boll, to fight your way to the proper height. I can hear your chest heave, your breath force itself in and out, and yet it must carry you to the first window at least. How did you put it last night — a little morsel of air travels downward and the pavement grows red with Boll's blood?

BOLL (*sits*): Yes, that is how it was to happen, that's what I predicted — my breath . . .

GENTLEMAN: Your breath presented a brilliant description of your plunge — but the plunge itself . . .

BOLL: We — shall — come — to — terms, my breath and myself. I thank you. That's that. The door, after all, is open?

GENTLEMAN: No, I'd rather follow you. I have the time and I would like to serve and further your plans. Don't delay, it becomes more difficult with every second's hesitation.

BOLL (*jumping up*): Sir, what an accomplished Satan you are! What impudence you assume!

GENTLEMAN: As long as you've regained your strength — you obviously have — make use of this bright moment. Don't consider the nothingness I put before you, Mr. Boll — Mr. Boll!

BOLL (*makes for him, gasping*): There's enough, oh, it will do. You shall know for what! (*He shakes him.*)

GENTLEMAN: Very well, I am punished. There was enough. But it cost you, I fear, the last bit of strength. Can you still carry it through?

BOLL (*leans against the wall, then pulls himself together*): Let us now again recall the rules of courtesy — let us outdo each other. So — after you! (*He motions toward the door.*)

GENTLEMAN: Time has run out. Too late, Mr. Boll; for everything has its time. The becoming that a plunge from the tower means, this primitive becoming, you know, you've missed. Does it make sense to begin with an ending?

BOLL: But how could you have the nerve, how could you wrestle to a point or, if you prefer, to brace yourself, to compel me so outrageously?

GENTLEMAN: Shsh! I dared it confidently, confident in the other Boll, that Boll who stands above the old one and who ventures beyond him to a new beginning, who rejects and forbids an ending. You know what I mean. You know that I am right in saying Boll has wrestled with Boll — Boll has judged Boll, and he, the other, the new Boll, has asserted himself.

BOLL: Then Boll has judged Boll? You mean I may live on?

GENTLEMAN: Live on? No, certainly not. But make a fresh start — yes. That has been demonstrated. You must — Boll must bring forth Boll, and what sort *he* will be — *there* lies a better chance of becoming than by a plunge down from the tower. Excellent chance, because there is substance and striving in you: to suffer and fight, good sir, are the instruments of becoming. Already your breath comes calmly and evenly and will suffice, I promise, for a successful fight and will have strength to carry burdens. Boll will become by means of Boll — and becoming, sir, becoming unfolds unexpectedly and delay is only its foolish sham. All this be offered to your insight — for whatsoever is more than this cometh of evil. (*Off.*)

BOLL (*beating his arms about him, falls on his knees, then slowly raises his head and looks up at the apostle*): Did *you* say that? Did *you* keep your mouth shut so long in order to make the word ready? Then Boll must? *Must*? Good — I *will*!